DOCUMENTARY
FILMMAKERS
SPEAK

LIZ STUBBS

ALLWORTH PRESS
NEW YORK

THE SURREY INSTITUTE OF ART & DESIGN

07 06 05 04 03 02   5 4 3 2 1

Published by Allworth Press
An imprint of Allworth Communications
10 East 23rd Street, New York, NY 10010

Cover design by Mary Ann Smith, New York, NY

Page composition/typography by SR Desktop Services, Ridge, NY

Library of Congress Cataloging-in-Publication Data
Stubbs, Liz.
    Documentary filmmakers speak / Liz Stubbs.
        p.   cm.
    Includes index.
    ISBN 1-58115-236-1
    1. Documentary films—History and criticism.   2. Documentary
films—United States—History and criticism.   3. Motion picture
producers and directors—United States—Interviews.   I. Title.
PN1995.9.D6   S853 2002
070.1'8—dc21   2002005830

Printed in Canada

To my dear friends Mark and Susan Solomon and Leila Garcia, who, with their creativity, passion, and empathy, inspire me to honor my goofiness and feed my artist.

To Mark and Susan Solomon, who feed my starving artist with creativity, passion, and empathy.

To my parents, Ann and Irving, who provide unflinching support—the kind money can't buy.

To Ruth Leitman, whose persistence as a filmmaker gives substance to the sentiment that if you believe you can do something, you can.

To James Jernigan, whose insistence on seeing possibilities instead of obstacles is a light at the end of many a dark tunnel.

Thank you.

Contents

Introduction

Passion. The inextinguishable fire.

Lives of passion are monumental in this world. They shine among us, reaching always for paths without compromise.

As with everything in life, there are no guarantees. There is no promise that being true to your passion will bring success, financial or creative. And in that sense it can be a scary road to travel. Those around you may be on more traditional paths in their careers and in their personal lives. And when you look around at your contemporaries to take a reading on how you measure up, you may find that you don't—on those terms. You might not be married, with 2.2 children, with a four-bedroom home, with a couple of retirement plans in the bank, or on the higher tiers of conventional success ladders.

But passion and its pursuit have payoffs far greater than numbers you can deposit in bank accounts.

The light in their eyes. The smile in their voices. The understanding and compassion that comes from having lived in worlds that are not normally open to most people. The intoxicating exuberance of one who doesn't utter the phrase, "I can't." The comfort and serenity with which they speak about their lives. As if all the awards and famous friends and critical praise of their work is of little consequence in the grand scheme of things. They wear them as easily as old jeans. The prizes, the accolades—Oscars, Emmys, Lifetime Achievements—they are simply what happened when these filmmakers made films about which they were passionate.

The voices in the following pages are widely varied in terms of style, experience, and critical acceptance. But they all are imbued with love for filmmaking—their craft, their art. They live and breathe it. Literally.

Albert Maysles is one of the founding fathers of the American version of verité filmmaking. His revolutionary film, *Salesman*, remains captivating decades after its creation. This is perhaps one of the most telling portraits of the American heart: You are in the scene, the emotions are tangible, and all this is captured without anyone directing events or subjects.

Completely in love with the craft of verité, Albert's longtime collaborator, Susan Froemke, was nominated for an Academy Award for a film she did on the present-day legacy of slavery in the land of cotton. Her love for filmmaking imbues every frame with palpable empathy. She is a master at capturing humanity and the layers of struggle, spoken and unspoken, that brew beneath our façades.

D.A. Pennebaker is one of the reasons these filmmakers can make films in the field. He was one of the primary engineers to design cameras both to have sync sound and to be portable. He and his partner, Chris Hegedus, have lensed energetic and raw films of some of the most legendary musicians and politicos of our time.

Ross McElwee paints intensely personal portraits of people and self as he travels through family events, states of the union, and states of affairs. His commentary from behind the camera adds levels of query and contemplation to his work that involves us on myriad levels.

Nick Broomfield's unique filmmaking style gets him behind doors that remain closed to most. Indeed, perhaps it is the inclusion of his pursuit of some of the most infamous and elusive pop-culture icons that illuminates them in a way that they would not consciously allow.

Truly a household name, Ken Burns is most famous for his love affair with American history. His examinations of events and people of our past have engaged viewers for hours upon hours, and his work has reawakened many to documentary as an engaging form of film. With archival footage, photos, and writings, we are taken on a journey in time to better know our subjects, yet we are taken on a timeless journey in which we discover, perhaps, more about ourselves.

Allie Light and Irving Saraf push the envelope in their filmmaking, exploring ways to express emotion and past events in recreations and emotional equivalents. Truth, after all, can be expressed in many ways.

Liz Garbus's innate sense of social justice has found a voice in her films. She tells stories of humanity in inhumanity, reminding us that crisis and redemption are not simply black and white.

Barbara Kopple points cameras where others might be intimidated to go. Union strikes, labor disputes, and even filming at gunpoint have earned her the reputation of being fearless. But she says she just keeps looking around the next corner.

Bruce Sinofsky and Joe Berlinger have collaborated on films that engage the viewer in the dialogue of right and wrong. Often, their films are of people in times of extreme crisis, and they craft their stories in such a way that we are there with them as the story unfolds—questioning innocence and guilt in the process of discovery.

Obviously, nonfiction filmmaking by nature is a different animal from fiction filmmaking. And, by process, they are worlds apart. Going into it, you have no finite end date on filming nonfiction, as you do with fiction. You could spend years in the field getting your story. You could likewise spend years in the editing room as you try to keep your project funded by doing other films, applying for grants, or looking for a sale. Being away from family and friends, finding backers for your film, dealing with subjects who don't want to be in your film: there are many levels on which nonfiction filmmaking is not just challenging but also difficult. It is not for the faint of heart. It is for those who don't honor the phrase, "I can't;" for those who burn to tell the stories, who can't imagine doing anything else.

And why would they? They capture the poetry of every day. The pain we'd rather not acknowledge. Zealousness that we either appreciate or fear. Grays in our black-and-white world. Moments of unguarded humanity, sublime and appalling and everything in between. Moments we often lose in the drone of our day to day—their eyes capture and immortalize. And we are richer for them.

These filmmakers display their passion in every frame of their stories. The honor with which they allow their subjects' stories to unfold, the dedication they pour into every minute of every year spent making each film, the beauty of the cinematography, the honesty of the lens in capturing lives—it's visceral. We as viewers live the journey the filmmakers took on each story. And we aren't the same people when the credits roll. We know something we didn't when we first sat down to watch. We glimpse lives we otherwise would not have seen. And we view ours somewhat differently as a result. Thanks to their passion.

Chapter 1: The Road to Realism

The motion-picture camera made its full-fledged debut in 1895, courtesy of Frenchman Louis Lumière. Others, including Thomas Edison, invented versions that predated Lumière's camera, but his was the only portable all-in-one unit that served as camera, film processor, and projector. A few years after coming onto the scene, D. W. Griffith lensed his full-length epic *Birth of a Nation* (1915) with the new technology, opening up a new world of possibility for film as an art form. Short films and silent films abounded in this early period. In 1922, American Robert Flaherty pioneered the first great documentary or nonfiction film, *Nanook of the North*, in which he recorded the lives of Hudson Bay Eskimos. And, thus, the art form of the documentary was officially born.

But first, let's take a step back. Realism was an artistic movement in eighteenth-century Europe. Realists would portray life as accurately and objectively as they could, rejecting the more classical romantic notion that life was more emotionally pleasing than it really was. Realism took hold in painting and literature and then found its way into motion pictures in the twentieth century. Italian neorealist cinema, such as *The Bicycle Thief* (1949), found prominence after World War II—turning the lens toward common people rather than actors and opting for actual locations rather than stages or studios.

Cinema verité—literally, film truth—is a movement in nonfiction film that grew from realism. Jean Rouche and other French directors are credited with developing the cinema verité style in the 1960s. *Chronique d'un Eté* (1960) is considered to be the first verité film. As its name implies, cinema verité does not rely on actors, narrators, props, big budgets, or special effects. The movement was a radical departure from the traditional studio films that dominated the 1930s and 1940s. These filmmakers filmed real people in their actual surroundings, living their lives unadulterated by directorial interference—capturing life as objectively as they could. They shot with available light, on location, and with lighter-weight cameras that were small enough to be as unobtrusive as possible—a characteristic that prompted these very filmmakers to craft equipment better suited to their style. Verité was able to emerge because of the technological advancements that people like Bob Drew and D.A. Pennebaker engineered—their sync-sound-recording equipment enabled filmmakers to capture high-quality audio on location.

Styles similar to verité evolved somewhat simultaneously in England, Canada, and the United States, going by several monikers—direct cinema, observational documentary, and free cinema. Albert Maysles and his brother David, Richard Leacock, and a few of their contemporaries are considered to be the fathers of direct cinema, the American version of verité. *Salesman*, the Maysles' landmark film about four Bible salesmen from Boston, had a realism and immediacy that hadn't before found its way to the screen. Pennebaker's legendary rock documentary of Bob Dylan, *Don't Look Back*, was also the first of its kind, giving us a backstage honesty never before experienced.

Direct cinema has since evolved into a variety of offshoots, straying from its strict no-involvement-with-the-subject origins. Nonfiction filmmakers find their voices now in a hybrid of documentary styles that continue to push the form and bring to the viewer worlds and truths and humanity we may not otherwise have known.

Chapter 2: Albert Maysles
Father of Direct Cinema

Lauded as the father of direct cinema, an American parallel to the French vérité style, Albert Maysles is a landmark figure in nonfiction films. With the revolution of sync-sound and portable film cameras, Albert and his brother, David, shot films handheld, with very little, if any, interview interaction, simply allowing life to unfold before the camera, capturing more truth than would be possible if they attempted to "direct" subjects and situations. Their style and their films are legendary: *What's Happening! The Beatles in the USA* (1964), a look at a Beatles visit to the States; *Salesman* (1968) chronicles four door-to-door Bible salesmen and is often heralded as the classic American documentary, reflecting one of the richest portraits of the heart of America; the cult classic *Gimme Shelter* (1969), a portrait of Mick Jagger and the Rolling Stones on their American tour that ended with a killing at the Altamont concert; and *Grey Gardens* (1976), a portrait of a very unique, eccentric mother-daughter dynamic in their secluded, decaying East Hampton mansion.

Albert and his films have garnered awards not just for their merits but also for their contributions to their times. *Salesman* was honored by the Library of Congress in 1992 for its historic, cultural, and aesthetic significance. And Albert has been honored for lifetime and career achievement by such entities as the International Documentary Association, the American Society of Cinematographers, the Guggenheim, and, in 1999, Kodak recognized him as one of the world's one hundred finest cinematographers.

Albert heads up Maysles Films today and continues to be a prolific filmmaker—most recently with *LaLee's Kin* (2000) and a series of filmmaker portraits for the Independent Film Channel (2001).

How did you get your start in film and documentaries?

I'd been a psychologist, teaching at Boston University. I worked in a mental hospital as a research assistant, and I also headed up a research project in Massachusetts General Hospital. I mention all that stuff because in 1955—as I was still teaching and one has a summer vacation—I decided that it being only two years after Stalin's death, it would be very interesting to go to Russia. Maybe I could get some sort of impression, record my experiences in some way to fill an enormous gap that existed at that time. People had no imagery, no way of even comprehending in the slightest, because the media was so deficient in this regard—you know, what it was to be a Russian, just an ordinary person—we had no basis of common ground for understanding because everything was speculation about activities behind the wall of the Kremlin.

So with that in mind I thought I would go there and do something that I knew something about—namely, mental health. And I decided I would try to get into mental hospitals, which was a tall order, but I've always been an adventurer. And the more wild the adventure, the more interesting it would be. Every documentary is sort of an adventure into the heart and soul of certain people. At least, that's what it should be.

And so, it's a long story, but I managed to borrow a movie camera, a 16mm camera from CBS. I just walked in there, just a total stranger, told them I was a psychologist and I was hoping to get into mental hospitals, and they took me at my word. And they gave me a roll of film—at that time, it was just a hundred-foot roll, three minutes of 16mm film—and said, "Just shoot something and allow us three hours to process it and we'll give you a critique." That was my training. So up I went and two days after I arrived in Moscow I crashed a Romanian embassy party, met all the top Soviet leaders. One of them got interested in me. He came back to me fifteen minutes later with a telephone number for me to call. It was the head of psychiatry for Russia. Of course, he was notified I would be calling and that paved the way. So I made my first film that way; that's how I got into it. So my interest has always been in, I suppose, finding and recording how people tick.

How did your style evolve?

I have an interest completely different from Hollywood's way of doing things. I'm not at all interested in what's called high production value. It's the bane of our existence. To me, of course, the high value is not what makes it expensive, but the high value comes in capturing another person's experience as directly and as interestingly as possible. Now some people, perhaps even most documentary filmmakers, don't think you can do that with any kind of full authenticity. They'll say it's all a point of view, and it's a manipulation, and you're always selecting. I don't agree with the downgrading of the truthfulness of what one can do in a documentary. It's been

Albert (left) and David Maysles filming Grey Gardens. *Photo credit: Marianne Barcelona.*

thirty-odd years now since we made *Gimme Shelter* and it's a very truthful account of what took place—should be good for another five hundred years, I'd say.

Do you find the presence of a camera or camera crew changes people's reactions?

It can. But it depends on how it's used. In my own work I think that it's not a serious factor. That is, it's not a serious factor in making what I do any less valid, nor do I think that the fly-on-the-wall approach is at all useful, because the fly on the wall is an instrument without a mind or a heart to control it. But then, of course, people say, "Well sure, the mind and the heart already are getting into something very subjective and you're getting away from reporting reality." But the way I use the instrument, the way I use my emotions, let's say, is, I think, to get closer, to get closer to the truth rather than distant from it. And I think, perhaps, the determining factor is I empathize with the people I film.

Now, there are, in our culture, influences that would belie what I'm talking about. People say, "Well, love is blind." Okay, so in a way that's true and in a way it isn't. I mean, the more you love somebody, the more—if it's genuine love—the more you are open to discovering good, bad, whatever, without making any negative judgment. And if it's somebody that you can't find an affection for, you can still make a film of that person, and be fair to that person if at least you try your best to understand them. Okay. So if you're trying your best to understand them, that's another way of saying you like them. So much of it hinges on your ability to empathize. It's an essential ingredient, and if you don't empathize somehow or other, I can't explain it, but you can see it in your results. The photography lacks a heart, and too many people who are skillful technically in their camera work—too many of them—just don't give it the empathy that draws the emotions of the scene, draws it out, evokes it, and gets it on film. Without that process, you end up with a lifeless series of images. Too often, an Academy Award winner will make exactly that kind of film. Technically superior but without a heart and soul.

You have these two things. There's subjectivity and objectivity, and for me the thing that makes both possible is the affection, the empathy that you put into it. In true love, you're not trying to do somebody in. In true love, you're not trying to make the person look any different—better or worse—right? In true love, you fully accept the person exactly as they are. So I think it comes back to this empathy factor.

Another thing that goes along with that—we're talking about gaining access, as well, because if you haven't got the access then people will be put off by the presence of the camera. I find that I can gain access, more often than not, immediately upon meeting somebody. Another factor that goes into it is how you look at the person. It's called the gaze. So with the empathy and the gaze and good luck you can get access to just about anybody.

You have another thing working for you, and that is, with that kind of access, with that kind of application of empathy and the gaze, you're able to do something for that person that would never otherwise happen. That is, you're paying attention to that person, you're giving access to that person, you're fulfilling for that person a very basic need that we all have, the need to be recorded exactly for what we are. So in a way you're doing a service of giving that person not a biography, but an autobiography, and again, there's so much misconception about that sort of thing, even among filmmakers. They give themselves director's credit? Come on, give me a break—you start directing a person or the situation, and it's no longer a documentary. The very essence of the filming is not controlling, but uncontrolled, a lack of control on the part of the filmmaker. It's not just the fly on the wall. You are using various skills that allow you to do all this stuff, but you don't try to change anything.

Is anything verboten? I never hear your voice in your films. Would you ever do anything to create drama if you felt it was lacking? To what extent are you hands-off?

Just about 100 percent. But, it's funny—it's not quite 100 percent because, how should I say, you use your presence to allow that person to be an uncontrolled subject.

How do you choose your subjects? Do they come to you or do you do your own ideas for films?

It varies from one film to another. Like somebody might call me up and tell me of something that should be filmed that may not ever have occurred to me and I think, "Oh yeah, that's great, let's do it." That's how my brother and I made the first film of the Beatles. We got into that because we got a call from Granada television asking us if we wanted to make the film, and they had the money, and the Beatles were arriving in New York in two hours. We rushed out to the airport and four days later we had it shot. So that's how that happened. Each film happens in one way or another, usually in different ways. *Salesman*—we just got that idea on our own and went out and, at our own expense, at our own risk, made the film.

Let's take *Salesman*, as an example. Can you know before you start shooting what your story might be?

Well, two things. One is, you have some sort of an idea, but you're ready at the same time to abandon that if it doesn't happen or if something better, something else, comes along. When we made *Gimme Shelter*, we knew that the concert stuff would be interesting. What we didn't know was whether there would be more than a concert film. We didn't know, but we wouldn't have made the film just as a concert film. We thought some other stuff was going to happen. Just what that would be we didn't know. If you asked us to guess, we probably would have thought it would be more positive than it ended up being.

But we were determined as always, as John Lennon put it, let it be, which is in contrast with the way *Woodstock*, for example, was made. When they made that film there were a lot of interviews. We don't do interviews.

Albert (left) and David Maysles work with Charlotte Zwerin, editing Gimme Shelter. *Photo courtesy Maysles Films.*

When you do an interview, the answer is your question, so it's a setup every time, and you're getting away from what documentary, I think, should do and what is its divine right or responsibility, which is to film people's experiences rather than set up an artificial situation where you're pumping them for information, information that is probably better recorded in literature rather than in cinema.

And so, when *Woodstock* was made, the filmmakers thought, "Oh boy, everything's coming up roses. Isn't it wonderful, the flower generation . . ." and you ended up with a film that wasn't really the way it was. There were all the seeds of Altamont at Woodstock—not all, but so many of those seeds were there. How many people were at Woodstock? Several hundred thousand? Okay, wouldn't you think that even now probably there are fifty thousand, at least, people from Altamont—the same number probably from Woodstock—who, even today, are still suffering from the effects of bad drugs? And that film, *Woodstock*, gave you no indication that anything bad was happening and it was only six months between the two, only six months after Woodstock that Altamont took place.

At some point in your filming do you discover your story, or is that something you discover in the editing process?

It can work either way. In *Grey Gardens* we were with them six weeks and we still were waiting for some culminating moment perhaps, but if it didn't happen, okay, well, it didn't happen. But it did happen one day when the mother and daughter were not in their bedroom, but they were in an adjoining room, which we called the pink room because the walls were pink, and it's when everything exploded. And there are little explosions and little manifestations of love as well as recriminations, but it culminated in that scene, and so, we had it.

In *Salesman*, it was a storm that was gathering all the time with Paul's evident decline, and it's interesting—the way the film was put together, you could read it in his face the first moments in the film. This guy had various human qualities that were very nice, but he was going to have a hard time making the sale.

Do you edit or do you hand over your footage to editors?

I don't edit myself. I've tried it and it's not the way I make decisions. With the camera I can make decisions, and I think the right ones instantaneously, but if I sit down and edit I can't make up my mind—and I'm not forced to do so.

So are you involved in the editing process at all—do you look at works in progress?

Yeah, but I'm really not on top of it that way. If it's something that I see should be done or shouldn't be done then I bring it up, but I'm very lucky that I've worked with the best. While my brother was alive he was in control of the editing. He supervised the editing, and we just about always saw eye to eye on everything.

How does the changing technology affect how you make films?

Oh, enormously important.

Do you still shoot film or have you moved to DV?

I was just with Paul McCartney about a month ago. You know, Paul was heading up that event at Madison Square Garden—a bunch of rock stars got together to celebrate New York in consequence to events of the 11th of September. So it was a big event where they raised some $25 mil-

David (left) and Albert Maysles—fathers of direct cinema. Photo courtesy Maysles Films.

lion at Madison Square Garden. And a week before it took place I got a call from Paul McCartney, whom I had filmed thirty-seven years before, and he said, "Look, remember what we did before? Let's do something now, and let's do it as we did before in black-and-white film." And I thought, "Oh, okay, sentimental reasons if nothing else." Already, I was trying to wean myself away from film.

I had made with Susan [Froemke] a film called *LaLee's Kin,* and, in fact, I got the cinematography award for it at Sundance this past year. But even then I was beginning to think, "Well, what about this new video stuff?" And since then, I've made a series of four half-hour film portraits of filmmakers, all with a little video camera. The Independent Film Channel is showing these four film portraits. Scorsese was the first one, Wes Anderson is the second, Robert Duvall is the third, and Jane Campion is the fourth. And I did them all with the little video camera.

With a digital video camera?

Yeah. Mini-digital. Some of them were with the PD100, and later on I began to use the PD150 when it appeared on the market. I couldn't be happier with it. In fact, even when I was shooting the [September 11 concert for] Paul McCartney I was thinking to myself, every time I picked up the camera, "Well, now, if I had the video camera . . ." So during the course of that week I sat down and I made note of what I thought were the advantages of the PD150 over the 16mm camera. I came up with twenty-seven points. And all these points are very, very important.

Do you prefer to shoot with digital video?

No question about it. I can serve all the purposes that I've always had much, much better. Like we spoke of eye contact. Okay, well, when I'm filming with the PD150 I can look at them and they can look at me and that's very important. And that gaze and being able to continue that gaze at any time, it's very important. You might be filming a moment where . . . it's kind of touchy, like maybe a moment of embarrassment or whatever, and so it's quite natural for the subject, perhaps, to look at you for reassurance and there it is—they can look right at you. Your eyes tell it all without saying a word. Twenty-seven points is quite a big advantage.

Digital video is much more inexpensive than shooting with film. Do you shoot more because of that? Is your ratio higher?

You do shoot more. But then, of course, we've all heard, editors especially complain about that. And then there is the notion that since you're shooting a lot more, you're not being as selective, right? And so, my answer to that is Henri Cartier Bresson. Would he have been any better off had he shot with a Rolleiflex, which has twelve pictures, rather than the Leica, which has thirty-five? Because the Rolleiflex gives you a higher production value—it's a bigger image, $2\frac{1}{4} \times 2\frac{1}{4}$, right? But you can't hold it up to your eye. You gotta hold it below so the camera is always looking up, and Henri Cartier Bresson wanted to make every picture count. And if you looked over his contact sheets, you'd see that each one was maybe not the best but it was important that he got that one. Each one was right for him at the time and so he had three times more chance of not running out of film. And in the case of the digital camera—sixty minutes versus . . . well, you can shoot it with sixty minutes or forty minutes with the same tape. But even with the forty minutes, you've got four times less likelihood that you're going to run out of film or tape at an important moment, and that's crucial.

What keeps you coming back to making films? You mentioned being an adventurer, so that's an appeal. What is it for you that keeps you enmeshed in film?

I remember addressing a group of filmmakers, and as I was thinking of what I should say I suddenly thought my first words were going to be, "Oh, what a terrible thing, what a terrible thing, what a terrible thing." I repeated it three or four or five times and I said, "The terrible thing is that there are so many people who never found in their work what they really want to do." And it's not likely to be that way if you're making documentary films. It certainly hasn't been that way for me. I have felt always that I was doing some good.

And also, the thing that drives you on is that there's no end to it. Each week many films are being made—and still, it's infinite. The well is not gonna dry up; there's always another one to do. And I don't think any of us feel that we've made the perfect film yet. There's a film that I've wanted to do for some time, which I think will be my best and I'm still hoping to do it. I've begun to do it, you know; I hope to get it done one of these days.

And what is that?

I get on long-distance trains in different countries. The reason I want to make it different countries is I want it to have a kind of epic quality, not just one country or culture—it'll be cross-cultural. People of different walks of life will be in this film. It'll be four or five or six major stories that will be spontaneous. So what I'll do is I'll get on half a dozen trains in different parts of the world and I'll roam the train until I find somebody where there's a story evolving, usually by virtue of why they're on the train. So I get off the train with them to film their story.

I took a trip across the country going from Los Angeles to New York several years back, and as the train pulled out of the Pittsburgh station with a new group of passengers, I was in the cafeteria coach when I noticed a young woman sitting alone at a table and looking kind of nervous, her two kids across the aisle. I could read her face; something was going on, so I asked if I could join her. At that time I had the 16mm camera on my shoulder, my soundman next to me. And I said, "I'm making a film of people I'm meeting on trains. If it's okay with you, maybe I could film from time to time." She said, "Oh, sure, that's okay." I started filming right away and she began to tell me her story. When she was three years old, her parents broke up in an ugly divorce and her father got custodianship over her, which is unusual, but, anyway, that's what happened, and he vowed that her mother would never see her again. And she's never seen her mother since then.

The night before she got on the train she got a call from a woman in Philadelphia. And this woman said, "Look, there's no time for me to send you a photograph or for you to send me a photograph of yourself, but get on the next train and I'll be waiting for you at the train station in Philadelphia." I got all this stuff on film. We got off the train and I continued to film and she looked around and there was no one at the platform. And then, as she walked up the stairs, there was a woman at the top of the stairs, a woman who threw her arms around her, and they talked. And then, finally, the woman, who was her mother, put her head over her daughter's shoulder and turned to me and said, "Isn't she gorgeous?" Well, that's why I make movies, and that's why I make them this way. It's the truth, so you have to believe it. Anyone seeing that stuff is not gonna have a shadow of a doubt that this was the real thing and I'd gotten very, very close to the experience of these two people. So that's just one story.

I have no idea what else I'm going to encounter. I took a train across Russia all the way to, almost to the Chinese frontier and returning from Novosibersk, which is very far, the east end of Russia. Again, I walked through the train and noticed through the compartment window what appeared to be a family. And I was with somebody who was translating for me. We knocked on the door and they allowed us in. It turns out that it wasn't a family. It was an aunt and uncle and two children, niece and nephew. And as I discovered, the reason they were on the train was that the two kids had just lost their mother, who had been killed by their father. And the aunt and uncle were taking them to their home way the hell out in the western end, in the Ukraine. That's why they were on the train. So that's another kind of story.

So I haven't decided just where; I'm very likely to go to India. The fanciest train in the world is the Blue Train, which is in South Africa. But most of it is just ordinary people chosen only because there's a story that's taking place that's interesting.

When we made *Salesman*, we'd broken through into new territory. I think it's safe to say that *Salesman* was the first real feature documentary film. And so, if you take literature as a parallel arc, there's the nonfiction novel that Truman Capote made and then around that time, maybe a year or two later, we made *Salesman*, which we could call a nonfiction feature film. Now, what other parallels are there to literature that would inspire us to do something in another form, but still a documentary? There's a collection of short stories, okay? And usually a collection of short stories is by one author, okay? Okay, so that's the case here, there's one author and what makes it so, well, what appeals to me so much is that it's not just a haphazard throwing together of stories. They're all unified by the metaphor of the train itself. Which is a metaphor for life as the train goes from station to station. And also, it overcomes the problem we have in documentary in that it's very difficult to film anything but what's contemporary and so you don't go back. It's hard to go back into a person's life in filming actuality—get photographs and maybe home movies or whatever, but that's not the same as the material you can get that's contemporary. So this is an epic film, the train film, which doesn't go back in time or forward in time, but extends itself laterally by being in different countries, different cultures.

Do you have favorite films that you've done?

Yes, yes. Well, there are the three that I've made into DVDs, *Gimme Shelter*, *Grey Gardens*, and *Salesman*. My brother and I, because I wanted to do the train film, my brother wanted to do one of the family. Actually, really of my father and a cousin of mine. Both of these people, my father was a postal clerk and my cousin was a fighter pilot in the Second World War, so they were both heroes, although of different character. Both of us, my brother and myself, we went as far as to make a fifteen-minute piece sort of as a trailer . . . so people could see what the film was going to be about. But then my brother died, and I don't know, someday I may go back to that, as well. I have several other projects, too, that are very much from my heart.

Unfortunately, the way things go in documentary, if you're going to get money for something it usually is from somebody that wants a particular idea for a film. It's an issue or something of topical interest or whatever. Who the hell would ever put up money for *Salesman*? Nobody. And, in fact, even after we made the film nobody wanted to show it. It took over thirty years to finally get the film on television. PBS—I remember we used to go to PBS. One day I remember they had a new guy in programming. So I called him up and I said, "I'd like to show you a film," and he said, "Yeah, I've heard of you. I'd be glad to come over." So he comes over, we put *Salesman* on, and I go into the room to change the reel and I can see he's been crying and he says, "No, I've seen enough." And I thought, "Well, this guy's so moved by what he's seen that it's a sale without even seeing it all." And he says, "No, no, it's too depressing. My father was a salesman." So there is an association somehow between a film that is a meaningful, profound engagement with the viewer that is depressing, or there's some kind of resistance, especially on the part of programmers, to show that kind of thing. You think we had an easy time with *Grey Gardens*? No one showed it. It took us twenty-three years before it finally got shown on the Sundance Channel. No one would show *Gimme Shelter*. But with commercial television it has to be theirs or it's not gonna show. And not like with the Independent Film Channel, when they said, "It's all yours." As I say, that's not the way it usually works.

Is funding easier to come by since you've become established?

I don't think it's any easier for me than anybody else. I haven't gotten a cent yet for the train film. You see, part of it also is the criteria for news or entertainment—it's almost necessary that someone get killed. What I mean to say is, look at television. What is it, something like twenty thousand or forty thousand people get killed every year on television? How many times have you seen a story like the one I described to you of that woman finding her mother? And if I took that stuff and went to television they'd say, "Well you know, Al, it's not exactly entertainment and it's not news. You know, we don't do that stuff."

What about the Independent Film Channel, Sundance Channel, Bravo?

My understanding is that so many of the cable networks, they have their own format. I wouldn't want to submit *Salesman* to Bravo's format, or even Lifetime. The heart of the matter is that the best way for an artist, documentary filmmaker, or whoever to work is to come up with a film that comes from the heart. Some early images, or cravings, maybe of another person, but it really turns out to be a story of your father or a relationship that you've got to get off your chest somehow or another that lead you to put it into some artistic form.

Can you imagine Shakespeare as a documentary filmmaker? He'd go to CBS and he'd say, "Look, I've got this great idea. The guy's name is Hamlet." And they'd say, "Well, Hamlet. What kind of a name is that?" "Well, it's Danish." "Well, we don't do foreign stuff. You know, you have to have subtitles, we don't do anything from another country." "Yeah, but this guy's so interesting he can't make up his mind." "He's interesting and he can't make up his mind and you expect people to watch some kid not making up his mind for an hour and a half? How long is it going to be?" "Well, maybe an hour and a half, two hours, you know, it's a great story." "Yeah but, no, no, no, it's not for us."

There's another thing, too. We spoke of the nonfiction novel and the nonfiction documentary, then we spoke of the short stories that are documentaries. What about poetry? I'll give you an example: I'm sitting on a bus. The same bus I take to work every day. It's a ten-minute journey. I have seen things on that bus that are the most beautiful, potentially video pieces of poetry. For example, I saw a very, very heavy black woman. She must have been a good three hundred pounds with a big hulk of a head on her shoulders. And I got to looking at her, but in a way that was somehow kindly and understanding enough that she wasn't put off by it. She had no reason to feel that she was some kind of an object of my staring. But I got so taken in by this woman and maybe some kind of anticipation that something was going to happen, I don't know. Anyway, I nudged the woman next to me who was white, middle-aged, and now the two of us were looking at this woman.

And suddenly the kid sitting next to this woman, this kid had to be her daughter, she gets up, slips around in front of her mother and nestles her head in between her mother's enormous breasts and falls asleep. Well, it transformed everything, as a poem can do, without any purpose . . . it's a poem, that's all. It doesn't have to justify itself. And if I'd had my little video camera in my hand I would have gotten it. But as it stands right now, there'd be nothing I could do with it.

But, you see, I'm getting into another problem that we have and it's very crucial, and that is, too much of what the media wants is not what's in our heart. They want stuff that has, if it's anything like what I'm talking about when I say poetry, they say, "Come on, but that's not what we do. It's gotta have a purpose. Is it on abortion? Is it news? Does it have anything to do with September 11? I mean, how can we justify showing it?" And some of the most important subject matter—just nice people doing nice things, but not just doing nice things, basically acts of good will and acts of kindness—that's all off-limits somehow.

Do you think that's changing since September 11?

It changed at least for the time being on two pages of the *New York Times*. Even in the Sunday paper nowadays I believe there are one or two pages that have ten or twenty portraits of families that suffered from

September 11. So it's a portrait of the guy and his family, or the woman and her family. Suddenly, in the *New York Times*, suddenly these human portraits burst forth. Except that this happened with September 11, you'd never hear anything about those families. But now, suddenly, you're hearing all the human stuff that went on and was disrupted by this event. That's probably just a temporary thing. But it does show you that that kind of information can make good material for a newspaper, but it's quite an exceptional case.

When my daughter was four years old—she's now twenty-five—I used to take her to pick up the *New York Times*. And so, one day we walked down the street, got to the newsstand and the paper hadn't arrived yet. I don't know, maybe the truck had broken down, or there was a strike, I don't know. But my daughter turned to me, age four, and said, "Daddy, the people haven't been killed yet." That tells it all.

I sat in the audience where there was a panel discussion amongst important filmmakers. Actually, they were all fiction filmmakers. The topic of discussion was violence and sex in the media. And so, when the panel was over, I was the first one to raise his hand and I told that little anecdote of haven't been killed yet and a ripple of "Oh my God" went through the audience. I then elaborated on it and pointed out how there was a gap in content and surely people can complain about violence and sex, but nobody is getting to the goodwill and kindness that exist in people. And so, a panelist said, "Well you know that stuff is not dramatic. You have to have a conflict, and if you don't have conflict then you don't have drama." And do you think anybody else on the panel differed? No. They all accepted that. I was the only one that disagreed.

Have you ever done or thought about doing fiction films?

No. I have been approached. In fact, my brother and I met up with Orson Welles. We met him at Cannes and then he invited us to spend a week with him in Madrid. And we made a little film of him talking about a film that we would make together. It would be somewhere between a documentary . . . as he said in the film we were making, "I know exactly what the film should be. I have a script and everything, but I'm throwing away the script." And so, I mean, I'd be able to make a very good contribution to it, there's no question of that.

And then, on another occasion, I filmed a twenty-minute sequence with Jean-Luc Godard called *Paris Vu Par*—Paris as seen by several French film directors. So he set the scene and I didn't even know what was coming up, and I just filmed it the way I do a documentary and it worked just beauti-fully. So I can see applications. And, in fact, as I was making these half-hour film portraits of filmmakers and one of them is Jane Campion. I filmed her as she was preparing to make her next film, and she asked me if I would like to do the cinematography for her next film. Some of what I've done has been seen by fiction filmmakers and some of them have taken that and gone somewhat in that direction. I know that, for example, remember that televi-sion show the *Monkees*? Well, Bob Rafelson was the producer of that and he's an old friend of mine. And he said, "You know, I got the whole idea of doing that from having seen your Beatles film." So the whole style of that filmmaking came from the Beatles film.

What would you do if you didn't make films?

If I didn't make films, well, I've never had that decision to make since I started. I'd do something where I'd be able to care for people. I think that when you make a documentary, people are putting themselves in your hands and you have a responsibility to take care that that responsibility is met. And not everyone feels that way, you know, but I feel it very strongly. And it's interesting, I've noticed. I have three children and I've never told them what to do professionally, but this is a very strong factor in what they do—take care of people. One of my kids, she's twenty, she spent four months recently in Nepal taking care of Tibetan refugee children. There's all kinds of ways that we can take care of one another and so I'd find anoth-er way of doing it, I guess. Maybe, I don't know, maybe as a therapist.

Well, your background is in psychology...

I guess I must have cared for people to begin with. And also, I was very lucky that I came from a family where my parents gave my brother and myself a great deal. They were immigrant children. And around the turn of the century, as a child, my mother somehow found an organization in Boston. It was called the Saturday Evening Girls. And the woman, a philanthropist, the woman who headed it up and paid for the whole thing wanted to make poets and writers, artists out of Italian and Jewish immigrant children around the turn of the century. And so, my mother got a lot of inspiration and train-ing in those areas and became a schoolteacher and a very ardent social- and civil-rights person. It's funny, one of the people she always wanted to meet was Eleanor Roosevelt, and I don't know how she did it, but just like me, she managed somehow or other to get to her and she spent a whole day with her.

And then, many years later, after I came back from Russia and made my psychiatry film, I read in the paper that Eleanor Roosevelt was going to go to Russia to look into social services there and she was hoping to visit mental hospitals. But she had heard that they didn't exist. So I called her up. I don't know how the hell I got her phone number, and I said, "Well, I made this film," and she said, "Oh, I'd love to see it." So I brought my projector and film and showed it to her. That was 1956, I think, and I hadn't yet got my hands on a sync-sound camera and I was completely out of any money so that by the end of the day she said, "You know, I'm leaving in three weeks. You're most welcome to come along." But I couldn't because I didn't have the equipment or the money. But she was taken that much by what I had to offer.

Did you or do you still have any anxieties about the process of filmmaking?

Well, what happens with me is once I get going on it, as soon as something happens, then it's just out of this world—a scene that is so telling that it propels me through the rest of it. I think it was a year ago; we had a screening of the Beatles film at the Film Forum here in New York. Because I had to introduce it and give a talk afterward, I sat through the film. I hadn't seen it in a long time and I noticed that I was moving around in my chair as though I was operating the camera all over again and I was zooming and switching shots. But I can tell you that if my way of doing it were any different, you know, then I would have felt, "Oh my God, I didn't do it right that time." But all the way through I felt, "Oh yeah, that's right. I got it right. I got it right. I got it right." So the satisfaction never ends.

You make a film from a script, a fiction film, and in a way that's the end of it because those lines never existed in reality anyway. But the lives of people in documentary, they still go on, and if you've done a decent job of it, they're still with you. And I get letters and telephone calls, which I return, from Little Edie Beale[1] all the time.

And with *Salesman*, as you can imagine, Paul became a lifelong friend. One of the reasons we did *Salesman* and did it so well was that in many ways the whole thing stemmed from our heart. We were Jewish kids brought up in an anti-Semitic environment. We were in fights with Irish kids every

---

[1]Little Edie Beale died in her Florida apartment in January 2002 from coronary-related issues. Her mother passed away soon after *Grey Gardens*'s theatrical release in 1976.

single day, so the time had come to make a reconciliation. It wasn't just by accident we chose these guys who were from Boston, all of them Irish. And so it was a turnaround that sort of had to take place at some time, some way, and that's the way it was with that film. With someone else doing it, it could so easily have been a diatribe, piece of propaganda, pro-Communist, pro-capitalist, goodness knows, anti this, pro that. In fact, I like to tell this story: When we finished the film, we made it primarily to get it in movie theaters, but no exhibitor was interested. So we knew that the only way to get it into the theater was to rent a theater. So we needed money for that, so we had screenings where we hoped to get people to contribute to our fund where we could rent a theater. It ended up actually that we had to rent it from our own money, but in the meantime, we had all these screenings. Maybe a hundred people would come. At one of those screenings I noticed that as people filed out and congratulated us, there was one woman who was still seated, the last person to leave the theater. And as she got up and turned in our direction, I noticed that she'd been crying. And I also noticed that she was really quite attractive. And I elbowed my brother and I said, "She's for me." And that's my wife—that's how I met her.

And also, there's another thing that my parents gave me—this very romantic and positive view of life. My mother told me the story of how when she and my father were engaged they would meet for lunch at a certain street corner in downtown Boston. And my mother would arrive at noon, and my father would arrive five or ten minutes earlier and place himself across the street behind a window and just look at her. And then he'd slip around back and come down the street. So he could do this every day. And when you have images like that, really indirectly somehow or other—I mean with images like that who knows? Maybe that's why I looked at that black woman anticipating that something beautiful might happen. That's the instinct that you have to follow. The market, the money be damned. You've got to do that to do your best.

Chapter 3: Susan Froemke
Celebrating the Craft

Longtime filmmaker with Maysles Films, Susan Froemke has been Albert's primary collaborator since his brother David died in 1987. Froemke came to Maysles after a brief stint with WNET in New York. Over two decades, and four Emmy Awards later, she is one of the most respected nonfiction filmmakers in the field. With Maysles, she has crafted close to twenty nonfiction films, including *Christo in Paris* (1990), *Soldiers of Music: Rostropovich Returns to Russia* (1991), *Letting Go: A Hospice Journey* (1996), and *Concert of Wills: Making the Getty Center* (1998). With Albert, Froemke recently completed an HBO production, *LaLee's Kin: The Legacy of Cotton*, an unflinching look at two stories of seemingly unbeatable odds: present-day poverty and illiteracy in the Mississippi Delta. *LaLee's Kin* won the Cinematography Award at the 2001 Sundance Film Festival and was nominated for a 2002 Academy Award for Best Documentary Feature.

What was your beginning? How did you launch into filmmaking?

When I came to New York City, it was before this huge phenomenon of film schools, and almost everyone I knew who came here was an English major. And just by luck I landed at WNET in New York. It was then called the National Educational Television. It was a place where ideas were constantly bouncing off the walls. It was a real think tank kind of area. I stayed there for six months. That's what really got me interested in filmmaking.

Filmmaking as a profession in the early seventies didn't really exist—at least if you grew up in Tallahassee, Florida, where I grew up. I came to New York City looking for something that would be a little bit different and more interesting and more challenging than the kind of job opportunities available to women in north Florida. So I fell into film accidentally. I think so much of what happens to people in terms of professions is accidental—you don't anticipate what you end up doing.

Then I landed, just by chance, at Maysles. I was waiting to get onto a documentary about the Loud family, the *American Family*, the first cinema verité documentary series. I knew the producer, Craig Gilbert, from NET and he wanted me to work with him as his production assistant. I was waiting for that funding to come through, which kept being delayed and delayed, and I got a call from a friend at NET, who said the Maysles were looking for someone to fill in for just two weeks. This was just after *Gimme Shelter* had opened. And, of course, I was more interested in hoping to meet Mick Jagger than to meet the Maysles brothers. I came down and met David Maysles, who was very eccentric. I remember he was dressed in pink pants and a baby green shirt and scarves and everything, you know, the seventies. What can I say? He was very intriguing. And he hired me. It was just going to be a two-week job while the secretary was on vacation.

I really loved being at Maysles and they liked me right away. We bonded very quickly. The last day I was there I got in early and there was a telegram on my desk. It was actually from the secretary who was on vacation in Switzerland. She had broken her leg in a skiing accident and was going to be in the hospital for over a month. I felt a chill go through my body when I read that telegram. I knew that this was destiny, that this was meant to be. And I was going to be a documentary filmmaker—I mean, I just knew it so clearly—I was going to be a documentary filmmaker.

I remember reading William Wordsworth, in college, about the spontaneous overflow of feeling present in his poetry, and that phrase has always stuck in my mind. In a way, everything at Maysles, in terms of filmmaking, seemed like that—so spontaneous and so emotional. And so, I didn't really know that much about Maysles films other than *Gimme Shelter*. Of course, as soon as I got there I saw *Salesman*, which I was profoundly affected by. And I felt that I really wanted to learn how to make these kinds of films. One thing about Maysles (now, remember, this was right when film schools were starting to come out of the woodwork everywhere), the Maysles never wanted anybody who had a film background, never. Because they did not want to retrain anyone who'd been taught to write a script or think about using narration. In a way, the best person to come to Maysles is someone who just loves people or who is a psychology major—like Albert was a psychology major. The idea that you didn't have any film training was very appealing to the Maysles, and I fit right in.

I wanted to learn, and in those days, because it was still 16mm, thank God, you could really go into the back editing room. I remember learning how to sync up myself with the outtakes of *Gimme Shelter*. I would just put the old sync reels on the Steenbeck, throw it out of sync, and sync it up again. Learned how to eyeball sync, which is crucial here, because we almost never use slates. You never have time to get a slate the way we shoot, and we certainly don't head slate anything . . . if anything, a tail slate . . . but by then you have a camera run-out so there is no slate.

What's great about Maysles is that, in many ways, it's like a university. You can learn here. That's why everybody wants to get their foot in the door for a brief period of time, because you learn so much. In those days it was really just me and the Maysles brothers. It was the aftermath of *Gimme Shelter*, and they were totally in debt. I had to answer the phone, but at that point I had a very deep southern accent and I could charm the debtors for a few more months. We were so broke, which was classic Maysles, and what's classic of independent film, I think, is that you . . . no matter what it takes to make the film, right? You spend it and then you just worry about how you're gonna pay those bills later.

You have to have this tremendous belief, I think, in the subject that you're filming, that there's a possibility of a film there. You may not see it in the beginning, and it is a sense of discovery that you go on as you're making the film. You see the film in your own mind take shape through the actions of your subjects. But you do have to have nerves of steel. I was so lucky because I got to see the Maysles do it. I got to observe them doing it and see how it was done and never question the fact that you wouldn't have a film at the end. I would always know there was going to be a film, by hook or by crook. They were going to pull a phenomenal film out of this footage, and somehow pay for it. And that's basically how I started.

I was very lucky in that one of the earliest films I worked on was *Grey Gardens* (1976), which, of course, is—I think all of us knew at the time that this was a special film—would always be a special film and that it would be very hard to ever work on a film like that again.

But in terms of learning how to make a film, I'd see the way the footage would come back, and watch both the Maysles brothers. Whether they were filming *Grey Gardens* or filming a messenger who had come to deliver a package to the office, they were excited about whatever they filmed. Every time they would come back to New York, and we would look at the footage, there would be such a sense of excitement. But also, you could see they didn't know exactly what the film would be. There was a lot of talk of what is this film going to be? Is Edie going to leave? Is Edie going to stay? That was also some of the early stuff. You only had to be there for a few more weeks to know that Edie was never going to leave, that it was a totally different story that was actually happening inside the house. But seeing how that unfolded in a very organic way and never questioning what footage you were getting and never coming up with preconceived ideas of what you wanted, that taught me a lot. David always felt like whatever he was filming was enough—that's what he wanted. He didn't want anything else. He was always happy with what he got.

But then, also seeing that he knew when to stop filming—I think that's one of the real skills: when do you know you've got it in the can? So how lucky could I have been? I came in right after *Gimme Shelter* and before *Grey Gardens*. Also, I was working with one of the most phenomenal verité editors, Ellen Hovde—she and Charlotte Zwerin had both worked on *Salesman*. Charlotte Zwerin's one of the directors of *Salesman* and *Gimme Shelter*. These women were, in my opinion, geniuses. They are the foundation, they are the backbone of Maysles in terms of who made these films, because so much is structured in the editing room, and that's why the editing is so fascinating. And that's why it takes forever, too. Because you're working it out—the structure, the writing that would have been the script— you're working that out after you've shot the footage. It's a very hard way to make a film. Whenever I do a commercial where I have a script . . . oh my God, it's so easy. I didn't realize in the beginning how difficult it was to make a cinema verité film.

Dealing with all the unknowns keeps you on edge—being out in the field for an unknown length of time, money woes, etc. . . .

It does. That's why I say you have to have nerves of steel. I said to someone a few years ago that you really have to believe in the process and believe in the technique. And he said, "You sound like a religious cult figure or something like that . . . you believe in the Maysles philosophy." I said, "Well, whether it's the Maysles or cinema verité, you have to really have a belief that you found the right subject." You have to spend a lot of time finding your story or you have to know in your heart that this is the subject you want to be concentrating on and that this subject is film-worthy.

Sometimes you go on these journey films. . . . We did a film in the early nineties where we went to Russia with Rostropovich. It was his return there after sixteen years of exile. We had met Rostropovich and we knew he's a great subject as a personality. He's also a man of conscience; we knew that because he had taken a stand against and had been exiled by the Brezhnev government. We also knew that there would be terrific music because the National Symphony Orchestra was going with him on this historic tour.

And, we knew that it was a journey he was taking back into his past. So, in a way, you know that there's going to be a narrative structure of a journey.

But in this film we just finished, *LaLee's Kin*—where you're taking the subject of poverty in America at the end of the millennium—how do you begin to even shape that into a film? And how do you know at all what you're going to end up with and how in the world can you budget how many shoot days you're going to need because there's no clear-cut story at all? It's totally different. That's where you'll really have to feel your way as you

Susan and Albert in Russia. Photo courtesy Maysles Films.

go. I had a thread of a narrative when I started that film, with the school superintendent in the Mississippi Delta. We went to one of the most depressed areas of the Mississippi Delta where illiteracy is rampant. It's intergenerational—we're filming the descendants of the slaves, so you're seeing the repercussions of slavery even though it's four generations later, but you're seeing it every day in the lives of the people there. So here's this school superintendent whose school is about to be taken over by the state of Mississippi if he cannot pull his school district off probation. The only way he can pull his school district off probation is if he can get the kids to pass the ITBS—the Iowa Test for Basic Skills. And how can he do that when most of the kids are illiterate? He's having to educate the children of illiterate parents. So right there is tension; right there, there's the narrative. That was the only thread of a narrative I could find after looking at many impoverished areas around the nation.

We were looking for a film . . . that was not just going to be following welfare stories. And then I looked to find a character whose life—her life and her children's lives—would interact with the school district, and that's how we found LaLee. Still, when you're filming poverty, there's not a lot that's happening. We thought we would be shooting for two years—in fact, we ended up shooting over five years. And that's where budgetary problems become enormous, and how you are going to afford all that extra filming is a challenge.

Did you have funding for that?

We were commissioned by HBO but they gave us a finite budget. Now, luckily, they gave us a generous budget, but it was a finite budget, and they only gave us seven months of editing. But compared to other companies, that is a lot of editing time. Some companies will say you should be able to cut this in five months. *Grey Gardens* took almost two-and-a-half years to edit because even when you got the footage, what is the footage telling you? You have to really spend an enormous amount of time cutting scenes and going back and forth over the footage and to really understand what is the relationship between Big Edie and Little Edie. That was big in our minds as we were editing it. And in the end the film really is like a balance of power. It's a very codependent relationship that's presented.

And then, how do you structure the material so that there is a narrative structure? In many ways a lot of our narratives are a more emotionally driven story line. I would say even though in *LaLee's Kin* we've got the school-district story with the school superintendent, who's luckily a charismatic character, the real heart and soul is LaLee's emotional arc and her relationship with her children. And so that's how we structured it—and it's the same thing in *Grey Gardens*. It's a psychological arc dealing with Little Edie and her desire to leave. At the same time, she's so trapped that she's not ever going to be able to leave.

Do you know what the big picture is when you finish shooting, or how much do you discover in the editing room?

We make the film in the editing room. I think this is true for most of the films . . . we know what we're editing towards. We know what our ending is. What we never know is our opening—how do you get into the film?

That's the hardest part. But we usually cut the ending first—if we have it. When David and Albert stopped shooting *Grey Gardens*, it was soon after they had filmed the pink room scene—there was a fight in a room that we used to call the pink room—where the Beales were going to have a luncheon. Then both of them began to get on each other's nerves. Edie has a kind of emotional meltdown and a lot comes out about her unhappiness and what she feels she sacrificed. And David, I remember he called Ellen Hovde up that afternoon at Maysles and said, "I think we've got it." He said, "I want you to look at this footage first thing in the morning, or as soon as it's possible." In those days it would take two or three days to get it back from the lab. And so, that was the first scene Ellen cut. So you know you have an ending, you know you have a climax. We often do it that way, but then getting an opening . . . just . . . oh . . . impossible. Film after film—it doesn't matter what the film is—it's always that way with us. How do you get into it?

What kind of ratio do you shoot?

We had about seventy hours to a ninety-minute film. In the old days people were always saying "Wow, you shoot so much, you shoot so much," but when I was at Sundance this year with *LaLee's Kin*, we had maybe seventy hours to ninety hours. From what I understand, *Startup.com* was four hundred hours. There was a filmmaker who told me he had shot seven hundred hours.

It had to be video.

Yeah, it is video. That's why I like film so much more than video. I feel that when you're shooting film—one, I love the discipline of having to change film every ten-and-a-half minutes because it gives you a chance to think. When you're changing film it gives you a moment to stop and think about what you're doing, where you're going, what you're getting, and also, you're very aware of how much money is going through that camera. I think it puts you on edge or at least brings a different tension, aside from the fact that I love the look of film so much more than video, but I actually like that discipline.

How do you think technology, like having mini-DV or DV accessible to anybody, has changed filmmaking?

Well, to me it's changed a lot just with the Avid. I love it and I hate it. I don't totally hate it. But one of the problems with the Avid is that it changed how editors and assistants work. Once I learned to sync up film, I could be an apprentice editor and then I could advance to an assistant editor. During this process, I worked with these phenomenal editors. I saw how films were made. I heard discussions. I was in the room touching film, seeing how an editor crafted a scene, seeing how a structure was built. I learned it all that way. I was then given small scenes to cut. And luckily I did a good job and so I got more scenes to cut, and that's how I became an editor, and then, that's how I became a director and a producer. Nowadays there's not that apprenticeship because the Avid technology is so expensive that we have our assistant editors come in at night when we're leaving. And then all they're doing is digitizing or cleaning up or putting the Avid through Norton to see where some problem lies. It's like there's no apprenticeship. I have worked with younger editors now who say that they've edited film. They don't know anything about structure. They don't even know how to organize the material in a filmic way—in selects and super-selects and things like that. And I think it's really, really tragic to say that there's no longer this apprenticeship that there always had been. I think that's a real shame.

I feel very blessed that I've been at Maysles all my professional life, which has allowed me to work on tremendous subjects and films that I absolutely love. But I have a lot of independent filmmaking friends who are very hand to mouth. They have to work for a few months to earn money in order to work on their own films. It's always a struggle. So to see them with the mini-DV cameras, able to make films on less money—it's great. But, I've also been a juror at many film festivals and I've had to see so many self-indulgent personal films, made by people who should never have been given a video camera, only because it's so affordable. And it's just torture, some of these films.

I'll tell you one thing: When you're shooting film, you make sure you come back with that shot. You make sure you're coming back with a scene. I shot a film recently on a DSR500 (DVCam) camera and I didn't really like the way it looked, but I have shot one other time on DigiBeta and I thought it looked better, a lot more like film. And I'm sure that when we actually start shooting with an HD camera it will start to look much more like film and the look will continue to improve—the texture and everything.

The other thing that the video technology has created is that it has knocked film budgets down so low that all you can do is shoot in video. The budgets that you used to get—not that we ever got huge budgets—but every aspect has been so diminished in a way because video is so much less expensive and you can edit and finish on the Avid, and now you can edit on and finish on Final Cut Pro.

How to structure a film is something you learn in verité. When I was talking about the apprenticeship, I meant seeing how to craft a cinema-verité film in the editing room. And you also have to start with great material. How you get a scene in verité is very important—the Maysles were very interested in getting scenes, not just doing interviews. We don't want to be doing interviews, although interviews are unavoidable in a lot of our films. Like *Grey Gardens;* you would never call it an interview film, but if you look at it carefully, Little Edie is always turning to the camera and doing a monologue. And in *LaLee's Kin* it's the same way. When I found LaLee she reminded me a lot of Edie Beale because she had a way of just turning to the camera and just telling this very witty story or a very edgy story. She always had a lot to say. Well, you gotta have a subject who's got a lot to say; otherwise, you're really in trouble.

So that it doesn't become an interview film or just all talk, you have to be able to craft scenes, and, to me, how you get these great scenes is by really spending a lot of time with your subject and just waiting for things to happen. I feel you can get the trust of your subject quite quickly—but to get intimate material takes awhile—being incredibly patient and spending time to get to know the subject, having them trust you implicitly. And being able to craft a scene while you're shooting is important, too. I don't think anyone even thinks about these things when they're teaching. Well, I don't know, I've never been to a film class, so I don't know. But when you're shooting a scene, you must think while you're shooting it: do I have an opening for this scene? Realize at the moment that this is a great scene. And do I have everything I'll need to explain it?—sometimes an incident will be happening and you realize you need something to set it up. You know what you have already shot, you know what you'll need to edit, and so you have to be able to nudge your subjects to get material out of them so that you have a beginning, middle, and end of that scene, so when you go back into the editing room it can be as great a scene as it was in life. I think there's a certain talent to that as well, which is uniquely cinema verité.

Ethical boundaries—what happens when you nudge your subjects?

I would never nudge something to happen. Like in *LaLee's Kin* . . . at the end of the film she finds out that her son is going to jail. The way it all transpired is that she was very upset when we arrived—a neighbor had come in and given her this news—and I knew there was no way to explain it, so I had to say when the scene was first starting, "Well, what did you hear?" Something like that, just trying to get it in her own words so that I knew what happened—I needed her to say, "Eddie Reed's been arrested and sent to jail," so we would know what her emotional outbreak was about. I needed that line. That's what I'm saying. I'm not asking them to do something. It's just trying to get some strategic line so I can open the scene. You could maybe find a different way to open it in the editing, but you have to come back with a couple of different options. That's what I'm saying in terms of knowing. Or at some point, just in a very conversational way, asking how they feel, or what's going through their mind. I went through, I would say, five very unsuccessful years of therapy. It didn't do any good for me, but what was interesting was when you lay down on the couch the therapist would say, "What's going through your mind?" And so I started doing that with my film subjects. That's the only question I like to ask: what's going through your mind at the moment? And it's always amazing—people really want to be listened to.

That's the whole key to getting the magic material—we're great ears—we're great therapists in a way. We're listening to these subjects who have never been listened to before. And I'm not talking only about this incredible family in the Mississippi Delta. I'm also talking about the directors of the Getty Trust who were very nervous about what we'd film for the documentary that eventually became *Concert of Wills: Making the Getty Center*. For that documentary, we filmed once or twice a year for fourteen years. I went to their office on each visit and said, "How are you feeling right now?" or "What's going through your mind?" And all of a sudden it was like a floodgate opening and all this amazing material would come out. Hopefully it's not like a Q&A session that's happening. We are always trying to keep our own personas out. What can really trip you up is going down with some agenda and thinking you're going to do this kind of a film and not seeing what is really there and letting all that reality happen. What really is happening truthfully is always more interesting than what you might manipulate.

But on the ethics, I don't really have any problem with doing that. I mean, no one's that pure anymore in the field where you never say a word to your subjects. Listen, at Maysles we always say we are not flies on the wall, and we don't want to be flies on the wall. We are very involved with

Susan and Albert film Steve Rountree. Photo credit: Jack Gould.

our subjects. We try to keep our personalities out of the filmmaking, but we are living with our subjects, so you've got to be talking to them.

Al and I have worked together for years, so we can sit around in a room and wait and wait for things to happen, and we even talk a little bit. But sometimes, if you bring in another cameraman, or another soundman (usually it's me taking sound and Albert shooting), and then they start talking to the subjects; it does change everything. All of a sudden you've missed something; the kid comes in from school, but they're talking to the subject so the interchange is missed. That's why I think so much of it is intuitive, timing and just knowing when you can talk and when you absolutely have to just be in the room, not making eye contact with anybody.

I used to always watch David Maysles when he shot, if I was able to be on the shoot. He would never once look at the subjects. If the subjects would look towards him he would always look down at his feet. I do the same thing. It's just amazing how quickly you can . . . by looking away from them or looking down, pretending you're fiddling with your Nagra and stuff like that, you can get them right back into their own real life. The other thing, too, is that nothing looks worse than when you are looking at them and then they're looking around the camera to talk to you. That looks so horrible.

What is the level of your involvement with your subjects in terms of giving them money? What if your subjects are going to be evicted if they can't pay the rent?

You've got to look at *LaLee's Kin*. There's a perfect example of that in that film where, to me, it's one of the most moving moments ever filmed in any of our films, where these kids—all of the grandchildren—are being dumped on LaLee all the time by their absentee mothers. Part of it is cultural, but part of it is just that the mothers are out on the street. It's the first day of school and LaLee is taking her youngest grandson, Redman, to register. And at the school she finds out that all her grandchildren need to have pencils, paper, magic markers, color crayons, and paper towels, and she freaks out. And you could see the expression on her face—where is she gonna get all this? And so she takes Redman back home. Then she goes around to try to find some money. This list of supplies becomes big in her mind; these white people gave her this list of things she needs to get.

Then the next morning, Granny, one of her granddaughters who's supposed to be going into the sixth grade, is crying on LaLee's porch. Her mother didn't take her to school. LaLee asks, "Well, what did your mother say?" And Granny says, "She says we can't go to school because we don't have any pencils and paper." Then this whole scene evolves where LaLee says, "Well, I have some nickels and dimes and I can give those to you. Maybe that'll do you 'til tomorrow." And then she tells the story about how her sister, who cleans floors in Chicago, picks up pencils and sends them to LaLee to give to the kids—pencils that she cleaned up from the office floors. And she brings them out and the kids are touching them like they're gold bars, these pencils. If we had sat there when LaLee is first at the school at the registration and said, "Oh, here's five dollars, LaLee, so you can buy the kids' supplies," we would not have had a scene—nor would we have had the truth.

You can never, I don't care what it is, you cannot get involved at that point. I've never been in a situation where someone's about to be killed or anything like that—then you might get involved. If you get involved, first of all, you're not going to make a very powerful film, because you're not going to see the reality of what it is really like to be really poor and illiterate and desperate. And this scene gives you the scale of what we're talking about in the film. So if we had in any way stepped in, it would have damaged the purity and the beauty of what we captured and the profound nature of their poverty. You just can't do that.

The same thing happened when we did this film on hospice. We were filming people who were dying. We were filming the last days of their lives. We had this wonderful story about a young black woman, forty-seven years old, who was dying of lung cancer. She and her family thought she would really not die because she would be saved through her prayers and trust in the Lord. Then, when she's actively dying, her children don't want the hospice around and they are really having these enormous crises in religion. They kept sobbing, "What were all the prayers about?" And if we had said, "You know, you've got to call up the hospice nurses and get them over here," we would have had nothing close to the truth.

There's this whole debate about whether the camera changes the reality. I think that's overblown. If you've got the right film crew, I don't feel like the camera really does affect the reality. And I feel very strongly that the crew can only be two people. You get a different kind of footage when it's just a sound and camera team than you do if you have a director hopping behind doors to get out of the shot. Just different. I think you get beyond that so fast and if you've got the right subjects. And we always tell our subjects anyway, "If you don't want us to film something, all you have to do is tell us or look at us or something." We always give them that, but rarely does someone ask us to stop. We are there and we are listening to them, and we are certainly sympathetic listeners, so it's very enriching to them in a way. So you are involved on that level.

But in terms of changing actually how they are living, you can't do that. I will say this: on *LaLee's Kin*, seeing the kids hungry and not having enough food to eat really affected me and Albert tremendously, more than anything that we'd ever filmed before. So at the end of each trip to Mississippi, we would go to the grocery store in Clarksdale and drive all these groceries down to LaLee. We knew that for the next month the kids would have food and LaLee would have food and then when we came back . . . let's say it was six weeks later, two months later, the situation would be exactly the same again. That's as involved as we've ever been.

But in terms of paying your subjects, we've always paid our subjects. We have never not paid our subjects. We always do it after the fact. When David and Albert began making *Grey Gardens*, I believe that we paid the Beales right up front. They knew what they would be receiving. With LaLee, we paid her afterwards. We weren't paying a lot of money. What we did do is buy them food—and we still do. In August, I sent a big box of school clothes and school supplies to them. These characters will never be out of our lives. But the truth is, you're never going to see your subjects with the regularity that you saw them when you were filming. On the hospice film, we lived through the deaths with these families, and it was incredibly difficult for us to say goodbye. That was seven years ago, and now, we just send Christmas cards to each other. And I know that's gonna be the reality. We still are in touch with Edie Beale. And I'm sure we will always be in touch with LaLee and her children. But it is really, really hard. I think most documentary filmmakers really do keep up with their subjects.

Documentaries can become many things to the filmmaker. They could be a journey of self-discovery. They could be tools to effect change. What's your reason for making films? What keeps you coming back?

We don't make the kind of films that are almost journalistic in terms of social issues. What's so amazing with *LaLee's Kin* is that it has the potential to be a vehicle for social change, which is a wonderful feeling, to think that you've made a film that might be able to have an impact on the education debate that is about to start in Congress. That is wonderful. But we are not journalists at Maysles. We are more interested in telling stories, almost in the literary sense. We are much more akin to nonfiction literature than we are to journalism. What we're always interested in is, what is the dynamic that is going on in this family? What is the psychological truth here? Who are these people? It's really more of getting to know our subjects—getting underneath their skin is what's interesting to us. And then for me, on top of that, just the craft of filmmaking and the challenge of doing cinema verité films is endlessly fascinating.

What always hooks me is the structuring of the film. And as I said before, it's really hard to do and sometimes you find yourself up against the wall. And it's always fascinating to me—if you can finally let go of a structure you've been working on for a year and shake things up—how, all of a sudden, things change—repositioning scenes, reediting scenes—and all of a sudden, you come up with a whole new structure that gives your film life. It's just amazing to me how that happens. The creative process is what I get really excited about. There's nothing more exhilarating than when you're in the editing room and you've really broken through the wall and come up with the right structure. It's just as exhilarating as when you're filming a great scene in the field. Al and I will look at each other and we just think, oh, we're so lucky. I can't believe this is what I get to do for a living.

How do you find your subjects?

Many of our subjects, since *Grey Gardens*, have been commissioned. We spent many years paying off the debt from *Salesman, Grey Gardens,* and *Gimme Shelter.* If it were not for that, we might be generating more of our own film ideas. Since the late 1970s, we've pursued a lot of corporate work so we could keep the doors open. Luckily, we've stayed in the documentary business because we have been commissioned by a lot of wonderful people who've given us great topics and good budgets. The Getty Trust, for instance, came to us to document the building process of the Getty Center in L.A., and hopefully, at the end of the shooting, to make a Maysles film. And that's what happened. It turned out to be a fourteen-year commission and a very difficult film to make. Oddly enough, it was the hardest one to get the right kind of access to [subjects were difficult to get on camera].

Nowadays, it's a very sophisticated population that you're filming. It's funny—I was just up at the Double Take Summer Institute last summer and they were showing *LaLee's Kin* on the same bill as *Titticutt Follies* (1967), Fred Wiseman's film. It was amazing to see that film again, because you realize it could never be made now. Institutions are so cautious and it's so hard to get access. To get access into a correctional ward with inmates suffering from mental illness would be almost impossible to do nowadays. You'd have very limited access. They'd let you go in and film for one day, where he filmed for obviously a period of time. The Getty Trust, they knew too much, they were very cautious about what we were allowed to film.

How do you deal with the fact that you're making a verité film, yet you feel like you're being censored?

The Getty Trust did control when and what we could film for *Concert of Wills: Making the Getty Center.* They were the client, and they were the subject, and that's not always the best combination. So they would invite us to Los Angeles to film a certain event and sometimes we would get there and they would say, "Well, some people don't want to be filmed, so you can't film." And I thought: what are we going to do? So I started doing what I call these updates, where I would ask the subject, "Do you think I could come up to your office for ten minutes and just talk to you?" And that's when I would say, "What's going on with . . . What's going through your mind?" and eventually they got to the point where they really liked the filming. We would arrive and they'd say, "Are you going to come and see me?" Once again, it's about getting trust.

The other thing that really worked for us is that we befriended the architect, Richard Meier, during the filming. This is a historic building, probably one of the most ambitious building projects of the twentieth century. He realized this and gave us a lot of access, which helped tremendously—just over time, getting to know him and the problems he faced. Nonetheless, in the editing room it was a very complicated film to make because we had twelve years of footage.

How many hours did you have for that?

I think maybe two hundred. It was a lot of footage. What I saw emerging after about six years was this aesthetic battle between Richard Meier and John Walsh. We saved the interview with Richard Meier until the last year of filming. And then, in that interview, Richard really let loose and talked about how he always thought that John Walsh, the museum director, would be won over to Richard's own aesthetic.

And here's something interesting. We interviewed John about a month or so later, and he also talked about the fact that it was almost like a marriage with Richard. I felt that on one level we had an ending—aside from

Susan and Albert film Richard Meier on the Getty film. Photo credit: Jack Gould.

the fact that we had a natural ending because the building was built—but now we had an ending to their story and their debate. I think Getty [the Getty Trust] thought that we were going to be making a film about how many stones go into making this and that, and be much more technical—even though they wanted a Maysles film. I think they were a little surprised about how much the camera did pick up.

Do you have a moment when you know it's the end?

I think you usually do—I did with *Concert of Wills.* I was worried about how we were going to end the film other than the building project being completed. And then we got this magic moment from Richard and then an equally magic moment from John. Carefully edited, it created a very charming and poignant moment.

The difficult part about *LaLee's Kin* was that every time I would go down to Mississippi, a new chapter evolved. You could keep filming forever. In the film there's a wonderful scene where LaLee says she's never been in love in the romantic sense—she doesn't even know the concept. And you realize that's the whole nature of living this impoverished life—it's about survival. There's nothing romantic about it. She loves her children, even though she's tough on them most of the time—they're not doing this, they're not doing that. But she loves them deeply. There's this wonderful phrase she says at one point, "You want to love your children, but don't love them too hard." The only person she allows herself to love unconditionally is her son. When she gets the news that he's gone back to jail because he was selling crack, she has an incredible breakdown. While we were filming this scene, I felt like we finally had the end of the film. In a way, we had a truth coming out of LaLee that we hadn't seen before and we had a climax to her emotional arc. As we left her trailer, Al and I looked at each other and said, "We got the film." That was a great moment. But you're sweating bullets until it comes, and you've got to keep going back until it happens.

What kind of corporate work do you do?

I do a lot of infomercials.

You've done Wal-Mart commercials, haven't you?

Yes—we produced some of their earliest campaigns. We've done hundreds of commercials, and we have a whole division now, Maysles Shorts, that does nothing but commercials by directors who are not part of the

Maysles alumni but share their sensibility. They're very much a part of Maysles Films, but they didn't grow up through the ranks of Maysles like most of us did.

Are you working on anything other than documentaries?

Oh, yes. I direct commercials, infomercials. I recently directed a series of three different infomercials for the Fannie Mae Foundation. What was nice was that they very much wanted a Maysles film. Even though they're just half-hours, they're all people-driven and nonscripted—we work it out in the editing room, telling real stories—they're really interesting, and it can be a very effective way to sell a point.

Funding—is it easy now that you have such a reputation?

We're terrible at fundraising. And I'll tell you why. People think that Maysles is rich because we've been in business for almost forty years. But even though we might get into the finals of a grant, after all the grant-writing we can't tell you exactly what film we're going to make. We try to anticipate what we might be telling, but it's such a leap of faith you have to take. We get into the finals and then people will say, "Well, we know you'll finish this film without us, we know you'll get this film made no matter what, and so we're gonna give the money to a first-time filmmaker instead." In this way, our reputation hurts us in terms of getting grant money. It's never easy. . . . Like right now with the economy, it's just completely grim and the commercial business is down, and documentary budgets are getting lower and lower. I don't want to be shooting in video, but I guess I'm going to have to succumb. It's all these kind of choices you have to make.

Luckily, we have clients like HBO commissioning great films from us. We coproduced with HBO a film on abortion, one on hospice, and now one on poverty. These are great themes that we can sink our teeth into and keep making Maysles films, so that's been wonderful. I've just finished *LaLee's Kin* and I've just finished a film on recording the cast album of *The Producers* with Mel Brooks, Nathan Lane, and Matthew Broderick—a wonderful job that came in through the same client with whom we had made many classical music films a decade ago. Certain clients come back through the years with wonderful films to make. So we're lucky that way; that's where our reputation helps.

But of course it's never enough. It's very difficult to keep a small independent documentary company going. We're working hard at it . . . at least we have a company that's like a family. We're all in it together and we're always cheering each other up when we're having a downtime so at least it's a communal world here. I think it's so hard for the one-person company or the couple that's a documentary filmmaking couple going through those things alone.

What have festivals done for documentaries?

Obviously, if you're in some of the big festivals. . . . Sundance can be tremendously powerful and whether you want to admit it or not, if you get your film to Sundance, it will be noticed. So it's tremendous what Sundance can do for a documentary. Their documentaries are terrific. They have two sections now, the competition and the American Spectrum, and I think even other sidebars, too. What's also great about Sundance now is they have this whole House of Docs program where all the documentary filmmakers can congregate and network, which is fabulous. And they do all these round-table discussions where anyone who has a film, or if you're a judge or what-ever, you can come and participate in them, and it's a great way of sharing stories and getting information. So it's tremendous that way. Hot Docs in Toronto is a terrific festival where your film will start to be seen more inter-nationally and they have this forum now, which is a great way to pitch your ideas. It's similar to the Amsterdam forum.

Festivals are a great way to network and I do think that it's a great way to have your film seen and get a little buzz going about your film because it's so hard to get a buzz going about a documentary. So I do feel they can be quite fruitful, but on the other hand, they're time-consuming and they're expensive. Every festival doesn't pay your way. We've done it with *LaLee's Kin* because we believe so much in the film and it was a difficult film to make and it's a film that we absolutely love, and we want it to be seen by as many people as possible. And if you get the good reviews at the film festi-vals, that's what it's all about. That helps tremendously.

Where are documentaries going stylistically?

About the reality television programs, it's not the least bit documentary. It's prime-time entertainment. We went to a panel at the Museum of Television and Radio and they had Alan and Susan Raymond, the man who made the *Farmer's Wife*, Johnathan Murray from the *Real World* (the MTV one), and Mark Burnett, producer of *Survivor*. At the very beginning, Mark Burnett said they were not doing documentaries—they had a staff of three hundred who were story-writing all the time—that they were not making films like the Raymonds, that they were using people for prime-time entertainment. He said it's very different. And so, basically, there was nothing to discuss after that. At least there's no illusion on his part that he's doing anything that's socially redeeming, if that's what a documentary has to be.

I think documentary filmmaking is more popular than it has ever been because everybody in the world thinks that they're making a documentary. When we do these Q&As, I cannot tell you how many people come up to me—like ladies in their late sixties coming up to me saying, "Can I call you up because I've made a documentary about a man who assaulted me." Unfortunately, it's all too easy for someone to call themselves a documentary filmmaker.

Chapter 4: D.A. Pennebaker and Chris Hegedus
Engineering Nonfiction Cinema

D.A. PENNEBAKER

Pennebaker began in film over forty years ago. With a background in engineering from Yale, M.I.T., and the Navy, his expertise made him extremely instrumental in developing equipment for recording sound synced to the pictures captured by a film camera. Together with Albert and David Maysles, Richard Leacock, and Robert Drew, Pennebaker developed the first fully portable 16mm synchronized camera-and-sound system, revolutionizing the way films could be shot. Now they didn't have to rely on voice-over narration, but could go in the field and capture life as it happened. With this ability, Pennebaker, Maysles, and the others developed the nonfiction filmmaking style of direct cinema, or cinema verité, in the United States. One of the first of this sort of film he worked on, *Primary*, an account of the 1960 Democratic primaries, established Pennebaker as one of the leading documentary filmmakers in the country. His legendary films, such as the 1967 Bob Dylan documentary *Don't Look Back* and the 1969 concert film *Monterey Pop*, are among roughly fifty films in his filmography. With his partner, Chris Hegedus, Pennebaker continues to be prolific—with such films as 1994's Oscar-nominated *The War Room*, a look at Clinton's winning presidential campaign, and 2001's *Down from the Mountain* and *Startup.com*.

CHRIS HEGEDUS

Hegedus joined Pennebaker in the mid-seventies and began editing with him on *Town Bloody Hall* (1979), a document of the dialogue on women's liberation between Germaine Greer, Norman Mailer, Diana Trilling, and other feminists. She and Pennebaker have collaborated on countless films including many rock music and music-oriented films. Their recent *Only the Strong Will Survive* follows several legendary rhythm and blues performers such as Isaac Hayes, Wilson Pickett, and Carla Thomas. With Jehane Noujaim, Hegedus codirected 2001's *Startup.com*, a chronicle of an Internet company's meteoric rise and fall during the height of the dot.com mania.

Who are the filmmakers that you most admire?

D.A.:

There's a couple of obvious ones. Ross McElwee is a very good one. Fred Wiseman—probably most people think we and him make the same kinds of films, and we think far differently. But we probably do make, in many ways, the same kind of film. Anyway, I know that the kind of work he does on them is really hard and, truly, it's driven by a real understanding of how to do it. But remember, he doesn't use a camera himself—while he does sound on most of his things, he uses a crew if he can, or at least he uses a cameraman so he doesn't see the same movie that Chris and I might see where one of us is behind a camera.

There's others who didn't quite make it until now in terms of high pro-file—Joel DeMott and Jeff Krienes. They moved down to Alabama because it got really hard for them, and I think Jeff now deals in equipment a lot. But they are two of the best filmmakers of their kind that I know—any-where in the world. And when certain kinds of things come up we go right straight to them. I'll give you an example. We did a film, *Depeche Mode 101* (1989). Actually, we love the film.

But in the beginning, everybody thought we were gonna make a film like *Don't Look Back* (1966) about these four guys [in Depeche Mode]. Well, they're just not Dylan, and there's no way you could ever make them look like Dylan. We wondered how to do this film for a bit, and then we decided to put together a trip. A bus trip, by a group of fans, and that was gonna happen because the band was going to go out on their tour and end up at the Rose Bowl and put on their final show at the Rose Bowl, and the fans would get to go for free. Somebody would select the seven or eight fans. Well, those two [Jeff and Joel] went along on that trip and made just an absolutely marvelous film, which saved our film in many ways. [Adding the bus journey story to our footage] made it funny and about something; whereas, just about the band it wouldn't have been much. And the band even recognized this early on and said, "Those are the celebrities." There are people like this [Jeff and Joel] who know how to do this, and some of them keep doing it and some of them just get worn out by lack of money and by lack of interest and lack of places to sell it.

Chris, who are the filmmakers you admire?

Chris:

In some ways I started not thinking of documentary filmmakers as people I admired. I came out of an art background. I was first introduced to European cinema, and my hero definitely was Fellini. I liked Godard. And the whole European movement I was very inspired by. And then, by following the art movement, I liked filmmakers—I remember Maya Deren being very influential to me because she was the first woman filmmaker that I ever came across. It was my first realization that you could do this as a woman. And then, of course, I saw the early work done by Penne [Pennebaker] and Ricky [Richard Leacock] and Al Maysles with Drew Associates and that was extremely influential to me. Especially the film *Jane* (1962) done by Penne, because it seemed almost like a fiction film because you had an actress in it, and the story was very dramatic behind it, very strong characters, and seemed very much to me that you were making a fiction film, but with real people. Those were my early influences.

The movement that Ross [McElwee] was part of up at M.I.T. doing personal cinema—Ed Pincus was a big influence for that whole group up there in Boston doing the diary films. And I've always loved the diary film. I don't have the courage to do the diary film myself as of yet, but I love what Ross does. I love what Joel and Jeff have done, and Pincus was an early influence in that style for me, as well as people like Michael Moore.

D.A.:
And Nick.

Chris:
Nick Broomfield. I think they've all added their own personal kooky twist to that style. You know who I love? Barbara Kopple. I think she's been a real role model for women filmmakers and has taken risks with subject matter that other people haven't gone near.

D.A.:
Yeah, she's fearless.

How do you choose your topics, or are you mostly commissioned? How do you come to your films?

D.A.:

It's peculiar. They kind of come to us, which isn't to say we stand out in the street and wait 'til an idea hits us or a person runs up with a script. Because they're not scripted, very little initial work can be done on them before you actually even decide to make a film about them. And somebody who sees one of our films . . . people would come to us and say, "This is a terrific film. Why aren't you making this film?" Usually, you say, "Well, we don't have any money and we don't have any access." And if they can provide either or particularly both, you take it seriously and you consider it.

How did *The War Room* come to you?

Chris:

We'd been interested in making a film about someone running for president, which was really the initial idea for *The War Room*, and Penne had

D.A. Pennebaker and Chris Hegedus, filmmaking partners since the 1970s, shooting The War Room *at the Democratic convention.*

actually tried to do it with Robert Kennedy when he was running for office and, of course, was never able to complete that film. And the election before *The War Room*, we had put out proposals, tried to do that election, follow a man trying to become president.

D.A.:
We even went to a TV station—WGBH.

Chris:
We went all over the place. GBH . . .

D.A.:
. . . offered us $25,000. For a ninety-minute film.

Chris:
That's it, so in the end we couldn't afford to do it—take that risk at that point, so we didn't do it. So the next election came up with Clinton, and several people came to us that year with different ideas of the same thing—watching the election—and none of them really followed through. Then Wendy Ettinger and R.J. Cutler—two aspiring filmmakers who had been working in theater and radio—walked in the door and said they wanted to do a film about his election. They had actually gone to the Museum of Broadcasting and watched Penne's film *Primary*, and they heard about us from that and they landed on our doorstep. And we basically said, "Yes, we'd love to do a film, but the two things we need are money and access. And why don't you go out and see if you can get that and if you can, come back and see us." So we sent them away.

We all were gonna try in the access—it was gonna be like that thing where everybody's connected in some way, so we were all calling up anybody that we knew who was connected. I think about a week later they came back in and said, "Well, we've done it. We've got money and access." Wendy had gotten $60,000 or something—her own family money she was going to sink into it, and access basically turned out to be . . . the Perot campaign denied they were running; Bush wouldn't let them in. But they got access to the Clinton campaign staff and that was basically it. At that point Clinton was a very unfavorable candidate in New York City. People didn't like him here, especially on the Upper West Side where we lived. So it kind of seemed like you were getting the booby prize. But there was a little money there, which is always enticing for independent filmmakers, so we decided just to jump in and see if we could continue getting into the other campaigns.

Most of the film was James Carville and George Stephanopoulos in the War Room, which was very risky because if they lost, the value of a film about the losing campaign staff wasn't going to be too salable for us. There is a risk in any story where you're following real life and you don't know what's going to happen.

Tell me about *The Energy War*.

D.A.:

Ross McElwee worked for us really long ago on a film we made called *The Energy War* (1978). We had three crews, and they all had to maintain poetic silence because we were so afraid the Republicans found out that our people [filming] the Democrats were talking to each other and they might have a fit [if inappropriate information fell into the wrong hands]. So we met in secret enclaves and talked on the phone in dark of night. That was a terrific film to do because we were on it for about two years. We went deep into the heart of darkness with cinema verité, believe me, with all those politicians.

Chris:

It was almost like if we had done *The War Room* part two, where we went to the White House and followed Clinton trying to pass a bill. That's basically what it was, but it was with the Jimmy Carter administration. And we followed this bill where the story line was—you'd think it was a boring subject, like their start-up in government. This was a bill about natural gas, but it ended up being the fiercest battle in Congress ever with the longest filibuster ever—it was fascinating.

Do you find you need to be personally interested in your topic to make a good film, with all the time that you have to put into one?

Chris:

I think you have to envision that the subject has some kind of dramatic arc to the story, and you have to hope that the characters end up being interesting characters. But sometimes you don't know that right off because quite often you're just meeting them for the first time and you have to go by an initial sense. Certainly, that was the case for me meeting Kaleil

[*Startup.com*]. I felt he had a certain sparkle and charisma. I thought he seemed photogenic and definitely, in terms of the subject matter, it seemed like what they were doing was going to be a very big, ambitious idea.

How long were you filming for *Startup.com*?

Chris:

Startup.com, we filmed a year and a half.

D.A.:

Sometimes you might have an abstract interest and not even know if there is a story or have any idea how to proceed. I've been interested in doing something on physics and I've talked to several physicists. I know something about physics since I was trained, in a way, in physics in college as an engineer. So I had this sense that there is some story, but as yet it hasn't jumped in the window and announced itself. It's just an idea, which may never happen. It might not even make a good film. But it is something that I'm interested in.

A doctor came to me once with a pair of twins and one of them was brain damaged and blind and the other one they weren't sure about. And they didn't even know if they were paternal twins, and he wanted me to spend time with the two of them and see, if by looking at what I filmed, they could figure out, because they didn't get much chance to study them. And at the beginning, the idea of a brain-damaged child, I thought, was just a terrible idea. I didn't want to do it at all. But I got so intrigued by this child and so engaged that it really was an enormous learning process for me. I never try to prejudice myself in front whether I think it's interesting to me or not, because usually, if you stick with it, you're gonna find out something you didn't know. So it's a peculiar thing.

The process, the filming process, is very much revelatory—it's like a research program in something you didn't think you needed to know about—you end up getting really into it. It itself is a reward beyond whatever the filmmaking is, and I think when that happens you're able to make the film better. It's easier to do the kind of work—because it is hard work—and the concentration and the focus is easier to maintain if the thing gets to interest you, whether it starts out that way or you don't even think it's gonna. If it was totally uninteresting the whole way through, I think it would be a very hard film to make.

Would you do a film you were commissioned for if you weren't initially interested in the subject, trusting that, in the process, you'd get interested?

D.A.:

Well, you might get interested in the money and the money alone. We've done things like that where we needed the money to do another film—to finish another film, and it was with joy that we greeted that money. And in the end that showers off on the film. We did one in Germany with a rock star there—the film would never emerge from Germany—and we had a great time doing it and we got to like the guy a lot. But it was straight for money. There was no question in our minds. And we tried to put him off three or four times, and he wouldn't be put off. In the end, there's always something about the process that you can take joy from a little bit.

Chris:

I think there's always something interesting to be learned in every situation if you just go at it like that—and, especially, if you do it with a friend, which is nice about doing it with Penne as a partner. You can make it your own adventure in some ways and it definitely is an adventure that's less painful if you aren't getting paid for it. We usually have done these films with very little budget.

Does funding get any easier?

D.A.:

I was going to ask you the same thing. Should I get off the bus now? Or is it going to get better? It's like writing long poetry. You just don't do it for money. Like winning the lottery—some people make a film and it goes on to make a lot of money. But you find if you study a detailed following of what happens, the people who initiated the film very seldom realize a lot of money in the end. I think Michael Moore is one of the few I know who actually ended up with some money, and he's busy spending it on other filmmakers to try to get them to make more films. But that was a one-off and a peculiar thing, and don't expect it to happen again. And you don't make any judgments by it because it doesn't hold up for what you're really doing. Every year, you make one or two films and they take all of your resources and energy and sometimes a lot out of your family life, but you kind of are obsessed and you do it.

Chris:

I always say no one asked me to be a documentary filmmaker. You're doing it for other reasons. But in terms of the funding aspect, there's always something new that's changing in terms of the market for these films because of the technology and the exhibition of it. Digital technology is really changing the whole exhibition of feature films and the making of a feature film, as well as documentary films, because the technology has been put into the hands of so many people now that the prices for these shows has come way down and there's a saturation. It seems like if you're in this field long enough, there's always something like that. I remember there was a really big fear when home video came out that that would take over films being projected in theaters. And then again when cable came out there was all this hope that there would be all this new programming opportunity, which really didn't happen for the documentary filmmakers. But things shake up. There's always something new.

D.A.:

We have an old film that's in 16mm and it's never going to be a big moneymaker. It's a film called *Town Bloody Hall*—it's Norman Mailer, Germaine Greer, Michelle Johnson. . . . Well, that film, I mean, it's played in Europe in theaters in 16mm, which you try not to think about because it's such a terrible way to show a film. But you think, "I'll just put that aside and when I come back it'll be over." But in this case, we have somebody downtown at Cowboy Releasing, at their screening room, and he wants to run it as a film. Well, we aren't going to do a 35mm blowup of that film for one little running, which is an experimental running, but we can show it in video. We happen to have a PAL video we did because BBC paid us to do a PAL video from the print. Actually, we had to go back to the original film to do it, so it was not inexpensive. We probably lost money on the BBC deal. But we now have at least a PAL video, and this guy is willing—in his theater, he has a setup for video projection—he'll show it in video. That's a big jump for us. That means a lot of our stuff, if we can ever get the money up to get it out of film and into a video format, we can get it theatrically shown without having to go that next step, which is so expensive and so wasteful, to make a 35mm print for projectionists all around the country to wreck at their expediency. So in a way, I already feel the thing changing underneath me, and it gives me hope that a lot of stuff we've been sitting on for years, if we can just get around some of the things like music rights, can be shown theatrically because television has always been pretty much cut off for us. They don't buy from us. They make their own.

Chris:

We can sell things for television after we make them.

D.A.:

Yes, after. They buy them as theatrical films. For us to do programming for TV, it doesn't seem to work out that way. Even Europe, where we've always had a market—that's kind of drying up because they have cheaper sources now and they really don't care as long as the stuff is documentary and can be proven to be so. They're not that interested in where it comes from or who did it. So you have to face the idea that it is a market that could dry up on you and then you'd be left with no place to sell them. I think these kinds of films are always going to be someplace that will show them in some fashion. You're not ever going to be cut off—it may get more expensive and you may have to figure out cheaper ways to do it.

Startup.com was shot in digital video, yes?

D.A.:

Yes, and so was *Down from the Mountain*.

So you embrace DV?

D.A.:

Yes.

How do you think DV will affect documentary filmmaking?

Chris:

I think it basically puts it into the hands of the masses. Almost every single thing we did as we made any other film, in terms of the digital film-making, I mean. The camera's little, but you're not going to make your movie—unless you do narration over it, that type of movie—unless you have professional sound equipment and that equipment remains the same size if you're shooting in film or if you're shooting in video. You have to do that same type of be-on-top-of-your-character and put the mics on, so that part of the process is very similar. You have to carry a lot less and it's certainly a lot less expensive. It gives people the ability to just go out and do it, which is great. It's a liberating thing.

D.A. :

You're able to do a lot more damage quicker with that new equipment.

But I don't think films are made with the equipment anyway. They're made in your head. I think you can give people who make one kind of film, you can give them any kind of equipment you can imagine and they're gonna continue to make their kind of film. It's not gonna change the film. But I think for people who are looking to get closer or maybe even get beyond the edge of what they've always seen as a kind of a wall as far as they could go, I think digital gives you a tremendous leg up. And shooting recently myself, I've seen things I can do with a small camera and it's not just the size. It's the difference between a pistol and a rifle. I would be surprised if I did any film for a while or ever again.

Chris:
We had to pull him kicking and screaming to video, but now he doesn't want to go back.

With DV you are probably able to shoot more than with film?
D.A.:
That's one aspect of it, yeah. Not necessarily an advantage, but in some instances it is an advantage. It's something you play off against other aspects, but I think the real work on the film is in your head. And the thing you've got, if you can spend less time loading it with whatever you're shooting with, then I think probably your headwork is more efficient.

What is your shooting ratio, and when you're shooting, are you aware of the big picture of your film, or does it evolve in the editing room?
D.A.:
You make it in both places. But the editing is when you see better what you've made. When you're shooting you're not sure what you're making but you know when you're getting close. It's like you're warmer or colder. You can sort of tell by the relationship of the people you're shooting.

Chris:
I always think of it kind of like an investigation in some ways. The process of finding your story while you're making it because you don't really know what it is while you're going along, and there's a lot of that same process of finding the story in the material because when you condense material in the editing process you form character in a way that you really didn't think you had because everything's so stretched out. But when you

put the dramatic situations together they reveal the character and start creating the story for you, so both of the processes have a lot of exploration in terms of what the story is.

What do you think your shooting ratio is?

Chris:

I think we shot somewhere around forty hours for *The War Room*.

D.A.:

There's sort of a point where you get bored, and it's usually about forty hours. I think the film *Don't Look Back* was forty hours, but some films where they have a little repeat built into them that you didn't expect, like *Moon Over Broadway* (1998), they kept changing the script so we'd have to reshoot all the rehearsals because we'd never see the old ones again. [*Moon Over Broadway* is a film chronicling the opening of the Broadway play, starring Carol Burnett.] So that took a lot more film shooting than we may have thought we would do, so you're always prepared for that . . . always prepared a little to be surprised. And then *The Energy War* took a lot more, because it just went on and on. They couldn't get the goddamn bill through either the House or the Senate, so it went on forever. But some, like *Company: Original Cast Album* (1970), were lovely. [*Company* is a film about the cast recording of Sondheim's musical.] It all happened in one night, except for one more roll. So in that time you can only shoot so much. You shoot as fast as you can load. Certain stories have limitations built into the story.

Chris:

For *Startup*, we shot an incredible amount of video, mostly because we were bored to just sit around, and it's kind of fun with little cameras so you might as well shoot. This was one tiny aspect of it, but I think we shot around four hundred hours so you can see it's amazingly different, but also because Jehane felt like she just wanted to shoot anything. That was her first film.

D.A.:

But also I kept telling them she was sort of setting off on a Proustian voyage here, and in the beginning I thought maybe I should discourage her. I'm sure I kept saying, "You just can't shoot that way." And it's true—you don't have time to even edit that much material; you have to wade through it and get rid of material. You don't have that much time to do it. So it's got drawbacks, but, at the same time, it had a peculiar quality of examination that I thought was amazing, and the more I saw it the more I saw what she was doing, or the two of them were doing. I realized that that was the only way to make that film, and that it was a new kind of film for us. And we had to find the physics rules that applied to something with that much material because you don't want to keep going back and making the same old film. They were going off into new ground, which I thought was really fascinating. I think you could make a ten-hour film out of that; that would be interesting to a very limited audience, but limiting nonetheless because it's so, it's like Proust. It's so real and it's so new that I think people would be intrigued to find out what there is to find out there in that world.

With such a low usual shooting ratio aren't you afraid you're going to miss something?

D.A.:

You're not afraid. You're convinced you've missed something. You edit these things thinking, "This is impossible."

Chris:

We miss things all the time. It wasn't a matter of courage. We had limited access and George Stephanopoulos did not want us hanging around the War Room all the time because his neck was at stake. We had to continually weasel our way into that situation. We would see discount fares to different cities and, lo and behold, Little Rock was one of them. And we'd fax George and say, "We've got this cheap fare and we're coming down unless we hear from you," and then we knew he wouldn't answer his fax by the time we got there. You kind of befriend secretaries and assistants who feel sorry for you, and you call up and they don't know you're not expected there and they let you in. So you do a lot of tactics like that to get in, but we weren't allowed there that often so we had to judge when something was going on if we could. And then we didn't have any money—we had this $60,000, which doesn't go a long way if you're shooting over a seven-month period or whatever it was, and your airfares and hotel bills, so you have to really limit how you shoot.

D.A.:

But long ago, when Ricky and I were first trying it on our own, when we left Drew, we would shoot a lot of very short films. There'd be things that we could shoot in a single day and we did a number of them—16mm black and white usually. We got very cheap black-and-white film from Dupont, and you could get it processed fairly cheaply. And you used practically everything that you shot because it was only going to be a ten-minute film and we only shot two or three rolls. And we did this a lot so you get in a habit . . . I remember in *Don't Look Back* there were a number of scenes in there where I could shoot them in one take, and I liked that idea—a scene that had no edits in it, so it was a real-time scene. When you start shooting and thinking that way you wait as long as you can, you shoot as little as you can, and you wait until the last minute, and you roll in and shoot something that completely exposes whatever you hope to expose, and then go on to the next. That kind of shooting we tend to do because it's easier. And it concentrates some things. Later, when you edit, you always find a way to make it work. I don't know why it is—things that people worry about there, I think they don't have to worry. Because by the time you know what happened and you know how your story should end, you can always get there; you'll find a way to get there.

Do you characterize yourselves as verité filmmakers?

D.A.:

Well, I don't.

How would you characterize yourself as filmmakers?

D.A.:

Movies. That [verité] was not our phrase—the French made that up—but it's always been applied to American films, which amuses them greatly. Jean Rouche was practically the originator of it. It doesn't seem to me that it's my responsibility to figure out names for these things, because they don't help me much in my work. I want to be able to do a scripted film or a fiction film if somebody brings me something that intrigues me. I don't want to feel that's not my business somehow. So I never think of it in terms of a limiting phrase, but I know that when you talk to people and you say documentary, that means it's got no actors in it. I mean, they know the difference is one's fiction and one's reality, and reality can mean so much to so many different people that I hesitate to even call our films reality films. Cinema verité is sort of an elegant French phrase and if people want to use it, fine. And sometimes I'll even use it because it's shorthand. I don't have to explain things. But in the end, I don't think it explains what our films are about because that's what the film is for. It doesn't help me much.

Are there ethical boundaries you don't cross—are interviews verboten; is it okay to become part of the film as a filmmaker?

Chris:

This is something that has evolved from being something that had much more of a strict censure to it, and I think it not only applies to our kind of filmmaking but also to journalism in general, where there was a journalistic code where you didn't step over this line or that line. And now I think journalism is a bit more blurry. And I think in terms of our filmmaking I don't have any strong rules. At the same time, I am interested in giving people the real experience that I felt in some way. But I know that these films are constructions and works of the imagination, so to say they're like film truths can't be true just from the nature of what we're doing, so I don't like to get pigeonholed into it.

And I think that the whole documentary cinema verité style has gotten a lot looser. People are using music. Barbara [Kopple] uses music in a very . . . almost television way, in a very manipulative way in her films, not in a bad way. And we are using music a lot more in our films, too. Things that I think weren't done as much in the sixties.

D.A. and Chris at the 1998 Sydney Film Festival. Photo courtesy Sydney Film Festival.

But, in general, I don't need to have strong rules about what we do. I think what we find works with our style is to let a story play out itself and have the audience be able to experience what goes on. We try to use little or no narration if we can, because I think it draws you out of the film in a different way. We tend not to interview people very much while we're making a film—in the beginning I tend not to do it because it makes people think that's what we want from them, because people are used to being interviewed—like, okay, do the interview and go away. And I don't want to establish that as the type of relationship that we want to have with our subjects. We want it to be, "Okay, we're just going to be there hanging out with you as much as we can, following you around." But later on, we interview if we want to because that has been established. But again, when you stick an interview in the middle of a film it sticks out. So you have to use that in a certain way. In certain places, like in a car, it's a very easy way to interview somebody, but make it look like it's part of your movie, so there are certain tricks that you can do to use those methods, but keep the film style.

D.A.:

I was always very affected by the way Flaherty just used the camera to watch. [Robert Flaherty's *Nanook of the North* (1921) has no conventional plot but tells the story of an Eskimo community through phenomenal black-and-white images of landscape and life.] And I know I heard stories about how he cut the igloo in half to get the light in it. I'm less interested in whatever tricks he may have had to do to give that quality. But just watching somebody do something that he does well or knows how to do, I think that's the highest kind of effort a camera can make. Because you can't argue with it. It's not like a writer telling you what it's like to be in the North Pole. You're getting it secondhand. This way, you're seeing it and you're feeling it even though there was no sound in it. You could just hear that wind and hear that whole feeling of being up there in that kind of condition. I guess I always wanted to use the camera in that way.

You know, it never occurred to me to ask Dylan why he changed his name from Zimmerman, and I'm sure that would be interesting, if you could get him to tell, but I don't think that that's my place. I don't see that as what I was supposed to be trying to do. I think that that extends pretty much to all our films—that it's more interesting—I think in the end you get more.

In *Down from the Mountain*, there's a lot of people in there and that's always a big problem for the documentary filmmaker, especially in a film where there is going to be a concert, or all the people are going to come together. Everybody looks alike in any movie, whether it's fiction or documentary, because you don't know them very well, so you confuse people—people say, "My God, how can you do that? He's blonde and now this guy's dark-haired?" Well, you notice certain things and not other things and you get them confused. People in television land, where they can't stand a moment's confusion, they put the names underneath the picture, so part of the picture is the name. Well, that's not a real picture anymore. That's a sign—like an advertisement of some sort, so I hesitate ever putting names under pictures, even though I know it's frustrating not to know who you're looking at. I sort of feel I'm not going to leave it to chance, I'll give every possible aid I can. I'm gonna take the best portraits of these people and put them in the beginning of the film—try to have it so before I even get on stage, you know the differences and you've got ways of remembering the differences before you're asked to sort it out. And I think a filmmaker can do that work; it's hard and it takes a lot of thinking to do it, but I think when you do it, it's a stronger film if you leave those names off.

I don't feel we have any moral high ground at all. I mean, there are things like where you ask somebody to do something again. I don't think that you've taken a lower folder. It's just that I think you lose; I think you give up something. The only reason for us for any of these rules is that in the beginning we didn't know how else to do it, and the rules were if you asked somebody to do something again, then you lost them. They didn't have time for your movie. They had time for their movie. So if they felt it was going to be their movie from the start, then they did whatever they wanted and you had to follow, and it was your tough luck if you missed it. The minute you start saying, "No, no, it's not my tough luck at all . . . this is an expensive process and I'm going to make you do it right because we need to have the shot," you've lost them and they don't give a damn about your process. They've got their own lives to live. I think most of the rules that came into this all probably came as a result of some sort of objective aspect of the filmmaking.

I'm also exploring the kind of character it takes to make documentaries. It's not an easy road. Funding is difficult to come by. You commit years to a film. What keeps you coming and making documentaries or films?

D.A.:

Life is not for sissies, as I always say.

Chris:

It's an amazing adventure to make films, and it's a privilege to live somebody's life with them, especially during a time that's exciting, like watching people elect a president and watching these two kids live through this dream and it ends up being this historic Internet bubble. It's hard work, but it's very rewarding and when you spend a lot of time with people and get to know them, to me it's very rewarding and I always learn something from the people we make films about. I can't think of anything else, really, that I'd want to do.

Do you learn something about yourself in each film you make? Is that part of the appeal?

D.A.:

It's hard to know when you learn something about yourself—you're so well disguised to yourself. It's like taking a trip where hardly anyone's ever been before. When you come back you're a foot off the ground and you're bejeweled in some way, and that's a great feeling. It disappears rapidly, but just the film itself, playing it before an audience, you feel like you're some sort of minor celebrity. It's that you've brought back some treasure that people didn't even know existed and it's always going to have your stamp on it and every-body is going to know that you were the one who found it. It's a great feeling.

Chris:

Penne and I like the mom-and-pop grocery store aspect of filmmaking. We do the whole process of the film. We're like a painter—we shoot the film, we edit the film . . .

D.A.:

. . . we carry them to the lab. We do the laundry afterward; there's nothing we don't do. Nothing's too good for us.

Chris:

So they become sort of like our children or something.

Do you have favorites?

Chris:

Definitely, there are films of ours that are more interesting than others at different times.

D.A.:
We love them all.

Chris:
Little ones have their jewels, too. There's moments in every film that I love. One of the interesting things, I think, about documentaries is that sometimes they're for a very narrow audience and they mean a lot to a certain audience and other people who are interested in peering into a different world can enjoy them, too. There's that aspect of films that aren't made for major distribution—they're just as interesting, especially to that narrow group, as a film that had a wider appeal.

D.A.:
And you acquire an entire Baedeker of lines that you can remember your entire life and we throw at each other occasionally. The thing is to remember the film it was from. They're lines you never would have written, you never would have thought up, that somebody said in extremis, and they haunt you for the rest of your life. They're kind of wonderful little bits of poetry that live on in these films.

In order to make the kind of films you and your colleagues made, you needed to devise a portable camera that was quiet and that filmed at a predictable rate. Take me through the invention of the Nagra/sync sound—what was the technological revolution that you were involved in that changed the face of filmmaking?
D.A.:
[The idea behind sync sound was that cameras needed to film at predictable rates so that] whatever speed it was, you could re-effect that speed later on a projector and whatever sound you recorded with it, if the sound could also be played back at the speed it was taken, they would be in sync together. The effecting of this kind of synchronism [synching sound with picture] took a little doing. [D.A. and his collaborators worked on developing a sync sound system in the late 1950s and early '60s.] And that was a big job and, luckily, Time-Life had a lot of money to spend on that kind of work because they were hoping to do what the History Channel now does, which is to put a program on every week, or every night or whatever, which is in their field. It would be candid filmmaking, as they had expanded on candid photography. So they had a big stake in it, they thought, and we

also were trying to get a camera that was quiet so you could be in rooms. Normally, cameras are pretty noisy and you can make them less noisy by wrapping blankets and things around them, but that doesn't make an inconspicuous object. So those were the two things.

Chris:

And the third thing was putting a handle on the camera and sticking it on your shoulder and having it really portable. I think the whole thrust of the invention movement that began cinema verité was really to separate the camera from the tape recorder and make them independent.

D.A.:

That's true, and of course that led to the two-person team. Usually, it was the cameraman and his girlfriend in the independent world. Now that you've got the little video cameras, people are beginning to see that one person can make a movie. The way we were doing it, it really took two. But the two gave the process a certain aspect that was interesting. It gave the basis of two people making judgment calls rather than a single person just doing

D.A. and Chris during the filming of The War Room. *Photo: Sonia Moskowitz.*

instantly what he wanted to do. And it led to a little more judgmental aspect in the film shooting and later, if those people worked on the editing, they consorted. It made a different kind of film than a single person would make.

Chris:

But how did the development of the synchronous camera come about? Which was the first film that used it? *Primary*, right?

D.A.:

No. First was *Balloon*. I had a camera that I had done some preliminary work on. I made it sort of synchronous—I was using my windup tape recorder that was handmade, but it was very rough and it was crude, and we could only shoot hundred-foot rolls. It had a lot of problems connected with it. When I went to Moscow, we had windup cameras and windup tape recorders if you can believe it. We didn't know how to shoot sync sound, but I knew that if I could take sound at the same time as I shot a windup that when I got back here I could find a way to sync them up. I didn't know how, but I knew we could figure it out. So that's how we were shooting sync sound, but then Ricky arrived with Leonard Bernstein and they were going to do this concert of this Shostakovich 7th and it was gonna be a big thing with the New York Philharmonic in Moscow, and they asked us—Al Maysles was with me—to help them shoot because they were using all the big 35mm cameras.

The Russians were going to film the concert but they had no way to film the audience. So we came in with our little windup cameras and a sync-sound rig. It had a tape recorder and a wire for the tape recorder to the camera, and then there was a wire from the camera to a big long microphone that was four feet long, five feet long, with a huge long stick, and that was wired to a big battery that you had to carry. It was about the size of a Volkswagen battery. So it really took three people to carry this mess—and then trying to follow Lenny down the hallways in the Kremlin . . . Of course, it was impossible, and we're falling all over each other and it got him laughing, so he says, "This is ridiculous. Get that thing outta here." And I could see that no matter how good it was at getting sync sound, it was impossible to carry it. It needed to be portable.

A lot of engineering had to be done on the process before we could follow people down halls and watch them play pianos, and follow them in the desert, follow them anywhere in the world and have one solution to the problem. We didn't want special solutions, one for this, one for that. And that's what I set out to do. That was in '59, and from '59 to about '63, Ricky and I and some other people worked on that problem steadily until I got a camera.

About in '63, when we did *The Crisis*, I had kind of a final camera, and later, when I did *Don't Look Back*, I used the same camera, but it was a little further modernized, and that camera was with me 'til the mid-eighties.

Chris:
But, backing up, the clue to sync was when you saw that Bulova ad or something?

D.A.:
Yeah, well, we didn't know how to get sync. We didn't know how to do it. And there were several possibilities. One is that in the air in New York— there's so much hum in the air. It's about sixty cycle—everything in New York is sixty cycle. You can put a little antenna up and amplify that hum and use it like a crystal to make a sync signal because it's sixty cycle. The trouble is, if you went to London it's fifty cycles. If you went to the desert, there'd be no cycles, so it's a special way of doing it. Then we started looking around for people that used sixty cycles or some aspect of it. Bulova had just come out with an Accutron watch. And the Accutron watch actually had a little tuning fork in it that produced 360 cycles, which you could use as a signal [a pulse to drive the sync between camera and sound recorder]. And if you mounted [an Accutron] on the camera and mounted one on a tape recorder and you used the one on the camera to drive what they call a flip-flop circuit, which, in a way, became a driver for a synchronous motor, which takes a lot of power, you have to carry a big battery to run it. And since it was the same driving signal—that is, the clock on the camera and the clock on the tape recorder—if they both showed the same time, you knew that whatever you shot on the two of them could be made to match, and that's what we used for a while. And later, they came out with crystals, which were more delicate.

The field expanded because they were doing the same thing for missiles, people getting to Mars and whatnot, so we got caught up in the jet stream of that and were able to get people in high places who had no business even talking to us to try to make stuff for us to experiment, and we did a lot of experimenting. I spent almost ten years trying to get a battery to drive these things, and I must have spent more money on that battery than the government did. In the end, it was impossible because they knew how to make the battery, but nobody knew how to make a charger for it. And they didn't care because they got the thing charged and they sent it up into space and they never saw it again, so they didn't worry about recharging it. But I have this constant problem of recharging these batteries, and that was a big problem for us. We had to be able to carry on our shoulders whatever we were gonna shoot with, which was a camera, three magazines, twenty rolls of film, whatever it was going to be . . . and be able to get in a cab and go to Hong Kong with the guy, if he decided at the last minute he was going to do that, and not question it. We couldn't go back to our hotel, we couldn't have it shipped to us, we had to have it with us, and we never checked it. We just used all our bodies, so anything we could take off that weight, that impedimenta, was a big help. I mean, we were crying. I remember when we were doing *The Chair* in Chicago. Ricky and I each got on the scale somewhere in the airport, and I think I had a hundred pounds of equipment on me. I said, "This has gotta stop." So we went back determined to shave it down even more, and we did over a period of three years.

And now, the DV cameras . . .

D.A.:

They're wonderful. I like it that you no longer have the curse of the heavy equipment.

Chris:

It's kind of a blessed thing, now that I'm older and it's harder for me to lug around all the heavy camera stuff, that they made something small for me in my old age.

D.A.:

There was a tape recorder that was half the size of the Nagra that was called the Stella Vox. I remember when I handed it to Chris . . . the look in her eyes, I will hold forever. It was half the size and half the weight, and it was just as good. In fact, I think it was better than the Nagra; it was also made in Switzerland, but it became subject to the uncertainties of commerce, and the company failed and went down.

DV changed the way films could be made.

D.A.:

It did. It absolutely did.

Chris:

The one film that Ricky made before they had this equipment that was just incredible—it's called *Toby and the Tall Thorn* [late 1950s]. It's kind of an amazing film. It's a very intimate portrait, but he lugged around things like this. . . .

Have you changed the way you approach filmmaking? Do you have more or less serenity or anxiety about the process?

D.A.:

We don't have such fierce fights anymore. We don't get divorced three times in the editing process like we used to. We get along better.

Chris:

I think it's the same. You still have those horrible butterflies when you miss things.

D.A.:

You hate to start. Oh God, that's the hardest thing, to start a film. I'll do anything to put it off. I even clean up my desk. I'll do anything to avoid it. I hate to start a film. It's horrible.

So it is an anxiety-producing process?

D.A.:

The need to fail. It gets harder and harder to face that.

In terms of the shooting, how do you know when you've finished, when you have the end of your film?

Chris:

It's different for every film. When you shot the film, or you shot until you ran out of money or got bored.

D.A.:

Or got tired of loading magazines.

Chris:

It was one or the other and, usually, it was, run out of money.

D.A.:

When you're bored by even thinking about it, for me. Boredom is the one thing I have to respect. When I get bored I stop shooting or I stop eating. My mind is telling me, "Don't pursue this anymore. It's not interesting." You always get caught in the coda.

Do you ever think about doing fiction films?

D.A.:

Sure. I've done a couple. I did some with Norman Mailer. I would do one under certain conditions. I wouldn't try to do what a lot of people can do much better and have already done much better and many times over, but I think you could do a fiction film kind of the way that we did with Godard. I think there's ways of doing a fiction film that would be kind of interesting. I think the Danish would be really interested if we did Dogme films, kind of maintaining the way we shoot and mixing it up with the concepts that would come out of imagined stories and made-up lines. I think that's possible. And I think it'll be done sometime very soon because you can save a lot of money doing it . . . to say nothing of bringing actors that otherwise are bored with acting in general, or the kinds of things they're asked to act; I think you could do that, sure.

Chris:

Every time we miss some major scene in our film, I always think, that's it, we're going to hire some actors.

D.A.:

I think there are a lot of surprises in the so-called documentary concept in the next ten years and the lines between documentary and narrative are going to get very unclear. I think that's good. The imagination always gets tired at the obvious.

How do you see the line becoming more blurred?

D.A.:

I think people will start out with their single little camera and their sound and start talking into it and start making up things into it, and pretty soon it'll be unclear whether it's a biography or a film. It's gonna get mixed.

Chris:

Also, I think that people start distributing movies in totally different ways because of the Internet and because of the accessibility. I think you can use them almost like letters, and they'll be traded online and sent to each other in whole different ways than we ever imagined.

D.A.:

I think films will get like letters in some ways. But made for one person, not made for big audiences, and later, they'll get seen by big audiences, like Browning's letters to his wife-to-be. They'll find ways of getting out into the public but, initially, they will not be for audiences of billions. Because that's a boring idea to begin with. Who cares about audiences of billions; how can you ever care about it? You're never gonna meet all those people, hopefully, and what are you gonna tell them? They're not going to respond to your personal life very well. I think there're gonna be many surprises—a lot of which I can only sort of guess at, but it's a great time to be making films because you're in the middle of watching them build the first airplane right in your backyard, so it's kind of interesting.

What are you working on now?

D.A.:

We're finishing up a tired old duck that's upstairs and it's almost done. It's for Miramax.

Chris:

We're doing a film on R&B music where we've gone around and found different musicians who are still out there and surviving and doing their thing. Everyone from Wilson Pickett to Isaac Hayes, Mary Wilson from the Supremes, to a whole group of musicians that were part of this famous Stax/Volt recording studio. Anyway, we're in the editing process of that.

Do you do anything other than documentaries right now to make a living?

Chris:

Well, we make our living by selling footage of dead rock stars. We've been very lucky because—Penne, mostly, but through the years both of us—

have been able to keep the rights to many of our films. One of the bad parts of funding these things by yourself is that you're poor when you're making them but afterwards, if you can sell them in a way that you retain the rights, or you can get back the rights, and not be a work for hire, the footage becomes valuable because it's part of history. You know, no one else has that footage of Janis Joplin or Jimi Hendrix, so you end up having these things to keep you alive. Basically, we do that. We haven't done many commercials. We never seem to be able to get the job to do the commercials. We have done music videos. We've been lucky to do a lot of long-form music films to make a living from. Like Penne was saying about this Westernhagen film, which was probably the largest concert we ever filmed—it was for this rock star in Germany that was done for Warner Brothers—it was a big deal, but you know it'll never be seen here because it's all in German. But this guy is basically the Mick Jagger of Germany. So, you know, we get hired to do strange things like that.

Are there any special challenges because you're a woman documentary filmmaker?

Chris:

When I first started film, there weren't very many women filmmakers and it was hard to find role models. Now there are women everywhere in filmmaking and that's very gratifying to see. I think women's stories are very suited to the filmmaking process, whether it's fiction or documentary, and it brings a certain sensitivity to it. It's wonderful that it's now appreciated and accepted. Recently, because I just worked with a woman, basically Penne functioned as a producer for *Startup*. Jehane and I shot together, and that was pretty interesting, for two women going into a situation where we were following all guys around. I think it worked to our advantage, actually, because we were not threatening to them. There were a lot of guys who were very alpha, very ambitious, so we were very unthreatening. I think it helped us get into a lot of the meetings and things that we did because we didn't look very threatening. We looked like two girls with a movie camera, so it worked to our advantage. So, if you can make it work to your advantage, more power to you.

Chapter 5: Ken Burns
Emotional Archaeologist

Perhaps one of the most recognized names in documentaries, Ken Burns's prolific filmmaking specializes in making the history of our country come alive in a notable string of PBS series. His first film, *Brooklyn Bridge* (1981), made with two college friends who started Florentine Films with Burns, earned an Academy Award nomination, paving the way for the litany of films that followed. He has traversed such complex and controversial subjects as *The Shakers* (1984), *Huey Long* (1985), *Congress* (1988), *Thomas Hart Benton* (1988), *The West* (1996), *Lewis & Clark* (1997), *Thomas Jefferson* (1997), *Frank Lloyd Wright* (1998), and *Not For Ourselves Alone: Elizabeth Cady Stanton and Susan B. Anthony* (1999), awakening voices from the past to illuminate those stories and shed light on our present and future. His love for his country and its people is abundantly evident in both the uniquely American subjects and in the extensive examination of their stories. In 1990 his eleven-hour *Civil War* series made Burns a household name and engaged multitudes of Americans in the notion that watching documentaries could be, well, fun. *Baseball*, in 1994, entranced viewers for nineteen hours. Most recently, Burns has regaled us with the very American stories of *Jazz* (2001) and *Mark Twain* (2001).

Which do you prefer, documentary or nonfiction [filmmaker]?

I usually just say, filmmaker.

How did you get into filmmaking, and how did you get into history?

Well, those are really two separate and distinct questions. I can't remember a time when I didn't want to be a filmmaker. From early childhood, I was so caught by movies and their power over me and other lives. My father had a fairly strict curfew but it was always relaxed and completely forgiven if there was an opportunity to stay up late and watch an old feature film on the late show, even on a school night. He took me to film festivals, and I went off to college absolutely convinced that I wanted to be the next John Ford or Alfred Hitchcock or Howard Hawks or whomever, and had already, by the time I was eighteen years old, read every book of film criticism, had seen thousands of movies, and kept reviews. But I chose to go to Hampshire College in Amherst, Massachusetts, where there was a complete lack of interest in the feature film, the fiction realm. They were mostly social documentarians, still photographers who did some documentary film work, and they exposed me to the great drama that is in what is and what was.

My own interest in history is completely untrained and untutored, but it's sort of like an artist who chooses to work in still lifes as opposed to landscapes, or chooses to work with oil paint instead of watercolors. Something happened towards the end of my college experience—I had an opportunity to practice filmmaking on a historical subject, and all the bells and whistles went off. It was love at first sight. And it became clear that I could take this very generous and specialized training by still photographers who really emphasized the power of the individual image to communicate complex information, unmanipulated and unfettered by layers of other stuff, and add it to this latent, untrained interest in history to try to tell stories that would have the same kind of dramatic impact, only they would be true. And the rest literally is history.

I've found, for the last twenty-six or more years, that the subjects in American history that I'm drawn to afford me the ability to investigate and represent an honest, complicated past that's unafraid of controversy or tragedy. But I'm equally drawn to those stories and moments that suggest an abiding faith in the human spirit and particularly the unique role our country seems to have in the positive progress of mankind. And that is what has animated all that I've done in the past quarter century.

I've noticed that there always seems to be a hero in your stories. Is that a conscious choice?

Well, it raises a pretty interesting question because I've called myself an emotional archaeologist. I'm not really interested in the dry dates and facts and events of the past, but more of a kind of underlying and abiding sense of the power those past events and individuals might have. The great danger, of course, when you mention the word emotional is that many people mistake that for an interest in sentimentality and nostalgia. They are, of course, the great enemies not only of good filmmaking but of good history, and I avoid them. However, I am not willing to place all my eggs in a kind of rational basket. I think there's something kind of super rational, and that

Ken Burns enjoys a cigar after locking the final reel of Mark Twain. *Photo credit: Robert Sargent Fay.*

is this larger, faster, quicker, in many ways more precise, emotional intelligence. Music is the obvious example that comes to mind. We often find ourselves unable to find the words to describe music, but that's not the failing of music. That's the failing of words, and that higher thing is a great emotional intelligence that I look for.

In saying that, another trap of history is a kind of hagiography, a hero worship. And while I believe firmly in the power of not only narrative, but biography to communicate even the complex theories, by no means do I feel myself taken in by the need to exalt heroes. I think the documentary is particularly susceptible, like most things in life—you know, we are all dialectically preoccupied—and the documentary, like anything else in life, is also dialectically preoccupied. That is to say, it spends time saying what's up or down, what's good or bad, what's in or out, what's male or female, black or white, and it forgets to select for a kind of mitigating and reconciling wisdom that might contain and see both. So while my films indeed have what you might loosely or superficially call heroes, they are, in fact, the examinations quite often of more complex heroism.

Heroes today in our superficial media culture usually means someone that we attribute a near perfection to, and are always disappointed when we find out that they come up short. That's the gotcha journalism, the disappointment, the wringing of the hands, and saying that we don't have any heroes anymore. But, in fact, if we'd listened to the Greeks and the Romans who have been dealing with heroes for thousands of years, heroes have nothing to do with perfection; they have, in fact, to do with a great and very interesting negotiation between very obvious strengths and very obvious weaknesses. And it is, in fact, the negotiations that make the heroism. So I've been interested in, say, taking an Abraham Lincoln and not only exalting him for his leadership, for the poetry in the speeches, for his attention to the survival of the Union, but also his tardiness on slavery and emancipation, for his own conflicting ideas. And I think all of human life is about undertow, about contradiction, and I look for that.

There is a purpose, and a larger purpose to any kind of art we make, whether it's a feature film or a documentary, nonfiction. And that is, it seemed to me, that we would want the whole to be greater than the sum of the parts. So if you're producing a film in which you're dealing with, say, biographical historical figures, there is sometimes a tendency to endow them with a little bit more than perhaps they actually had. This was certainly true in my film on Elizabeth Cady Stanton and Susan B. Anthony, where I was trying to exalt the two most important women in American history. Two women who, at best, get a footnote or a caption in regular histories, but who changed for the better the lives of the majority of American citizens. And what I've noticed over the course of twenty-five years is quite often the difference between who they truly are, and this little bit of extra is our own desires and wishes that we see in these people, the possibilities of our own improvement. And so we invest them sometimes with a little bit more than they have, as if it could be a goal, a potential for us. And I think if you approach this in a conscious way, what you're saying is not just fact, but myth is very much a part of story and history. And as long as your film doesn't lose its compass and doesn't forget to delineate the difference between the fact and the myth, it's often important.

Myths are hugely important in all genuine cultures. And since we don't have a genuine culture now, it's sometimes the place of those of us who are engaged in this sort of inquiry to remind us of what our higher aspirations might become. And often the easiest way to do that is to endow these people with our own wishes, and I don't mean my own personal, but a kind of collective sense—of what goodness is, for example, or what generosity is, or what sacrifice is. Higher things that make our lives enriched. It's the same thing when that painter sits down, having chosen to do a still life, and endows those oranges and those vases with more of their "is-ness" than they actually have. And what that is, is just a manifestation of a human inclination towards the divine.

In terms of heroes in today's society, the media will tell you there are none because they will muckrake through anyone's history and expose what they purport to be their . . .

Failings. Which then disqualify them as a hero.

Yes, they're fallible. Like Clinton, for example.

Is the classic example.

And had the media been so excruciating in their discovery of things when JFK was president or when FDR was president, I think there would have been different perceptions of them by today's generation.

No question about it. I think an even better example, using Clinton, is that, if you are disqualifying people for certain failings and, therefore, cynically not dealing with their very real talents and achievements, you then have to disqualify Thomas Jefferson, the father of our country, who slept with a teenage girl, and fathered children by her, and never once claimed or owned up to paternity. Or you could take a president in the twentieth century who was so imperious that he had few close friends, made the greatest assault on the Constitution in the twentieth century, slept with his wife's secretary, and when she found out agreed that he would never do it again, but when he died, he was with that woman and not with his wife, and who was so physically infirm that—in our media culture we have to have these bull-like automatons who can do the campaign cycle—this is a man who couldn't stand up on his own and yet we consider him the greatest president of the twentieth century. And by our current standards he would've been disqualified before he got to the primary process.

So showing the things we think are hero-worthy and the humanity are essential in terms of painting a picture of them. Do you think the country's perception of heroes since September 11 has changed and do you think there will be a shift in terms of giving people latitude to be human and to be heroes at the same time?

I don't really know if that is the case. Certainly, we have shifted our focus and there is a good deal of self-serving sanctimony among the media elite as we now find in our firemen and our policemen a sense of heroic behavior. And, of course, these people are true and real heroes, but I'm afraid the kind of judgmental process is at best a cynical one and doesn't have much of a half-life, so we're still very curious about what Madonna is doing, you know. We're still susceptible to a new kind of royalty, which is the tyranny of the televised over the great mass of us who are untelevised. And that's a huge danger in a democracy. And what I would hope is that we would examine heroism for a much more complicated dynamic and find [it] in existing people around us, particularly in politics, where you find fewer crooks per capita than in almost any other segment, but where the conventional wisdom allows us to lazily label everyone as essentially dishonest, phony, and a crook.

Has September 11 affected in any way what types of projects you'll do?

September 11 affected me more than any event in my public life, having lived through missile crises, fifties nuclear hysteria, assassinations and riots and the sixties, Vietnam and Watergate, and many other things. Nothing has been, in my life, more important than September 11. You're talking to someone who has spent his entire life trying to understand and love and criticize his country, and I took it extremely personally. And the effects in the weeks and months afterwards have been absolutely devastating to me, so everything is different. Only in a couple of cases have I really thought, among a wish list of projects that I'm considering, that September 11 would have an effect on whether I would actually do them or perhaps approach them differently. Specifically, I'm considering a huge project on World War II, and I think that September 11 will change the tenor of it—to deal with more intimate and personal aspects than to try to throw the same old gung ho itemization of triumph and victory and killing and brutality out for everyone to react to.

As September 11 happened, I had finished a film on Mark Twain. Sam Clemens's life was so filled with such personal grief and tragedy, and he wrote about it, that I found myself at first questioning whether there was any relevance to what I did, dwelling so much in the past. But Mark Twain has been a friend who has helped me to answer it with a resounding question. History is not just about the past. History is about the questions the present asks of the past, and so our historical pursuits are very much a

Ken Burns (left) interviews Hal Holbrook at the Academy of Music in Northampton, Massachusetts, for Mark Twain. *Photo credit: Robert Sargent Fay.*

reflection not only of what went on before, but where we are now. And history has a kind of revealing and, almost in a way, medicinal force. And when you have someone negotiating his own very real and personal grief, and Sam Clemens lost two siblings to early childhood diseases, a father very early, a brother, a beloved brother in a horrible accident in a steamboat explosion, then his own father-in-law, followed in quick succession by his own son and three of his four daughters, and his wife, before he died. And he went bankrupt after being the richest author in America in front of everyone and had to publicly earn back the money in a very painful European and worldwide exile that everyone in America was aware of. And he was able to continue to articulate his grief in a way that helps us all now as we struggle.

Twain is the most contemporary of all our writers, of all the historical figures I've gotten to know, the person who'd be least staggered by arriving in our very stupefying present day. I mean, he'd get it. He's understood the essence of what it means to be an American, but he's seen the universal in that, so he's our most widely read author around the world. And there was something very helpful about having to deal with Mark Twain, who basically said, "Get up, dust yourself off, and get going. You have something to say."

How do you choose your subjects?

The subjects choose me. I am so filled with many ideas, but, you know, there's no failure of good ideas or good projects. What it takes, I think, is a strange kind of emotional alchemy in which, suddenly becoming aware of a project, some bells and whistles going off, I just say, "I have to do this." And I never pick a project that I know something about. I pick a project that I want to share the process of discovery as I delve into that subject. Nothing could be worse than a documentary that is expository and merely the expression of what somebody already knows. What is so inspiring to an audience, and indeed to the filmmaker who works on it, is the idea of discovery, of process, of practice.

Quite simply, I've made the same film over and over again, asking the same question: who are we? And each subject, like a different arrangement of fruit on the table, provides that possibility to look into something more divine, or something higher. That's what I'm looking for. So I think that what happens is that these stories, these moments, these collections of ideas and events take hold of me, and I feel literally compelled to do it, and I've been fortunate enough that I have never had to abandon a project once I've really begun it.

In terms of the research for each of these projects, do you do the majority of your research yourself or do you have researchers?

That's a frequent question, and the assumption is that we have a legion of researchers and, in fact, we don't. It's a very small operation that expands and contracts in size to fit the particular grant-funded budget that we're working on. But there is a small nucleus of people. Traditionally, a researcher is the lowest on a production team ladder, and I find it the height of absurdity and terror to send that person out to an archive to look at images and say "Yes" and "No." Now, if they say "Yes" to an image, I'll see it, but if they say "No," I'll never see it. So we want that kind of selection to take place among a small nucleus of three or four of us, a couple of producers or associate producers, myself, and a writer, and that's essentially who does the lion's share of the research. We're really very much about discovering on our own. And even among people that I've worked with for twenty years there's still disagreements—"What do you mean you didn't get that photograph out of that archive? I think that's the best one." And so it is a very intimate and personal process of how we unearth this stuff. And we've come to know and love and respect each other in such a way that we can attend to this process, not so much as a business or a job, but as a family untethered by time. I think the greatest gift in some ways is that Friday isn't a day of joy for me. Nor is Monday morning or Sunday night a day, a period of disappointment for me. The days are indistinguishable, the lines between family and work are completely blurred, between friendship and staff are completely blurred, and that's the way it should be. I actually feel I have the best job in the country because it educates all of my parts.

Take me through the nuts and bolts of your process. Say you've fixated on a subject and you're going to start researching it. Do you shoot during research—is that your production period?

We do everything, as far as I can tell from the reactions of many of my friends and colleagues, completely ass backwards. First of all, we write a script with the right hand hoping that the left hand doesn't know what we're doing. We begin shooting almost immediately. We ask questions of the people that we interview without them knowing (A) what the questions are, or (B) having any idea ourselves what they might say or where it might fit into a script. In fact, we don't look at the script at that time.

But the script is written at that time?

No, it's sort of developing on a separate track. Conversely, we're out shooting archives, not with our head buried in a script saying, "Oh, we've got to fill up paragraph three of page twenty-seven." But because we're drawn to all of the images in the archive, we're fresher, we ask more questions. On the other hand, we're working on a script unconcerned with whether there are images to illustrate what we're writing because we think illustration is the death of documentary films. So what we end up having when we get to the editing room is a huge mess of interviews, a huge mess of script, a huge mess of archives, and quite often it's true that a whole bunch of stuff can't be used. And quite often we find ourselves with a scene that we love in a script for which there don't seem, at least at first blush, to be images. But what we end up doing in addition to reshooting and continuing to shoot until the very last day when we've locked the film, and researching and writing, is keep a developing process where we're open to new ways of telling stories.

We also don't add our music after it's locked. We go, in that early first process, and listen to dozens, hundreds, of tunes and pick out, say, fifty that we're drawn to, that are historically accurate. Or contemporary tunes that have echoes of the past moment we're hoping to bring alive. We go into the studio before we've begun a day of editing and work with session musicians laying down twenty, maybe even thirty different versions of each of those tunes, doing it based on the integrity of the music. And then we come back and we have music beds that are as rich, as organic an archival resource as the still photographs or the first-person voices that we've also collected hundreds of and read by three or four people dozens of ways or by the different script notes.

And then we start editing. And it is the most important, most difficult, painful process, in which we listen to this material and try to divine a structure out of what is essentially static moribund images, lots of testimony. So, to give you one example, any time you see the proverbial talking head in my film, that is a happy accident of trial and error and final placement. There is nothing that has been preordained. We haven't in any way shown the question to somebody or shown them a bit of script and said, "Can you get me to point A from point B?" Or, "That was great. Could you say it again?" We've just never done that. So everything has the chance to be organic, and invariably the film takes different directions and turns and, like a bucking bronco, we ride it and see until the end. And a script draft comes about when it gets so written up and so rewritten that we have to print it out again in a new form. And we're constantly doing that. The last day of editing, we're probably shooting an archive and making sure that I pan across in twelve seconds instead of fourteen, or we're adding a phrase to a sentence in our writing because it fits to the music that works so perfectly there, and rather than have the music be mechanically timed—scored—to a finished or locked or nearly locked film, instead, we're adjusting other elements so that the music has a chance to do what it does. So many of these things are ass backwards and create extremely complicated editing dynamics, but, I think, account for the success of the films, and account for that higher degree of interest and emotionalism.

Is editing the longest phase?

Editing is by far the longest. We don't really have delineated phases, we don't go from a research phase to a shooting phase. It's all going at the same time. As soon as we get footage back we start fooling around with it. But the editing is the most defined and the longest of all the things. It's where you prove the great truth that no matter how beautiful the images you've collected, either live cinematography, interviews, or the rephotography of still photographs and the collection of newsreels, no matter how beautiful that accumulation is, no matter how good on paper a story might be, no matter how compelling the interviews are—until you find a way in which they organically fit together, you have nothing.

Do you go through different versions?

It's an ongoing process. The first script that came out is an interesting on-paper narrative thing. But you'd be hard-pressed in the first draft of the film—you might wait twenty minutes—to recognize something in that first draft that is in the actual finished film. We're constantly designing and redesigning. We hear a story, it gets moved up to the opening. An opening quote that lasted for 90 percent of the editing of *Civil War* suddenly got taken out and, I thought, would be put into the last episode. There was never room there, and it has existed as one of my most favorite quotes not in our film. And that happens to music, that happens to images, that happens to newsreel footage, it happens to interview bites—it happens to almost every aspect of what we do, so our cutting room floor is not littered with bad things, but [with] things that didn't fit.

How long did it take to edit *Civil War*?

Civil War took more than two years of absolutely solid work, with ten or twelve of us working six days a week, ten hours a day. *Baseball* took two years, *Jazz* took nearly three years. It's a process, and I think one of my two skills in some way has almost nothing to do with all of the different hats that I wear as executive producer, producer, director, music arranger, and, sometimes, cinematographer—it really has to do with having a trust in the process, so that when, early on in editing, it looks hopeless, I know what to do next. And then later on as the stories are emerging and they're beginning to work, knowing how to see the material fresh, unencumbered from what I've already known about the subject. So I can be a warm body in the editing room as if I've never seen the material before, which is helpful. I can say things like, "But we don't know that. This makes assumptions that we don't know," and help to direct and redirect.

You know, I've made experimental documentary films, I've made cinema verité documentary films, I've made all different kinds in the years in college and immediately after, experimenting. I know of no form, at least for me, that is more complicated, more difficult, more multilayered than what we're doing right now, and the end result should look seamless and effortless as if that particular still photograph was meant to be our first choice. But at any given time, with a ratio exceeding 40:1, there's thirty-nine other photographs that are chomping at the bit to get in at that moment.

Your ratio is 40:1?

At least, yep. And quite often, when you take a subject like jazz, more than half the images have nothing to do with jazz. They have to do with African-American life, urban life, what the insides of concert halls were like, what street scenes were like, all of that stuff. And you quickly learn, while it might be nice to master the archival chops of your subject, you're also forced, because of the subthemes I insist on engaging—particularly race in most of the films—in an exploration quite apart from the subject of the film.

How do you choose your—I don't know if authority is the right word? But in *Civil War,* there was Shelby Foote; in *Jazz,* Wynton Marsalis seemed to be the strong voice. How do you come to those people in your films?

I don't choose them. They choose themselves.

So they emerge?

They emerge. In the case of Shelby Foote, I had assumed we'd do dozens and dozens of interviews. Shelby Foote happened to have been the first because Robert Penn Warren, the great novelist and poet, the first poet laureate of our country, called me up and said, "You have to do Shelby Foote." And it was a name I'd known as I was beginning to read Civil War literature. So being a dutiful student, I took my mentor's advice. But I had no idea that most of the other people we would interview would be so academic as to ruin the narrative of the story. You ask a professor, "Was it tough for the Confederacy food-wise?" And he'd say, "Well, '61 they were doing fine, '62 was a lean year, '63 was really worse, but by '64 and by the surrender, it was really bad." So that just takes you out of the moment. He just tells you the end of the story.

But Shelby says, "They ate something they called sloosh. They'd take bacon or ham and they'd fry it in a pan and they'd eat that and it would create a grease. So they'd mix in some flour with that grease and they'd make a kind of sticky dough and they'd roll it into a snake and they'd drape it over their ramrods and their bayonets and they'd cook it over the fire and make it kind of a fried dough and they called that sloosh. And they had to eat a lot of that." So that's the bite that gets in because it puts you right there at the campfire. So Shelby's in . . . I think it's eighty-nine times and there are only six or seven or eight other commentators who, at best, like Barbara Fields, who makes a huge appearance, is in seven or eight times, so [Shelby]'s a huge force.

In *Jazz*, Wynton Marsalis is not on camera the most. The honor goes to Gary Giddons, a critic who actually has many difficulties with Wynton's contemporary views of jazz. But since I'm doing the history, they can co-exist and it's just the compelling nature of that interview of Wynton's that makes him stand out among—I want to stress—the seventy-four other people that appear in the film, out of the more than hundred that we actually interviewed and kindly left some on the cutting room floor. So, yeah, we just allow these people to emerge.

What part of the process is the most challenging for you?

I think it's the editing. If I could turn it around, I have three things that just make me glad to be alive. There's a moment when I'm out shooting. It's usually late, late at night or early, early in the morning and you're carrying heavy equipment and suddenly the light is just so and you're able to frame a shot that you know will get into the film somehow. And there's a great exhilaration. It's not dissimilar to the same exhilaration when you're in a dusty old archive and you've got your easel, which we've been using for twenty-six years with little magnets from the hardware store holding up a still photograph. It's not even an easel; it's just a sheet of metal placed into a two-by-four with a groove in it that we made in 1978. And you're moving your tripod and the prime lens with a close-up attachment and you're inside a photograph and you realize you're gonna spend half a roll taking maybe ten or fifteen shots within that old photograph. Say you're at the Library of Congress—that is just amazing.

Then there's a second thing, which is really inspiring for me, when we're editing. These are all essentially detached static, moribund images. And we're trying to tell a story. We're trying to make the past come alive. We're trying to do a little bit of a sleight of hand where we can push through the raw materials that we're using—the newsreels and still photographs—into a moment where history is not was, but is, as William Faulkner says. And somehow, either the subtraction or the addition, the rearrangement, the getting rid of something that's a favorite, the moving something around, the rewriting of a line of narration to make it better, more poetic, the editing of a first-person quote into something that is streamlined, the rearrangement of a scene within the context of the fifteen or so scenes that might comprise an episode—it's something that in a moment coalesces, and what had been that morning an incoherent story suddenly gels and everybody looks at each other and goes, "Whoa."

And it's a process that our audience never sees. There's a kind of assumption I've divined over years of speaking in public, that people think you just go into the editing room and you just put in the pictures and you let it go. But we're talking about incubating and massaging and struggling and crying and taking out things that are great because they slow down something later on. I've just gotten through a Twain film where one of our favorite quotes of Mark Twain was one of the highlights of an early bio-graphical scene. When it was about twenty minutes later there was a kind of fatigue like, "Why haven't we gotten out of this early biography?" And when we took it out, nobody ever had that feeling. So we had to make the hugely painful decision to take out something that was so beautifully edited and so wonderful because, in the words of Franz Joseph in the movie *Amadeus*, there were too many notes, and you take out a beautiful note. So that is the second thing. When story and moment and art coalesce in the editing room seemingly out of nothing, and you feel a great deal of satisfaction and excitement about that.

And then finally as I intimated, I love the evangelical part. I love travel-ing with my film or even traveling alone to engage a public that is so bom-barded with so many other stimuli. To say, "This could be worthwhile, this might be helpful for you to learn about the Civil War or how wonderful a writer Elizabeth Cady Stanton is, or what a schmuck but genius Frank Lloyd Wright is, or how important Louis Armstrong is apart from *It's a Wonderful World* and *Hello Dolly.*" All of these missions become a kind of thing and when you're speaking about it, and proselytizing or evangelizing, I take great satisfaction, and you could have blown me over with a feather twenty-five years ago if you told me that that would be a hugely important part of what I did.

When you first began, did you take a vow of poverty?

I think every documentary filmmaker, if they're realistic and love their work, knows that you take not only a vow of poverty but anonymity. At best, your films are going to be shown at film festivals to a few hun-dred people, and that there might be a showing on public television that might bring in a larger audience, but traditionally even public television tends to marginalize documentaries. I was living in New York and shooting my first film on the Brooklyn Bridge and moved to the house I'm talking to you from twenty-two years ago in 1979 so that I could live inexpensively—remember I'm not getting investments; I'm writing grants and begging foundations and various entities to support my film with no possibility of return. And then all of a sudden, whatever it was in the particular alchemy of how we made films—the first film was nominated for an Oscar and people got starved for that sort of thing and the next few films so blazed a trail in PBS's schedule that they themselves initiated the American Experience. And then all of this is before *Civil War*, which was a flabbergasting thing when, all of a sudden, you go from being a filmmaker who's just barely now beginning to survive comfortably and feed the family on what you make from the sale of films and cassettes to something that is this huge public event, and I'm still pinching myself, and that was twelve years ago almost.

To the general public, the word documentary or nonfiction film is a narrow band. And we think that the feature film is this huge magnificent spectrum. But if you really look at it, the feature film is governed by a formula and laws of plot that make it, I believe, the narrow band in the spectrum. And it's the documentary, it's the nonfiction film, that has so many glorious possibilities. I work in one small corner of it doing a particular style that works for me. And style, of course, is just a solution to the inevitable problems of production that are authentic and organic. There's Errol Morris doing these highly stylized films. You've got films that border on the dramatic. You have the traditional classic cinema verité that continues to astound and reveal. You've got Fred Wiseman owning a whole peninsula of ways of approach and many, many other people that deserve mention that, I think, represent a vast, vast spectrum. So when we say documentary and we say nonfiction, we're speaking of some unbelievably potential-filled medium that has almost limitless areas of exploration and, more important, means of expression.

I love seeing every other form. I think the video revolution is helping. I think access to the Internet is helping. I think that we're pushing and exploring in lots of ways and I have only the greatest respect for those people who are outside the industry. And remember, Hollywood warns us about what they're really about by calling it *the industry*. We don't call documentary filmmaking *the industry*. We call it documentary filmmaking. They put palm trees in silhouette over their logos, but, in fact, they're smokestacks. This is an industrial project that doesn't get made unless somebody some-where thinks it can turn a profit. But the documentary has its soul firmly planted outside of the marketplace, and if, in my case and others, it actually has one foot tentatively in the marketplace, then that's good news. It just means there's an appetite and we've been able to awaken people to the commercial possibilities of this. But if you told me tomorrow that the film that I was about to do wasn't going to make any money, I'd say, "Okay, thank God I still live in New Hampshire." Where, although I'd miss the society of my colleagues, I am nonetheless protected from the economic slings and arrows that inevitably blow in the documentary world.

Are you ever tempted to try experimental documentaries again or to do fiction films?

I've always been lured by fiction film, which was my earlier love. But I had the desire to have carte blanche when I made my first documentary film. I didn't want anybody telling me to make it longer, shorter, sexier, faster, to use this talent, or don't use that talent, to do that subject or not that subject. So I can, after making documentary films out of college for twenty-six years, tell you that if you don't like my film, it's all my fault. And I never ever want to be in a position where I would say anything but that, that if you don't like my film, it's all my fault. And every time I've had some connection with Hollywood, I've realized that somewhere along the line I was going to be in conversation with you, or someone else, and say, "Well, you know, they really weren't too happy with the script they gave, and there wasn't enough money to do this, and they made me use this per-son as the star, and I would have preferred this person, and then when we had a wonderful film despite all of these limitations at two hours and ten minutes, they cut it back to one hour and fifty." That is not the case. And so I have run with my tail between my legs in the three or four times I've had opportunities to work.

Did you or do you have anxiety about the process of making films?

Oh, all the time. I try to bite off more than I can chew with each project and then learn how to chew it. And in the beginning, just the sheer fact of trying to make a film is so hard. And I have such admiration for people who actually get films done. I mean, we live in this world where our critical apparatus is so finely tuned, everybody's got the long knives out and we take a certain amount of delight and say, "Oh, Ken Burns, you know, *Jazz*. Nobody who really knew anything about jazz loved it."

And so I just remember something Shelby Foote said to me when I asked him about Ulysses S. Grant. He said that Grant had what you call four-o'clock-in-the-morning courage. That meant, he went on, you could wake him up at four o'clock in the morning and tell him that the enemy had turned his left flank, and he'd be as cool as a cucumber. Well, I think documentary filmmaking is about four-o'clock-in-the-morning courage. I wake up probably every morning at four o'clock. I sit up, I take a huge breath, my heart is pounding, and, if I'm in the editing room, I've got an idea of how to fix a scene and I write it down and try to go back to sleep. Or I get up and I go to the editing room and I try to make it happen. Or I'm working on a script and I find a better way of saying something. Or I realize that if we approach this foundation, they might be interested in what we do, if it's in the funding periods.

And that goes on now. I woke up at four o'clock this morning. My partner, coproducer on the Mark Twain film, Dayton Duncan, who lives about a mile and a half from me with his family, has the same thing. Quite often, we're out on the road and we're supposed to get up at four or four-thirty; we walk out at three and he's out there smoking his pipe, and I'm going, "Hmmm, I was just worried that the weather would be alright," or whatever. We're worrywarts.

I have never taken a full-time salary in the twenty-six years I've run my business. I have people who work for me that are full-time, but I get paid only when there's grant money and a line for the director/producer/cinematographer. If we run out of money, my line is the first to go. *Civil War*, I didn't get paid for the last six months. *Baseball*, I didn't get paid for the last year. The only difference, I have to point out, is that I own these films. And later on, if they sell cassettes or books or whatever, I can then benefit. But I am the last hired and first fired in all of my films and it keeps me remembering what it's about.

This kind of filmmaking is not easy.

No, it's not.

It's not something for which you have a prescribed start and finish date.

There's no career path, either, that people can follow.

You could be out in the field for an unlimited amount of time. You certainly can't predict that going in sometimes. It's difficult to get funding.

I know really great filmmakers, artists who I admire and take great sustenance from, who've had to, just because of the circumstances of where they live, the kind of projects they've wanted to do, they have to spend most of their time doing commercial work. I have not had that happen, in part because I could be in New Hampshire and live on nothing if there was not a grant forthcoming for my next project, but I've not had to take commercial work.

And it's also difficult on family or significant others because you are so devoted to your projects and you're gone for extended periods of time ...

It's very, very tough.

Is there a type of animal that's better suited for this kind of filmmaking than others, or what qualities would you say are important for this type of work?

Four-o'clock-in-the-morning courage. When I go to Double Take and other documentary venues and look at my colleagues, what I love is that we're so different. We're also, I'm sorry to say, a little suspicious because we're in such a difficult world, right, that sometimes I think people think that others are eating out of their dish. And I've had filmmakers come up to me at parties drunk and accuse me of taking the money that would have gone to them if I weren't already *the* Ken Burns. Which, of course, is nonsense. I work extremely hard. All that we do is extremely delicate and fragile. I think it's a kind of courage that everyone seems to have as I look across the whole wide spectrum of my colleagues, so different, male and female, black and white, straight and gay. Doing experimental, doing more classical constructions, everybody's struggling to do it right and do it well with motivations that don't begin and end with money. That involved in it is a certain amount of courage and a certain amount of sacrifice because, I think, you're absolutely right. Family life is disrupted. You go away for long periods of shooting. Editing is such a huge, almost constant twenty-four-hour-a-day thing that even when you are out of the editing room, you're sometimes lost in thought about how you figure it out. It's extremely difficult, and yet, there is some just indescribable satisfaction from doing something free of the marketplace that touches, reaches, moves, changes people. And that's great, because the doing of it has done that to you.

And you just hope—we used to have arguments in film class at Hampshire College about whether films actually did anything or preached to the converted. My first film on the Brooklyn Bridge came out, and a year later, they broadcast it on public television at the time of its birthday and there on the front page of the *New York Times* is a couple and their kids from Idaho walking across the Brooklyn Bridge, and I turned to the story deep in the D section. And about twenty paragraphs in they said that they decided to take their vacation in New York because they'd seen a documentary on public television about the building of the Brooklyn Bridge. And the first thing they wanted to do when they got to New York was walk their kids across the Brooklyn Bridge and tell them the dramatic and heroic story of how it was built. And I clipped out the article, my first film, and sent it back to my film teacher and said, "You know what, it isn't just preaching to the converted." Which had been the cynical consensus of those classes, but in fact people do learn something. And after *Civil War*, battlefield attendance in every Civil War battlefield went up, and when I did a film on Thomas Jefferson suddenly they were flooded at Monticello, and, you know, that's a good thing. People read more and think more about the subjects that I've done, and I love that.

It's the best kind of connection to people because they've given, in the case of *Baseball*, eighteen-and-a-half hours of their lives to something I've done. *Jazz*, seventeen and a half; *Civil War*, eleven and a half; some of these shorter films, four hours over several nights, in some cases, and they're willing to talk about it or sit down and write me a letter. I get thousands of letters a year. I'm just stunned, and I write back to each one of them and say thank you—I have to.

Is there a film that you've done that is a favorite of yours?

I can't. I'm the father of two teenage daughters who are up and out of the house, and I think I'd be remiss if I said I loved one child more than the other, and I don't. Each film has meant something to me, so one film like the *Civil War* might get more attention and more awards and more whatever, but that doesn't mean that the energy and love I gave to the Shaker film is any less, and so I love it just as much. Just as a child who went on to become somebody famous and celebrated—a doctor or a lawyer—doesn't get more love than a child who has a more modest existence. They're still your own children and they represent the best I could put in at that time, and that's the other thing that I've been fortunate enough to do. I haven't had to abandon, and I haven't had to change, and I haven't had to alter. I've been able to say, when we've locked the picture and rung this beautiful little bell as each reel of film is locked in the editing room, that we've done our best.

For some people, filmmaking is a personal quest; for some, it's a mission to effect change, or an opportunity to challenge themselves, or an opportunity to push something in the form. What does filmmaking represent for you?

It represents all of those things. I don't know where that history interest came from, although my mother, who died when I was eleven years old—there was never a moment when she wasn't sick when I was growing up. I remember commenting about ten years ago to a friend that it seems that I'm still keeping my mother alive. He just looked at me and said, "What do you think you do for a living?" And I said, "Excuse me?" And he said, "You wake the dead." And I said, "What do you mean?" And he said, "You make Jackie Robinson and Abraham Lincoln come alive for everybody else. Who do you think you want to wake up?"

So that is at the heart of my exploration of history and even my interest in race, because my mother at her sickest occurred when the fire hoses and dogs were being set upon innocent citizens in Selma, Alabama. And I transferred a great deal of my understandable anxiety from the cancer that was killing my family to the cancer that was killing my country. And so, I took to heart at the deepest level of my being not just an abiding interest in American history but an ongoing question about race and racism and slavery and equality in our country that's informed almost every film that I've done. And it's born of intensely personal things that would qualify it as mission. At the same time, I'm a filmmaker; I'm not a historian. I'm exploring how to push and change and solve problems and arrive at solutions that work in a medium, in a corner of a form of my medium. That gives me tremendous satisfaction.

Everyone has the ability now to buy a camera and chronicle the experiences in their lives. Does the accessibility of technology have any bearing on how documentaries will be shaped and how they'll be pushed?

It does indeed, but we have to remember that with every positive thing—and this is just the way the universe works—there's unintended consequences and quite often negative things that come with it. We love the new technology and the accessibility to everybody, that democratization of the process. But at the same time, we see, particularly with regard to the Internet and video, the way in which the technological tail is now beginning to wag the dog. I think we've lost touch with story, with narrative, and I don't mean that in a feature-film way, but I mean, just our ability to follow stories. And we still have to realize that this is a process that involves discrimination, in the best sense of that word, that we need to be able to choose. It isn't enough to throw everything up on the screen or up on the Internet. The great danger of the Internet is that the flood of information doesn't in any way indicate its relative truth or fact, so lies go around the world three times, the old saying goes, before the truth gets started. And the Internet speeds up the truth in that. So I think that we can look with a great deal of excitement at the democratic possibilities that these new technologies permit us all.

But the same laws as old as Aristotle's *Poetics* still exert their force on material that works, on art that's created. And these are things that will both bedevil and delight filmmakers and then audiences, as people struggle to come to terms with these new technologies. And so it's really important to be bold and to investigate and to explore. But it's equally important to be rooted in the old, very human verities of how you organize, how you structure, how you eliminate, how you discriminate, how you choose, and how you actually create. Because the great danger is that in all of this new stuff we'll forget to actually exert the whole reason why we're playing with this stuff at all, which is to create and to have messages that are a synthesis of parts that have in their totality more than the sum of those parts.

What's next on your drawing board?

We are in the process now of really making two films and planning several others, or in the earlier stages. One film is a rather light, funny film that is the story of the first transcontinental car trip done on a bet by a thirty-one-year-old Vermont doctor who was told that no car would ever be able to cross the United States, as indeed many earlier attempts had failed miserably, barely getting out of the starting blocks. And this young guy bet fifty bucks in a men's club in San Francisco and set out a few days later with almost no publicity, no preparation, hired a mechanic and promised to do it in less than three months. And it is a funny story of a country on the cusp of the automobile age, and this poor, unwitting, indomitably optimistic soul is the vanguard. His name is Horatio Nelson Jackson, and we are going to tell the story of Horatio's drive.

In addition, we're making a film on the boxer Jack Johnson, which is a very complicated story of race and sport and America in the first two decades of the twentieth century. Jack Johnson is, of course, the superb boxer for whom white people felt compelled to invent the term Great White Hope, hoping some way to find someone who could possibly beat him. And it was only through subterfuge and defeat that he actually was [beaten]. It's an unbelievably great story.

We're also working on two rather expanded series. One on the National Parks to try to do biographies of land—not just travelogues or pretty pictures, but to understand the land in time and the unbelievably new, and, to us, now obvious, clichéd idea that land could be set aside for people, not just noblemen and kings—that it could be set aside for posterity—and how those parks were born and the struggles they face, not just environmentally, but sort of humanly and historically. And then we're working on trying to see if we can put together a very personal, intimate bottom-up story of World War II so that at the end people know what happened in the larger aerial sense, but only through the experiences of ordinary people in ordinary towns as they try to come to grips with the greatest human tragedy in all of history. And other biographies that we want to do on Martin Luther King and Elvis Presley.

How do you find the time?

I have the best job in the country. It's so exciting. I love it. I live in this little village where any kind of notoriety that I have plus fifty cents gets me a cup of coffee. So you can't take yourself too seriously. It's like having a big sore thumb. When you start feeling like you're somebody, you sort of look and the thing is throbbing and you go, oh, yeah, you're just the same. There is a thing out there called a Ken Burns film, but a Ken Burns film is really just acknowledging an orchestra of people. I'm the conductor. I can't do it without the people who make it. So when you see *Mark Twain*, it's not a Ken Burns film; it's a Dayton Duncan film and a Jeff Ward film and a Paul Barnes film, and when you see the Stanton/Anthony film, it's not a Ken Burns film; it's a Paul Barnes film, and a Sarah Hill film, who edited it so magnificently. It's a collaboration, and the people that we work with not only work so hard and patiently; they have the great forbearance to watch their baby go out

Celebrating locking the final reel of Mark Twain *at the editing studio in Walpole, New Hampshire. Ken Burns (center, seated) and Dayton Duncan (kneeling to his right). (Left to right behind them) Debra Keller, Craig Mellish, Robert Sargent Fay, Patty Lawlor, Erik W. Ewers, Meg Anne Schindler, Pam Tubridy Baucom, Mark Twain, Margaret Shepardson-Legere, Christine Rose Lyon, and Susanna Steisel. Photo credit: Robert Sargent Fay.*

and get the shorthand tag of a Ken Burns film. And the only thing I can do is try to honor their contributions. They don't get made without everybody working. From the newest intern to people I've worked with for twenty-five years: they're not there, I'm not there. And what you like about my films, you can attribute to them, and what you don't like, please blame me.

Chapter 6: Ross McElwee
Personal Journeyman

McElwee combines a unique verité style with musings from behind the camera to create films that communicate and engage viewers on many levels. His films are unique among the voices here in that he not only captures slices of life, but he includes his connectivity to them and their experiences with very compassionate and personal commentary. From his first film, *Charleen* (1978), which was awarded Best Feature Documentary of 1980 by the Boston Society of Film Critics, to *Sherman's March: A Meditation on the Possibility of Romantic Love in the South During an Era of Nuclear Weapons Proliferation* (1986), which was awarded 1986 Best Feature at Sundance and runner-up Best Feature Documentary by the National Board of Film Critics, to *Time Indefinite* (1993), which garnered the distinction of best from several festivals, to *Six O'Clock News* (1996), McElwee takes us on journeys across America and across generations to paint unforgettable portraits of family, friends, and people along the way.

How did you get into filmmaking?

I came somewhat late to the profession. I came to it as a student who was not a declared filmmaker. I was an undergraduate at Brown and was supposedly writing a thesis, but during my senior year I became very interested in what was going on at the Rhode Island School of Design (RISD), which is adjacent to the Brown campus. There I saw people my own age—eighteen, nineteen, twenty—making movies, and that was a very engaging idea to me. I'd never seen the process before, of editing and dealing with film stock, making decisions about sequencing of scenes and length and duration of shots and how the finished films worked. I couldn't take courses in filmmaking there because RISD students got priority. But I did take still photography and then watched over their shoulders as they edited the films and saw these films being made from start to finish.

And, at that point, I realized that on some level ordinary mortals could make movies, and that was a very exciting notion to me. I should also say that this was a long time ago. I graduated in 1971. And the notion of being a film director, especially a documentary filmmaker, was an obscure thing to aspire to at that time. Back then, there wasn't the plethora of film schools scattered around the country that we have now. It was a totally different environment. Especially for documentary filmmakers. So it was uncharted water. The whole notion of what an independent filmmaker was, in fact, entirely uncharted. The phrase had not even been invented at that point. But somehow, I had a notion that I might come back to some version of the filmmaking I had first seen at the Rhode Island School of Design, which excited me.

And, for the meantime, I was going to continue writing, I was going to travel, and I was going to do still photography. I supported myself in a variety of jobs. I came back to Charlotte, North Carolina, finally, when I had no money and ended up getting a job at a local television station, Channel 9, WSOC. The job I was able to get was as a summer vacation replacement for someone who operated a studio floor camera for the six o'clock news. It wasn't the most exciting work in the world—basically, wide shot, close shot, medium shot, and do what you're told by the director who talks to you through the little headset. But it was a start. And then there was the opportunity to do church broadcast, Presbyterian Church broadcast, on Sunday. They let me do the balcony camera, and that was very exciting for me. Again, it was kind of telephoto shots of the choir, occasional shot of the preacher if the other camera's angle was not interesting enough to the director, who was buried somewhere in the bowels of the church watching what we were feeding him on the little monitors down there. But that's literally how I got my start. You know, looking back on it, it was not the most exciting way to get started, but it was a start. And the other thing I've noticed is that no two filmmakers ever get started in exactly the same way. Everybody carves out their own series of apprenticeships and internships.

What happened after that . . . I got an opportunity to work as an assistant cameraman for a producer for *Bill Moyers' Journal*, which was a different kind of PBS series insofar as they did a lot of location shooting with Moyers, and traveled and investigated issues around the world. And it was very personal in that it was Moyers's take on things as opposed to, maybe, a more objective point of view. He's since gone on to establish himself as, I think, someone who's earned his subjectivity. It was interesting for me because I got to travel a lot and, also, I could observe firsthand the mechanics of 16mm documentary filmmaking, which I had not been able to do at the TV station. That was a great job for me. I loaded lots and lots of magazines.

Filmmaker Ross McElwee. Photo credit: Adrian McElwee.

At that point, I realized I could do one of two things. I could either see if I could worm my way into the PBS system and try to find some way to become part of a production crew, and learn more about making documentary films, as PBS defined the making of documentary films. Or I could try to strike out on my own. And I'd had some interesting examples of other ways to make films thrown at me when I'd been an undergraduate. I had seen Fred Wiseman's *Titticutt Follies* (1967), and the other film that stuck in my mind was Richard Leacock's *Primary* (1960). We didn't really have film courses back then. *Titticutt Follies* was shown in a psychology course and *Primary* was in a political-science course, oddly enough.

What stuck with me about the way both of those films were made was their rough-hewn quality, the ways in which they seemed to be willing, shot by shot, to take a kind of risk by intersecting the real world with the camera. Something interesting, albeit a little frightening in terms of its unpredictability, could come out of this approach to filmmaking—that they were out of the studio, that they weren't really doing interviews per se; they were just filming what they could capture as it was unfolding. And I had a sense that that was the kind of filmmaking that I was more interested in than the more polished work that ended up on PBS. Somehow, I found out that Richard Leacock was coming to MIT to head up a new department in documentary filmmaking, and I said, "This could be interesting." And so, I went to Cambridge and met Richard Leacock and [Ed] Pincus, who was actually the one starting the program and had gotten Leacock to come and to serve as the figurehead to launch it since Leacock was so well-known. So here was the man who made *Primary* and *Happy Mother's Day* and all of these classic cinema verité films, starting a film school. And I thought, well, "This sounds perfect for me at this point in my life." I guess I was twenty-six then and had been bumping around the world for a few years since graduating from college, and dived right back into it. Graduated eighteen months later, finished up a thesis film and shot a couple of other films just to get some things in the can before they booted me outta there, so I could edit them at some point. In fact, I lingered around MIT for at least another six months, maybe even a year, sometimes as a teaching assistant, so I could do rough edits on the films that I'd shot. But that really is how I got started.

The first film that I made, my thesis film, was *Charleen*, which was a one-hour portrait of my former teacher, Charleen Swansea from North

Ross's longtime friend and film subject, Charleen Swansea, from Time Indefinite. *Photo credit: Marilyn Levine.*

Carolina. At MIT I'd been able to finish shooting and editing it, so it was picture-locked and sound-mixed, but I didn't have the money to print it. I received a Massachusetts Artist Foundation grant, $3,500 to finish the film. This was a real windfall, an amazing gift at that particular point in my career. And that enabled me to have 16mm copies of the print of my first film, and from there I could at least send it around. I made some copies of it onto video and began to try to propose other films that I might make.

How do you characterize yourself in terms of style as a filmmaker? Or do you characterize yourself in a particular way?

We've all been struggling for words and phrases for the odd approach to documentary filmmaking in which the filmmaker is not seeking to convey objective fact. Your objective is not to convey knowledge, it's not to proselytize, necessarily; that's my point of view—that you're after something different. And the closest phrase I've been able to come up with is, it's a kind of nonfiction essay filmmaking. It's very subjective. It owes something to cinema verité. But then I do have conversations with people from behind the camera, and I employ a highly subjective voice-over narration which, of course, cinema verité eschews. So I've just taken different things that have seemed to work for me and blended them into a style which also includes a kind of performance that sometimes I do on camera, where I talk to the camera at points that seem critical during the journey that the filmmaker's on. So it's a little bit of performance art, it's a little bit of classical cinema verité, it's a little bit of talk show, you know, where you're talking to people you meet and try to learn about their lives—it's all of these things.

In *Charleen,* were you a character?

I wasn't, but you hear my voice from behind the camera, and I state in a title card at the very beginning that Charleen had been my high-school teacher and has since become a friend. So I think the viewer clearly senses that there's a connection between the two of us. In fact, that connection becomes very important as the film goes along. It starts off being a portrait of a very dynamic and interesting and somewhat controversial high-school teacher in Charlotte and really shifts into a much deeper portrait of Charleen's personal life—her breakup with her boyfriend, the difficulties she's had raising her kids, and the problems she faced being a really individualistic, iconoclastic, highly idiosyncratic woman in a very conservative southern town. That's what this film ends up becoming about. Teaching kind of gets left on the margins even though it's a very important part of her life. I don't think that that film could have been made by someone who Charleen didn't know very well because they never would have gotten in with her.

So from the very beginning you have been a player in your films in some sense?

Well, I wasn't really a player in *Charleen*. But you did hear my voice talking to her, and it was clear that she and I had a connection, so in that sense, yes, I was a player, but the film was in no way autobiographical. And there was a film called *Space Coast*, which I made with another person, Michel Negroponte. It was a portrait of three families who lived in Cape Canaveral. And it was not autobiographical, although it's clear that we've established a strong rapport with our subjects and they do address us directly from behind the camera. So I guess you would say I wasn't a player there. But I definitely am not invisible behind the camera. I think what I was doing with both of these films was experimenting with what I liked and what I didn't like about classical cinema verité.

Your speaking from behind the camera and being in front of the camera has become a device that moves your films along. This is part of your style. Do you think you'll ever stray from this style?

I've done short pieces for television, the local PBS outlet, WGBH, here in Boston, which are not of that style, but I can't really make more than one film at a time. I think I'm simpleminded in that way. I have no idea if I'll ever diverge from the style that I've found is comfortable for me to embrace. It's possible that someday I could try a fiction film, but on the other hand when I see people struggling mightily to get scripts produced—thousands and thousands of people have scripts. And all I hear about is people waiting five, seven, ten years to get the funding for these things. I do sometimes become impatient with the style of filmmaking that I've evolved for myself—it is clunky. I'm doing everything myself—I'm shooting, I'm recording the sound, I'm doing the editing. I do have an assistant editor sometimes. But basically the onus is on me to edit these things. I do the producing of them. I basically ended up often doing a lot of the publicity afterwards. And now that I have a family and two kids, this has become untenable, so I do often think that something has to change, and maybe it's the style of filmmaking. Also, I just can't be on the road for a month at a time as I used to be able to before I had children.

So something's dictating a change of some kind here, but would I jettison the whole style? I don't think so, and I think the reason is, it still enables me to make films fairly simply that end up actually getting out into the world for relatively small amounts of money. And there's a great pleasure in actually finishing something. You know, sometimes it takes too many years to finish them, but at least they get finished eventually and they get out there on some level and they're actual films, rather than dreams. If I abandon my current approach, I've got to up the production ante and get a big crew and go to fiction and hire actors and actresses. Who do I think I am to be making a shift in career like this, and also, where's the money coming from? So I think not. I think I'll probably just keep doing what I'm doing.

At least now you have complete creative control.

For better or for worse. There's definitely a trade-off all the way down the line; when you have less control and more people working, you can finish films faster. You make more money. But I'm mostly comfortable with what I've set up for myself in this approach to making films. It's altering from year to year—a little bit here, a little bit there, but, basically, I'll keep doing it this way. It's certainly not the style for everybody, it couldn't possibly be—my way of filmmaking would drive most filmmakers insane.

It is not for the faint of heart. No one has said being a documentary filmmaker is a piece of cake. Do you think there's a certain type of person better suited for documentary filmmaking?

In some ways you need to be a misfit to make documentaries. I hesitate to make statements about what I think you might need to have to make documentaries. First of all, what is a documentary these days? We don't even know. Basic curiosity is an extremely important factor in making documentary films. And the willingness to be able to change your preconceptions about things and allow things that you encounter as you're filming to alter the direction of the film—to me, that's very important. Other documentary filmmakers will go and shoot films that are basically prescripted. They've sent out a production assistant who's done the preinterviews and locations. I'm sure that's how Ken Burns does them, and he does them in a very different way, and they're extremely polished, and they're meticulous. So I just can't possibly say what the qualities are that you need to make documentary films, because the range of what documentary films are is so broad.

Your films prompt self-inquiry. Is that something you set out to do in your filmmaking? Is it a personal quest that you're on when you're making a documentary? I'm curious about the genesis of your film ideas.

Well, it can sometimes be a very simple idea. With *Time Indefinite*, I just assumed I would be making a lighthearted film about getting married in the nineties from my own particular, fairly committed bachelor's point of view. And it would basically be advice given to me by relatives and friends, and people willing to share their experiences about weddings and marriage. And the preparations for the marriage my wife and I would be making, and then the wedding itself would be the conclusion of the film. And maybe it might include the honeymoon; maybe not, I didn't know. That was the general idea.

Of course, what happens in *Time Indefinite* is, my father dies suddenly and my wife has a miscarriage, which was totally unexpected. My father's death was totally unexpected because he had never had any health problems. And my grandmother died suddenly. So I had this triad of deaths occur in a very short period of time and I passed into a very dark mood,

A moment in the generational standoff between Ross and his father, from Time Indefinite.

and that mood leads me on a journey. I realized I couldn't make a light-hearted film about marriage. Somehow, I needed to deal with these events. I went back down to North Carolina, and I filmed people and events and places that somehow obliquely dealt with my father's absence, my grandmother's absence, and the fact that we'd lost our first child. And I came back with the footage I had and then realized, well, maybe it's not two separate films, maybe it's one film and it's gotta work. It took me another four years to finish it.

You asked me what my mission was. My mission was to make a fairly entertaining lighthearted sequel to *Sherman's March*. While *Sherman's March* had some serious themes, overall, it was a pretty lighthearted film, and that's what I think people really liked about it. I thought this would be the sequel to *Sherman's March*. But it became something altogether different. I guess my mission is to make a film that is interesting to me, but also, it has to be interesting to at least some other people.

When you're shooting, do you have a pretty good idea of how your film is evolving? Or does your film evolve in the editing room?

As I'm filming, as I'm on the road, as I'm shooting, I know after a certain point what I probably need to get to make the film work. But I think the real work occurs back in the editing room in terms of really knowing what the film is about and having that dialogue that you have with your footage, which tells you what the shot is saying, what the scene is saying. And then you start to discover what the structure of the entire film is. That takes me a very long time to figure out and it's more in the editing room that I discover the structures that I may have been only partially aware of when I was out on the road.

Do you have a certain ratio you tend to shoot?

No.

How many hours do you think you shot for *Time Indefinite*?

Time Indefinite had a very low shooting ratio and I think the reason for that was the wedding was a specific event that didn't offer up tangential stories or themes, really. I mean, we were in power drive toward the wedding day. When I was shooting the wedding preparations, I didn't have time to run off and film tangential stories that might or might not relate to this particular film. And then after my father died, I think I knew even more specifically what I needed, what I wanted to film in order to be able to deal with his death in the movie, and that was interactions with my siblings. And then to film some meaningful things that were occurring around the house. And, finally, a visit to my friend Charleen, who had also lost her husband that same year, so that was all pretty straightforward. I think my shooting ratio for *Time Indefinite* was 7:1, maybe 8:1. That's quite low for 16mm. I know for *Sherman's March* it was higher. It was, like, 16 or 17:1. I can't remember exactly, but that film had lots of tributaries, thematic tributaries that went off on little mini-film jaunts. Many of those didn't end up in the movie. *Six O'Clock News*, like I said, had all kinds of stories that I followed and some of them, tangential, ended up in the film and some did not—that also raised the shooting ratio quite a bit. I probably shot with *Six O'Clock News* maybe 20:1. Twenty to one is probably the highest ratio I've ever shot.

How do you know when you've got the end of your picture? Do you know when you're shooting? Do you have an epiphany when you know?

It varies from film to film. With *Sherman's March*, I wasn't very sure because I was new at this game of first-person autobiography-documentary-essay filmmaking. It took me a long time to figure out whether I had a movie or not, so that's a metamorphosis process. *Time Indefinite*, I knew what I needed. And *Six O'Clock News* was a little more wide open, but at a certain point in my shooting I knew I had what I needed there. *Charleen*, my first film, I definitely knew when I had the conclusion to the film because of the climactic final scene, which was this remarkable event in Charleen's life that provided a very strong conclusion to the movie, which nobody had seen coming. So there are moments when you know and moments when it's less clear.

How long do you spend in the editing process?

It varies from film to film. It takes me a long time to finish a movie, simply because I also do other things. I think it's measured more in years than in months, for sure. Sometimes I teach. All the time now, I'm giving a lot of time to the family. I'd say I'm home 30 percent of the time. I share time so my wife has time to do her writing and the things that she needs to do, and that's cut quite a bit into my editing time. That's a pleasurable thing to do, to spend time with my children, so it's not as if that's a burden, but it has an impact on my ability to work.

I think the editing process, for me, if I could sustain it and work straight through, in terms of forty-hour weeks, I'd probably finish a film in eight months. And you might say, why? It's only a ninety-minute film or an hour film. It shouldn't take that long, but so often, you have to find the film in the footage, and I think that's often what I'm doing. It takes a lot to find it.

How did your narration evolve? It feels like it's effortless.

I have a horrible time with narration, I don't know why. I look at the transcripts of my narration, ten pages, it's simple prose . . . there's nothing complicated about the syntax. It's intentionally unpoetical. Why is it so complicated or difficult for me to write? I can't explain it. First I write a draft of the narration. Then I make a scratch recording of the narration on a little handheld analog tape deck. Next I play the tape back while watching the film, to get an approximate notion of how the narration works with the film. Often what seemed good on paper does not work at all with the footage. So I have to go back and rewrite and rerecord. I go through dozens of generations of the narration using this process. Finally, when I am pleased, I record another test narration with a digital recorder, and then download the sound onto my hard drive so that I can place the narration precisely, in a way I could not when I was using the analog tape deck. Again, invariably, I find that certain portions of the narration do not work when I try to lay them in precisely. When I finally have a version that seems to work for me, I then have a test screening for a few friends or perhaps a small audience, and again, invariably, I discover things about the narration—not to mention the film as a whole— that are not working. So I go back to my laptop and start rewriting. This process goes on for months. It's a very mysterious process for me. I can't explain why it takes so long, but it takes me multiple generations, versions before I can get something that seems to work for me. I find it extremely hard. And I tried to give it the feeling of casualness or spontaneity, but the actual process of achieving it is quite the opposite.

Is there a part of the process that's more enjoyable for you than others?

Well, I get enjoyment from the different aspects of filmmaking, but I love shooting the most. And there are times when I can gain my momentum and really see progress that I'm making in editing a piece that's very, very enjoyable to me. But it's becoming increasingly difficult for me to have that experience just because of the rest of my life now. Shooting continues to be the thing that I enjoy doing the most.

Do you actually cut film or do you edit on nonlinear systems?

I cut film on all my documentaries except for the one I'm working on now. Now I'm doing nonlinear editing. But I'm still shooting in film. I processed the negative, made dailies on Beta tapes, and downloaded the Betas onto my hard drives. I edit on a system called Media 100.

How do you like nonlinear?

It's a good experience.

Do you do test screenings?

Yes. They're very valuable for me. I know filmmakers who don't do them, and I don't see how they can finish the films without doing them. I have to have them. In fact, I enjoy them a lot. I have a group of filmmaker friends and colleagues here in Cambridge and the Boston area that I rely on for advice and criticism, and I always show my films five or six times to this group of people to get advice.

There are different kinds of test screenings, too. There's when you do it for a small audience just to understand what's working and what's not. Often, in those situations, it's what you're sensing sitting in the back rows, as opposed to what anybody says specifically about how the film is working, that's valuable. I also show my work in progress to people one at a time, in the editing room. That's also very valuable because you can be much more precise about what's working and what's not. But I use both of those forms of audience screenings as often as I need until I get to the point where I feel satisfied with what I have.

Do you do any preproduction with subjects before you get them on camera?

Well, I almost never film without asking permission—at least in a cursory way. I think it depends on the person; some people are so self-confident and secure that nothing fazes them. But I always prefer to utter the simple phrase, "Do you mind if I do a little filming here?" if, in fact, I've walked into a situation where I don't know anybody and nobody knows me and something interesting is happening. I never do formal preproduction where I fly down and meet somebody and prep them on what I'll be filming and then come back a week later with all the equipment and do it—it's just not how I make films.

Basically, I think the most important thing to have is a sense of humor, a casualness about your approach; you get people to relax. It helps that I'm doing everything myself. I don't have a large crew of people pointing things at the person being filmed. It lowers the profile a bit that there's just one guy with a camera and microphone. And so, the issue of invasion of privacy becomes a little less prevalent, I think.

On the other hand, I think things have changed quite a bit with the plethora of reality programming shows on television and so forth, that people are now aware that almost anything that can be captured by camera might end up on TV. So they're a little more careful, probably. Sad sometimes, that people want to know what it's for. It used to be that nobody asked those kinds of questions. They just got into the gestalt, into this notion of being in a movie and, "Hey, this'll be fun."

There are areas of the country that are more open to allowing you to film at will—the South; the Midwest; to some degree, the West Coast. I find people are a little more restrained in the Northeast about the presence of cameras, as, perhaps, they should be. But the other thing I should say is that, actually, I don't end up filming strangers all that much. My films tend to be about my family and my friends, and people who know them, and so, in that sense, I have an entrée.

How do you feel about paying people?

It's almost never an issue. Once I gave some production money to a guy I'd filmed who'd been an earthquake victim. He didn't ask for it, but I could see that he was a person who needed money—he was quite poor and trying to support a family. He'd been crippled by an accident that occurred as a result of an earthquake. He was from another country and if ever someone needed money, it was this guy.

Are there any ethical lines that you will not cross?

I guess you could argue that I should not have given any money to the Salvadorian earthquake victim, that it was improper journalism. But, then, I do not think of myself as a journalist. And besides, I didn't give him money until I was partway into the filming, when it really occurred to me it would be tremendously appreciated by him and his family. I have absolutely no regret about having done it and would do it again. So that was my decision on that issue.

In *Six O'Clock News*, I met a lot of people who'd had terrible disasters befall them, and filmed their lives, and felt that if I had had to track them down, if I had been the first person with a camera to reach them, that this would be a film I could not make. Not so much from an ethical point of view: I can't do that kind of filmmaking where I barge in on someone who's just had a catastrophe and say, "Tell me about how you're feeling." But what I did was let the television crews do the dirty work for me—rather cowardly of me, perhaps. In a sense, they preselected people who were willing to go on camera and talk about catastrophic events that had occurred to them. And I collected vignettes of those people and selected people I wanted to contact to do follow-ups, and the very fact that they had already appeared on camera told me they probably would be open to letting me film them in more depth. Ethically, I don't think I could do what many television stations have to do, which is rush to the scene of the disaster and, somehow, get people's responses on the spot and follow up on it. But, perhaps, what I was doing wasn't really all that different.

Also, in general, I try as best I can not to present people as being ridiculous, but I'm sure sometimes I film people who say and do things that they may not be aware of as seeming silly. I suppose you could criticize that from an ethical point of view. So there are real examples of the nonstop dialogue that most documentary filmmakers have as to whether or not they're trespassing into unethical territory where you should not be.

You still shoot in 16mm, correct?

Yes, super-16.

Do you ever think about moving to digital video?

Yes, how can you not these days? Everybody's doing it. I think about it, and I may have to next time. It all depends upon whether someone's willing to once again provide the funding to shoot 16mm film. I think I'll keep shooting film as long as I can raise the money to shoot film.

Why is that?

Film has a different quality to it. It's getting harder and harder to justify as the transfers from video to film get better and better, but I still believe that projected 16mm film provides an image that projected transferred video cannot match. And the quality of that image is still very important to me in terms of resolution and luminosity, and the ability to hold blacks and the edging capabilities, the ability to convey motion from left to right or right to left without any kind of artifact.

Where does your funding come from these days?

Grants and combinations of funding from Channel 4 in London and WGBH here in Boston and sometimes ZDF in Germany and whatever else I can scrape up.

Is funding relatively easy for you to procure at this point in your career? How do you go about getting funding?

Well, I've had a wonderful working relationship with Channel 4 and WGBH, and it has often been fairly simple, just a matter of presenting an idea and getting enough money to get it started. And then being willing to show them a cut somewhere, midway through the process of editing or assembling the film, their approving it, then giving me a second installment of the funding. And then after the fine cut, I get a third installment to finish the film. So that process has been in place, but then the other side of it is, of course, that the bureaucracy of these huge institutions, like Channel 4 and WGBH, are constantly changing. And who knows if in the future these people will be there who have been interested in my work? And there's just no guarantee, no guarantees at all. And grants are grants. Most of the ones I've gotten, they just leave you alone until you finish it and they're really happy if you finish it, first of all, and secondly, if you put their name in the tail credits.

How would you characterize your relationship with filmmaking?

Love, hate, love. It's about a two-to-one ratio and it's in that specific order. I love it when I'm just beginning to film. I usually hate it when I'm midway through the editing. And I love it when it's done.

You mentioned *Charleen* as being your first film and you speak about it as though you like your first film. Is that correct?

Well, it's not a good film in many ways. It's shot rather poorly, although the shooting improves as it goes on. The editing is kind of atrocious in the beginning because I didn't know what the hell I was doing, but it gets better as it goes along. One thing it had, thanks to Charleen, is heart and soul, and I think that's what people sensed as they saw it—that it was remarkably honest. She's a remarkably interesting woman. It was a very fresh portrait of someone who was very, very willing to open up in front of the camera. And there was more than just talk going on. There was a lot of activity that was very filmable with her kids and the schoolkids she was teaching. So I think, as crudely fashioned as it was, people are willing to overlook the technical problems of a filmmaker learning how to make films and saw through to Charleen's wonderful presence in the movie. So, yes, I would say I like the movie, almost despite the movie.

Do you still have anxiety about the same things in the process? How has making films changed for you over the years?

Maybe they're slightly easier to fund, but making them is no easier. Each one is really, really hard. I always start off thinking that this one's going to be easier. It's more straightforward than the others. It's about something I'm really interested in. I don't have to deal with sad things in this one. And this one's going to be, not a piece of cake, but like sitting down to a nice dinner, with many courses—the courses will take me a while to get through, but I'll finish the meal, and I'll finish it in a reasonable time, and I won't be sleeping in the restaurant for the next three years.

It's never easy. It just always, for me, seems to take way too long, cost way too much and drive me insane as I'm working on it. And then again, as I said, towards the end of it I feel, especially when I see it projected and there's an audience and the audience is somewhat appreciative given the results, then I just fall in love all over again with the whole process of making movies.

Chapter 7: Liz Garbus
Confronting Humanity

A young eye in documentary filmmaking, Liz Garbus comes to the camera with a well-honed sense of social justice. And her films reflect that passion, focusing on judicial reform and youth issues. One of her first films, *The Farm* (1998), which she codirected with Jonathan Stack, won two Emmy Awards and captured the Grand Jury Prize at the Sundance Film Festival. Garbus's other films range from *Boys Village*, a look at four young men in the juvenile justice system, to *The Execution of Wanda Jean* (2001), a look at the last days on death row of the first woman to be executed in Oklahoma's modern history, to *Waxter Girls*, which was accepted at Sundance 2002.

How did you get involved in documentary filmmaking?

I started making documentaries in college. I don't really think I knew then that I wanted to be a documentary filmmaker, but I knew it was something I really enjoyed. Actually, that's not true. I made my first documentary when I was a senior in high school. I made a documentary of my last week as a senior. I took around a video camera, and I interviewed everybody. It was actually very funny because David Grubin, a well-respected PBS-type filmmaker—his daughter was a very good friend of mine, and she was in my documentary. So we had a little screening of it. I did a little in-camera edit, the most basic thing. And he lauded me with praise and said, "This is a great documentary. You have a future here." Which was very funny. Which I didn't remember until much later when I met David in a more professional context. And then he said, "I told you you were going to be a documentary filmmaker." That was my first verité documentary.

And then I made a documentary when I was in college, or I made a few. And then I started working with another documentary filmmaker here in New York, Jonathan Stack, who I ended up making three films with, including *The Farm*. He was very open to different ideas. I started working there as an assistant but ultimately ended up developing this professional relationship with Wilbert Rideau, an inmate in Louisiana, a relationship which ultimately led to the film *The Farm*. And so I was his underling, but I brought that into our relationship, and that's how I ended up codirecting that film.

Did you go to school for filmmaking?

No. I went to Brown University undergraduate, and there were a lot of video-production classes, which I took, but I never went to film school.

How do you think that's affected you as a filmmaker?

In the absence of having gone to film school it's hard to say how my filmmaking would be different. A lot of the documentary filmmakers I know didn't go to film school. Well, actually, that's not true. I know a few who did. I'm not overly concerned with formalistic methods. That may have to do with the fact that I wasn't ever taught them in any kind of formal way. I think my filmmaking has been much more influenced by stories themselves. And I feel like it's something I came to very organically, rather than with a lot of intellectual ideas about what cinema verité is or should be. And I think, therefore, the films that I make take part of a cinema verité style but they're certainly not strictly conforming to that. I'm happy to use what I feel works given the demands of the story and the characters. That's always

Liz Garbus. Photo courtesy Moxie Firecracker.

been paramount to me—the story and character. Subject matter is paramount to the formalistic concerns.

How do you choose your subjects?

For me, there's been an evolution from one film to another. And often, the films that are near and dear to me evolve from the last one. For instance, the first film that I directed was called *Primal Judgment*. I was talking to Wilbert Rideau, this inmate in Angola, on the phone. I wanted to make the film with Wilbert, which was ultimately *The Farm*, but I thought it was really more about Wilbert at that time. We were talking about it, but he said, "Okay, look, that can come later, but right now there is this story about a man who is gonna be executed in about three months. You should come here and make this because I have some serious doubts about the fairness of the trial. I think this is an important story."

We went down there with a DV camera and started making this film and ultimately Discovery Channel ended up giving us the money for it. Making that film, which was really this one man's story, Antonio James, I started to get exposed to this world of Angola. And I knew that with Wilbert's insight into this world and to all the different guys I was meeting, the inmates, the wardens, the different folks there, that there was this other film, and that ultimately led to *The Farm*. He'd been down there already a year when we started making this film. So the knowledge of the place was relatively rich and the relationships were very secure, which, I think, allowed *The Farm* to be a very special film.

And then from *The Farm*—so many of the men I met there had been in the juvenile system—I just felt this desire to go back to the juvenile system and find out what happened. Because so many of these people who had ended up committing murders were in the system as juveniles and had just been bounced around from place to place to place and had never gotten therapy and never gotten counseling. They had always just been returned to the place they just left. There was never any aftercare. And that led to this film called *Juvies* where I spent time with boys going through the juvenile justice system. The boys going through the juvenile justice system led to . . . I met a couple of girls who were in this very small program called the Secure Program in the state of Maryland. It housed about fifteen girls who committed the most violent crimes among the Maryland juvenile justice population. And I got to know some of these girls and was just struck by their character. In a similar way that *Final Judgment* led to *The Farm*, I got very comfortable in the place and got to know people. The contacts became very solid, and I felt that there was another film to be made, and that is a film I'm currently editing called *Waxter Girls*. So, in many ways, these films have led from one to the other.

And now I'm pitching a film about foster care. I'm developing it—what I see in the juvenile system is, these kids get bounced around from different foster homes. These kids who were doing nothing wrong end up going from foster home to foster home and end up committing crimes, probably out of a cry for attention. And now I want to go back there. I guess soon I'll be in the neonatal ward because I keep going back. So I'm not sure where that'll lead me.

You're getting to be an expert in this kind of field.

Expert, well, I have a lot of experience, and I have a lot of experiential knowledge.

Are those issues the things that attract you the most, or have they just been easy to go from one to the next?

I'm attracted to the issues. Growing up, my father was a lawyer; he is still a lawyer. Justice. The courts. He did a lot of civil rights cases early. He was the associate director of the ACLU in the late sixties, early seventies, so there was always talk in my home about issues around justice, around fairness, about disproportionate incarceration of African-Americans. He was involved in a police brutality case in the South. So it was always something that made me feel very incensed, very passionate, and that's certainly something that I get from him. I think that the issues have really driven it, which is not to say that I'm exclusively interested in those issues. I think I'm attracted to stories of people whose lives are in transition or in some kind of crisis and working toward resolution. And I find an awful lot of those within the criminal justice system.

Do you have a particular style or mission in filmmaking? Is documentary filmmaking, for you, a tool to effect change?

As a director, do I have a style? If [I do, it's] a combination of verité scenes with interviews. So it's not a purist Fred Wiseman approach. I use music, I use montages, I use interviews. But I generally find the most exciting filmmaking, the strongest scene, usually is a verité scene, and that other stuff works around to support it, to help out the narrative, to help the storytelling. Verité filmmaking is ultimately the centerpiece, the scenes that people walk away remembering. And the rest of it serves to construct the narrative; the building blocks are the spine of the narrative through which the verité films are the accompanying sort of centerpiece.

I also have a mission. I have a company and I executive-produce a bunch of projects, which are on all different topics. *Mission* is, maybe, a strong word, but I think that if I can expose people to the humanity of segments of the population that they're never exposed to, then I've done a really good job. Particularly in today's climate. There's so much passion for the death penalty. There's so much passion to try juveniles as adults. This is a monster, this twelve year old who killed another eleven year old—this is somebody who should get locked away for life. If I can put a face on that person, and show what that person went through, and show that this person can change—because ultimately that's what a lot of my films are about— people are not equal to their worst actions. There's going to be the occasional sociopath who probably cannot be rehabilitated and can never live in society safely, but that's really the minority in my experience traveling around jails and traveling around juvenile detention centers. Most people can change; there is hope for people, and there is redemption. And there should be forgiveness in society. I think that in all of my films it's part of my mission to work towards that—fostering a sense of forgiveness, and that people can change, and that healing can happen for both victims and folks who committed crimes.

You spend a lot of time in grim situations. Is documentary filmmaking a growth process for you through your films? Is there a personal journey through your films?

I think that's something I need to work on—my own self-discovery. I'm so immersed in my stories, I should probably do more self-examination to figure out how I'm changed by them. I know that through my filmmaking, as a person, the ability to empathize has developed and deepened. In my filmmaking, also, I approached, for instance, *The Farm* from the perspective of being around inmates. And then in a recent film I just finished for HBO about a woman who was executed in Oklahoma in January [*The Execution of Wanda Jean*], I spent a lot of time with the victims, and I learned an enormous amount about them. And I was totally bowled over by them at the end of the day and their ability to grow and forgive, even given what this person had done to their lives. I think I do grow, and I think each film is a process of discovery, and each character I meet becomes a little bit a part of me. With this film I'm making about these girls in Maryland, the line between me and them, in terms of whatever kind of journalistic separation I'm supposed to have, is. . . . Sometimes I can maintain that, but on this film these kids are . . . I got a call two weeks ago from a girl who is asking to come and stay with me in New York because things have gotten too hot for her in Baltimore. And that I'm still struggling with . . . what to do about that. It becomes so much a part of your life. I think I've been doing so much. It's been five years since I've been directing. I probably need to step back and examine this stuff in terms of my own self. I think that's what I do least, and that's why I think I should go to a shrink. But right now, it's just working on the film.

As a documentary filmmaker, you are chronicling their lives, versus you are a part of their lives. Is there a boundary that you try to maintain between the two, an ethical line that you don't want to cross?

In certain ways, it's a case-by-case decision. I think that any documentary filmmaker who tells you that there's a hard and fast line where you have to keep a distance, is probably not making the same kind of film that I am. There's a financial thing. If you're working with people who are poor, I think that there has to be a line in terms of money. I will take my subject out to eat. I will buy my subject a birthday present. If somebody comes and tries to hit me up for $500 because they can't pay their rent, there's a line you have to draw there because the relationship can become very distorted by money. And that's very tough, because you have money and they have none in many situations. And if you can give them $50 and their electricity isn't turned off, that's an extremely tempting thing to do, to help somebody you care about. But I do find that that's a line you have to hold firm with. I mean, with kids, I find if you work it out at the beginning of the process, you can give them sort of an honorarium—"Okay, you're gonna spend ten days with me and we'll give you $50 a day, and at the end of this thing you'll get $500 and that's your honorarium." And if you work that out from the beginning and it's a no-questions-asked thing, that's it. When I worked with teenagers, that's something I felt okay about.

But then in terms of the emotional, it becomes much more complicated. There is this young girl who lives in Baltimore who's in *Waxter Girls;* her name is Megan, and she was locked up. Now she's back on the street and she's trying so hard to do good. Her mother is a junkie and lives in her neighborhood. She basically has been in and out of foster homes and she has been sleeping on friends' couches. And given her horizon, the fact that she's staying off drugs and she's going to school is just extraordinary. She called and wanted to come up because she felt like things were getting very hot. Her mother was a mess. She was getting sicker and sicker every day. The pressure of Megan seeing her mother all the time was becoming extraordinary. Some people Megan had some former criminal activity with, friends, had gotten out of jail. Things were getting very stressful for her and she wanted to come up, and she called saying she wanted to come and stay with me for a couple of weeks. And I really don't know what to do about that. Maybe she'll decide she doesn't want to and I'll be off the hook. Or maybe I'll have to make a decision. Maybe I'll say she can come up for one day and supervise her, but that's the kind of thing that's very, very, very tough.

You really become close with people. I stay in contact with people from my first film, and people call and they want to talk. I guess it's not that tough for me because I've never made a film in which anybody's looked bad. It's not the kind of film I make. So there hasn't been a stress with, "What do I put in the film?" versus "What have I told them I'm gonna do?"

Liz and Megan during the filming of Waxter Girls. *Photo courtesy Moxie Firecracker.*

So generally all of those relationships stay very comfortable. But there is a tough line on this film I was making that I just turned in to HBO. I was dealing with both families—the victim's family and the perpetrator's family, and a lot of questions were asked. A lot of people became very dependent on me, and it's tough.

Giving money makes you a part of the story, does it not?

I think we affect the lives of our characters in our films no matter what we do—if we take them out to lunch, or if we pay their rent. I will draw the line at paying somebody's rent because it affects the purity of the story, in which they would have been out on the street, versus they would have been in this house, which is a huge difference. It also affects your relationship. There's a power dynamic. Is this person in the film because they think they can get money from you? Is this person going to continue to hit you up for money? And then if you ever draw the line, reject you? It will distort the filmmaking relationship, and it will distort the subject matter that you present to the world at large, and, therefore, taint the purity of the story.

But at the same time, us being there, us following them around with the camera always affects their story. I followed these girls who are in these detention centers. Did they get out of detention sooner because we were there? Very possibly. Did they get more aftercare attention because we were there and the Maryland department was concerned about their image? Very possibly. Did Megan's mother come back in her life because she felt like getting herself on camera being a good mother? Very possibly. So it goes beyond "are they on the street" or "are they on the run." People behave differently.

What I love . . . when I feel that I've achieved a really great relationship, and I'm looking at my dailies upstairs, is when people just totally ignore me and I can be rolling the camera and they have their back to the camera and they just don't even care. That happens after a year of filming in a place. But before that point, your camera is completely a character in the show. I think that, so long as you don't pretend otherwise, that's part of the territory.

And also, in the editing process, you hone an extremely complex reality into a story that you can follow with dramatic elements—into a three-act structure. That affects the purity—reality is extremely complex. You tell a story with a beginning, middle, and end. It's probably different from the way the person experienced their own personal arc during that period. We were in the editing room yesterday and there are these two girls who are the main characters in this film *Waxter Girls.* And Shanae is doing really, really well, and there's this scene where she's going to a party. And she's got this award and she's on the honor roll. And then there's Megan, who's sitting on a stoop, and there's nothing going on, and people are just hanging on the corner. This juxtaposition between those two scenes—you know, maybe Megan didn't feel lonely or sad or like she wasn't going anywhere that day, but when you cut from one scene to another it's certainly going to read that way to the viewer. So that is part of what we do. I think that as long as you're true to your characters and as long as you don't deceive them about what you're doing and you don't deceive yourself about who they are, and you try to present a story—you have to really trust yourself and trust what kind of story you're trying to tell. And maybe there's a certain arrogance which goes with that, but so far so good in terms of what folks have seen that I've done with them in films and how they felt about it.

How do you gain the trust of the people you shoot?

You definitely spend a lot of time with them before the camera is on. I do, anyway. I guess the general rule is that I spend many days hanging around with people before a camera is introduced, getting them comfort-

Shanae (left) and Liz during the filming of Waxter Girls. *Photo courtesy Moxie Firecracker.*

able with it. Oftentimes, they'll watch a film that I've made so they understand. Because I often find people don't really have any sense of what they could be getting themselves into—how much time I would want to spend with them—what it means. It's not just an interview—that I'm sitting down with them, that I'm actually there while they're eating dinner. So they'll watch a film with me and they'll be able to ask questions. There's definitely a workshopping, development period. People are really apprised of what's gonna go on. And then, when I call them and say, "I'd like to ride with you on your way to the doctor's," there's no, "Why do you want to do that?" I think that's one of the most important times.

And because I'm white and I'm also dealing with people in African-American communities, because I'm not locked up and I'm dealing with people who are locked up, there's always going to be a boundary and a divide. There's a leap of faith that folks will decide to take or they won't decide to take. In this film for HBO about this woman who was executed, her family . . . it took them a really long time to trust me. And people would tell them rumors that I was actually making a feature film and I was involved with Hollywood and this was just a pretense and I was writing a screenplay. I would walk into the house and people would be furious at me. And I would just have to sit down and say, "That is not true. You've seen the kind of films that I've made." It was such a high-stress point in their lives—their daughter was being executed—and I think that sometimes their anger or confusion was taken out on me. It was taken out on their lawyer. I often tell people if they don't want me around and they want to kick me out, or they don't want something on camera, I will respect that and I will listen to them. If people tell me to turn the camera off, I will. If you want to come back, you've got to do that.

In filming documentaries, you are often on the road or in the field for months, you have doors shut in your face, and so on. How do you cope with the frustrations and challenges of documentary filmmaking?

Premature gray hairs. I get about four per film.

What are the characteristics that you think you need to have to be a good, tenacious documentary filmmaker?

You have to have an immense belief in yourself. When people's lives are in crisis and you're in there and you want them to open up their homes to you, you're asking an enormous amount. You really have to believe in the integrity of your mission, believe that you're doing this for something bigger than just the fact that you're inconveniencing these people, and you have to hopefully have them believe that with you. And then, you have to believe enough in yourself and that you're going to do the right thing with this material and never compromise your goals no matter what somebody from the TV station or funding may ask you to do. You just have to be really strong and have a tunnel vision and not get distracted.

I'm on the road a lot and am exhausted a lot. When I was dealing with this film in Oklahoma where there were all these rumors flying about what I was doing or what I wasn't doing, I was just sleepless because I didn't know what I was going to walk into because I was dealing with folks with mental illness in the family. And I was with this family with mental illness in the middle of the most stressful time of their life. They were going to take it out on me, and they were going to take it out on their lawyers who failed them. I just had to believe. It was so appealing to walk away, pack up, and go home. And I really wanted to sometimes. But at the end of the day I said I believed I was going to make a film—I'm passionately against the death penalty—and I believed that I was going to make a film that was going to really move people. I just had to keep on telling myself that in order to not just go home, because I was definitely met with so much resistance. There was so much suspicion. That was terrifying to walk into. I guess I just had to tell myself that what I was doing was important.

Definitely having somebody in your life who understands that a little bit—my boyfriend, I can totally rely on him. I call him a lot after I'm done with a shoot and we'll go on and on and on about what kind of day I've had. Having that kind of support is really important. And also your crew. I'm very close with my cameraman, and we've gone through a lot together. I feel that's a really important relationship, personally, to have somebody who's in the field with you who you can really talk through stuff with emotionally, not just creatively.

Do you know what kind of ratio you shoot?

About 70:1, generally. Or maybe 100:1. I'd say 100 is more average for these verité films.

When you finish filming do you know what your story is?

Not always.

To what extent do you find that in the field or in the editing room?

I think there's a little bit of both, and it's also on a film-by-film basis. On some films, the beginning, middle, and end are really clear. On the film for HBO about this woman who's being executed, the beginning, middle, and end of the film were very clear. That was a film that I could have written a treatment for before I started editing, and it would have been somewhat similar to the finished product. On this other film that I'm editing now, which I've been shooting for three years, I really feel like I know. Right now, it's about ten hours long, and it will be ninety minutes. I don't know how I'm gonna get from here to there. Or maybe it'll be two hours. I think I knew going in what the major questions were that the film was seeking to answer, what my questions were, and what I felt the arcs of the characters' stories were. But how that was going to get told, the structure of the film, which part of the film would end up having to fall to the side, I really don't know. And that process is really in the editing room.

Then there's films like *The Farm*, which really didn't have a beginning, middle, and end—that film was tough to edit. There were six guys, and except for two of them, nothing happened. So how do you create a film which has dramatic tension? The film operated on philosophical levels rather than on dramatic narrative levels. Obviously, there was a guy who got executed and it has a narrative thrust that's clear. And there was a man who died of old age. But for the other four guys, they were just there. And then they were there. And then they were still there. That film was really made in the editing room. We edited it for quite a long time, and struggled and came out at the other end.

If you find yourself in a situation where you don't find a lot of dramatic tension, is it okay to create that in the way you present it?

I feel like my films have always had a lot of drama that's real. I don't know if I've faced that question head on. I think *The Farm*, for four of the guys, the drama was very internal, and we brought that out. I'm not sure if that's creating it or if that's just paring away the banality.

Do you do test screenings? Or, when you finish the edit the way you like it, is that the way the film lives?

Not at rough cuts. Once I get much closer to the fine-cut phase, I'll definitely show the film to four or five people because I think my films can often be confusing. One of the most important things for me is to figure out what's clear and what's not clear, because when you're so close to the mate-rial, it's hard to figure out. And then I always love to hear what people find most memorable and least memorable. So I'll do that with a very small group of people, but generally not until a fine-cut phase, because I'm really interested in clarity.

Is fiction something you'd like to do?

I optioned a book. A friend of mine wrote a screenplay, but it's one of those things that's pretty far on the back burner, unfortunately, because my documentary filmmaking is so challenging, so time-consuming. I think I'd like to try it. I don't think I'd ever want to cross over, because my life is so rich doing this, and I would miss my experiences in the field. But I have tried to think about ways to integrate or to combine fiction and nonfiction filmmaking. With a couple of these girls in Baltimore—because there have been all these experiences that have happened in their past that have been so extraordinary, that they talk about so much—I've been thinking a lot about how to combine those two things. And if I could figure that out, that would be something I'd be really excited to do. But that's just a kernel of thought in the recess of my head, that hopefully, when I get a week off, I'll try to bring up to the forefront. Just a new life experience. I have worked with actors before, and it's something I really enjoy. But I really am happy being in the field I'm working in, [with] the people I am working with. I know I would miss that if I was ever away from it for too long.

Is funding for documentaries easier as you go along in your career?

It's easier as you go, and I think that, right now, in television, there is such a need for programming—what we find works for these kinds of films is to find somebody within the system who wants to have a project which they see as unusual. They have to get x-number of hours on whatever their strand is, but say they want to have one special project that they're hoping will go to a film festival or will get some Emmy or Academy nominations . . . whatever it is. You need to find that person who will let you have that long shooting schedule, because often with television, they want something yes-terday. So you need to find the person who's gonna help you just let that one project you have go. Like, the *Waxter Girls* project is funded by The Learning Channel, of all places. They never do films like this, and they've been letting me go for two-and-a-half years. They call every once in a while and they say, "When's *Waxter Girls* . . . is it finished yet?" I'm like, "No, it's really good, there's all this stuff going on, and I want to keep on shooting." And I just have this executive who believes in me.

Also, HBO is a very special place. They really support the filmmaker's vision. They give you the support you need, and if your film wants a longer schedule because it's gonna be a better film with a longer schedule, they'll give that to you. They'll give you another year. And their notes are always so helpful and great. It was like heaven making a film with them. If I could make every documentary feature with them for the rest of my life, I'd be extremely happy. Other folks, I think, you have to convince or find that mentor within the place. HBO is really set up to accept that kind of model, which is unique.

What's your take on festivals?

I think that Sundance can be an extremely helpful festival for a documentary. It can really launch it and get it out from the margins of documentary-as-medicine to, here is something that's entertaining, that's in the public eye. When *The Farm* went to Sundance and won, it got a big fat kick out the door in such a way that people just started noticing it. And when it was finally on television, the television station promoted it saying, Grand Jury Prize Winner at Sundance, so that festival has a real brand that will bring people to watch your documentary that might not otherwise. Television programmers like HBO are so savvy in how they market their films that a lot of people will watch their documentaries without them ever going to festivals, and I think that's really great. I think for other films, where people aren't used to watching longer-form, feature-length, verité-oriented films, a festival with a stamp of approval can be very important.

Do you have heroes in the documentary world?

I think there are favorite filmmakers who have influenced me, and there are just favorite filmmakers. Errol Morris—I think he is a genius, and *Assembly Line* is definitely a film which inspired me to be a filmmaker. I don't emulate his style at all, but I think he's fabulous. And I'm a huge Wiseman fan. I studied Wiseman, and he definitely influenced me, but clearly, I've strayed from a strict verité fold. And then, Barbara Kopple, who I met early on in my career; just as a personal role model, [she] was very inspiring. She was one of the few women doing it. She's got kick-ass stories. She was never confined to what people thought was more female-oriented subject matter; I'm not, either. So that was very, very inspiring, that my subject matter wouldn't be limited by gender. Those are some heroes.

Are there different challenges or advantages to being a woman in this industry?

In the industry, people will often think of you for the films which have female subject matter, which is good because I like making some of those films, but that also can feel limiting. And the harder-edged subjects, you have to really make a harder sell for yourself. But for me, it's a little bit different, because the first film that I made which had notoriety was *The Farm*, which was so not female subject matter. I do think my approach to that film, in the editing and in the choice of music, has something of a feminine feel. I do think Lifetime Television will come to us to make specials, stuff like that. That's great, too, but I do think you have to sometimes sell a little bit harder when you want to deal with subject matter that doesn't necessarily ring immediately as female subject matter.

In the field, as a woman, it's a great advantage. I think that people are used to talking to women. They've always talked to their mothers. That was the person in their family they went to talk to. In this society, people are more used to talking to women within [their] families, so I think that's an advantage.

Is there a feminine facility in terms of connecting with people?

I think so. When you first meet people and your subjects are men, is there going to be a level of flirtation? When we first started making *The Farm*, because Jonathan Stack and I made that film together, you could tell . . . the interviews he got at the beginning were different; they had a different feeling to them than the interviews that I got because sometimes, the inmates were flirting with me. In that way, it was terrific to have both of us there. As time went on and we really got into it, those differences started to erase themselves, which was good. But that's life.

Do you see parts of your style in the first films you made in college?

Oh, yeah. The way I make films is so much about getting intimate with people, bonding with them, and having a good ole conversation. That is a big part. There's the verité, where I just follow the scene, but a lot of the other stuff is me in conversation with people. People who I feel intimate with, people who trust, people who I trust, people who I like, people who like me on a personal level, and talking to them, not only in an interview, but often I'll be sitting around with a character and her mother and I'll just be talking to them. And that will spark the conversation between them, which will ultimately become a scene. So yeah, there's definitely a fluency, a similarity throughout.

You're also working on other projects at the same time?

That's the only film right now I'm directing [*Waxter Girls*], but I have a company and we executive-produce projects and often have directors working with us, so there are other projects going on.

So you have multiple balls in the air?

Yes. That's how we pay the rent here.

Do you see documentary filmmakers and films pushing boundaries or moving into new arenas?

There are so many different things that are considered documentary, or considered nonfiction programs. There's been this terrible thing of reality programming. A lot of people think that that's what documentary is. It's not what I do. It's its own thing that has its own internal rules and structures that I'm not familiar with. And then, there's docu-entertainment that's on every night. There's the Biography series—those are all documentaries; the History Channel, filled with documentaries. I think people love information and they love being told information in a packaged way. Then there's a sort of risky, feature-length, often cinema verité documentary, that is having, actually, a terrific life. I think that, while the reality programming and all that other documentary programming is so different, it's also made it more palatable to a wider population, and, therefore, this documentary-as-medicine idea that the public perhaps had . . . documentary has become entertaining, and people who would not think they would enjoy documentaries are going to them. That's very exciting.

What keeps you coming back to it?

I'm going to answer a slightly different question. In terms of documentary filmmaking, what needs to happen in the industry, I think that the HBO model of films that are long-form, often cinema verité-inspired, films which can take on tough subjects—they have been doing so well—they have been winning Emmys every year, and Academy Award nominations. And I really wish that other networks would look to that model, because I think it can be successful commercially and critically. So many of these other outlets need the documentaries to be turned around tomorrow or they won't put their publicity or financial backing behind the films. And if you look at what's happened with those kinds of films, and those are some of the most daring documentary films being made, subject matter-wise and often stylistically, I hope that the industry will take notice of that.

What keeps you coming back to it?

The people. The people in the films. When I haven't been out in the field in a long time, as I've just been in my editing room for months and months and months, I start jonesing for getting out into the field, and hanging out with my kids. My life is so rich because of it. I'm in people's homes and they welcome me and we eat together and it's so rich. It's not work, really. That's what's amazing about it. When I'm in the field, I'm exhausted and I'm working really hard, but it doesn't feel like work in any kind of conventional sense. You just live a very, very full life and then you get to share it with other people. What a privilege. It's the greatest job. It's living life in the most full way.

Chapter 8: Nick Broomfield
Modern Adventurer

Recognized for his on-camera pursuit of elusive public figures, Nick Broomfield is indeed our window into worlds behind closed doors. His non-fiction films—*Aileen Wuornos: The Selling of a Serial Killer* (1992), *Monster in a Box* (1992), *Heidi Fleiss: Hollywood Madam* (1996), *Kurt and Courtney* (1997), and *Fetishes* (1998)—track his quest of characters who are in the public eye, yet shrouded in intrigue. Broomfield's style of filmmaking includes him as a character in his films—both engaging and entertaining us as he tracks his subjects. He has also delved into fiction, having directed *Dark Obsession* (1991).

How did you get your start in filmmaking and documentary?

I did some still photography to start with. I loved reading history books and things like George Orwell's *Down and Out in Paris and London*, socio-logical studies of different communities, that kind of thing. And my still photographs were that kind of stuff. Then, when I was at university, I did my first film, made with a little windup Bolex, which was set in the commu-nity in Liverpool and it was just a study of the community. So that was how I got into it. When I did my first film I met Sir Arthur Elton, who made a film called *Housing Problems* in the thirties, which was always heralded as the first cinema verité film. I guess, in a sense, it wasn't, but it was the first film with sync sound with normal people who were filmed in their homes. And I remember also loving the work of Fred Wiseman, which I saw at a later date when I was already at film school. I suppose it's more a universal interest in people, and documentary gives you that ability to find out about the world that you are a part of.

What is your definition of a documentary? Or do you think that docu-mentary can be defined?

I would like to think of my films in not a particularly sanctimonious way, but of sort of recording an aspect of our history and culture in a way that is representative of it and its time, and the people and their values, and

Nick Broomfield. Photo courtesy Lafayette Films.

just the way that people are and the way they relate to each other; it gives you kind of an insight into what it would've been like to interact if you had the opportunity to meet them. I think that's what, probably, I like most about so-called cinema verité or observational type films, that you get a sense as to what the people are like, what their humor's like, and how they are to be with; you just get a sense of them. I feel that that's kind of been lost. I find that as almost the most interesting thing. That's not to say that there aren't a lot of other films that aren't fascinating, too, in different ways, but that's my particular fascination, and probably these are the films that I enjoy the most in that particular style.

How would you characterize yourself as a documentary director? Is there a mission in your filmmaking?

No. I think I wanted it to be as accessible as possible to as big an audience as possible and to find a way of holding an audience. And I always thought that that was part of the riddle that it was important to be able to do that. I suppose I probably started off as a more overtly political filmmaker, but I feel that my films are all to do with that political situation insofar as that reflects the society we're in, and often, the main dimensions and battle lines; in a sense, even the contradiction. I think a work, to have any kind of real longevity, often needs to have that dimension to it as a sort of outer boundary—it needs to have that resonance. I think, at their essence, most subjects are bound to hit those distinguishing marks, those boundaries. It's almost like they need to be rolled back to that point because it's at that point that they have the greatest significance. They're not just about that one thing.

Do you feel that your films are an exploration as much of yourself as of your subject matter?

Well, I don't, actually. I think the inclusion of myself is more a device of telling you a fairly complicated story. I think in the earlier part of my career I made much more traditional verité subjects like institutions—things that had a kind of built-in boundary to them—that weren't particularly investigative, or they were more a portrait of a situation. I became more interested in doing different kinds of stories and, in a sense, moving back the boundary a little bit . . . also, being able to make films about subjects that weren't always necessarily cooperative. The most interesting subjects aren't cooperative—they don't necessarily want to be filmed; they have things they want to hide. Often, those are the real challenges, or those are the ones I become more interested in. And then, you have to think of a style that actually is going to encompass that and is going to make it possible for you to include the omniscient.

Often, people define themselves more by the things that they won't talk about than the things that they will, so you try and come up with a style that will accommodate that. And I've always loved the essence of the cinema verité style, which is long takes and allowing footage to play. There's nothing I love more than that, but I felt the need to contextualize it more. You need to set it up more, and you need to have some means of moving it from one point to the other. The way that I use is myself as this sort of honing device or this sort of detective that would take a way through it and would make seemingly disparate bits of information link. I've always thought that that was the vibe—it wasn't really a need to necessarily explore myself—but I'd rather explore other things.

Some have described you as a great adventurer. Do you see yourself that way?

Well, I think there are greater explorers who go up mountains and spend their time with wild tribes. Some of the people I've filmed are wild tribes, too. But, yeah, I would say that, in a way. It's more or less just telling a portrait of the world we're a part of, finding a way of telling a story that is insightful of that particular world. Obviously, if you choose a subject that is iconic and popular, it has a particular life to it that other stories might not have, but it doesn't make those stories any less valid. In fact, maybe they're more interesting, but you pay a certain price for that, too. I did a couple things in South Africa, but I haven't really done things completely out of my culture. Maybe because I'm not much of a linguist, but I also didn't feel that I knew enough about those other worlds. To that extent, I'm not a great explorer. I've just really been within my own . . .

. . . world?
Yeah.

What excites you about documentary filmmaking? Where is the passion for you, what keeps you coming back?
Well, I think it's incredibly hard work, and I don't think it's going to get any easier. It's an incredibly privileged position because basically, you're paid to document a world you are a part of in a way that even a journalist isn't. You can spend months and months and months on a film, and I can't think of anybody else who is in that position. You can do a much more competent story and you can find out things about every nook and cranny you want to. It gives you an excuse to question people and really find out about the world that you are a part of in a way that most newspaper articles . . . they barely scratch the surface. So, you know, you're just very lucky. I think that's what I love about it and why it keeps me coming back you just find out so much and meet so many amazing people. And some of those people you have relationships with afterwards and you have a key into all these different worlds. You know much more than most people you know. You almost know too much.

Also, it gives you an ability to mix with virtually anyone. I think good documentarians all have an ability to just get along with anyone; it doesn't matter who they are or if they're rich or poor or where they come from or whatever. You have to find a way through and you have to kind of be a listener . . . giving of yourself when other people want to give to you. It makes me feel very alive. That's what I really like. It also makes you kind of modest, I think, because you're dealing with real people, real life, real tragedies, and I know other people are much less fortunate than oneself, and it sort of puts you back in your box. So there isn't a lot of room to feel sorry for yourself or complain too much. I think that's healthy.

Heidi Fleiss and Nick. Photo courtesy Lafayette Films.

Anybody can chronicle reality. What does a documentary filmmaker bring to the table that makes a difference?

Well, it's all about storytelling—in the way you order it and the connections that you make and your ability to bring people out. Also, it's an overall shape you bring to the story or film that you're telling. That's the art . . . how you shape it, the fun that you have with it, the fun that you bring to the audience, the way you manage to encapsulate film. I think that's it.

Do you consider yourself a verité documentary filmmaker?

Well, I'm certainly not a traditional verité—I guess that's more almost observational. It's more in an anthropological way. I've never really liked the term verité very much because it sort of sets itself up to fall, because it's actually not verité—you change every situation by just being there. But I don't think that's really what it's about, anyway. I mean, I remember looking at verité films years ago and being powerfully influenced by them, particularly in anthropological situations where you realize people actually have a real language, they have a real job; they're not just sort of strange-looking people in grass skirts. They are actually people with a culture. I had an interesting conversation with somebody who was the controller of one of the television stations here. He had a job programming and was very in touch, I guess, with audience expectations, and he was saying, "Well, I think audience demand has changed. It's very hard to get an audience to sit through some of these things unless there's some edge, unless there's some other thing you offer them." I think, normally, that's true.

I personally love sitting through good verité films. It's a treat. But maybe people are more impatient. I certainly think audiences are impatient.

How do you characterize your style, as you have evolved from verité?

Well, I guess it's much more investigative. I hope they still have the adrenaline of verité films—you see things in a sort of rawness; you see the rough edges. I think it's important to see where people live. So many documentaries you see on the television, they're just like a studio interview. It's all to do with the person giving information. It's not to do with who that person is and their lives, and I always think that's such a waste. Why not just write an article? You don't need those people to be there. Because they're just a conduit for information, you're not really that interested in them in themselves; you're not interested in their back stories; you're not interested in how something really affected them personally. They're just sitting there as a mouthpiece. And I think that that's something that verité films are not about. They're about seeing people in those situations, and they're very . . . in a sense, they're more respectful of people. They're much more to do with the humanity behind the situation. And that's what I think is always the most interesting part.

I'm doing this film about Tupac and Biggie, and I don't know how many cuts I've done, but it became interesting when I realized it became much more about the way in which the lives of those two people and what happened to them had impacted all these other people. There was the policeman who resigned because he couldn't do the investigation he wanted to. It was interesting in its own right, the fact that he had a lot of invested prejudices because of who he was. And the way in which the bodyguard who was with Tupac on the night he was shot was so horrified that he became a born-again Christian, and that was his way of dealing with all the death threats that he was getting. And you just see all of these people who have ingested what happened in their own respective ways, and that's what makes it interesting, not that they're saying, "This happened then and that happened then"—but what it did to them, what happened to them.

There's excitement in the discovery of that, that I don't think is present when you have just talking heads.

Yeah, because otherwise, you're just running from one base to the other. And I actually really try never to use the same interview . . . to go back to it, because I feel that you've kind of gone backwards and the film needs to be a narrative construction where, if you have another visit, it's another visit, not to get more information. The one interview is about one thing, or that is a visit. That's what I like to do.

Do you ever have difficulty gaining your subjects' trust?

Yeah, well, often I don't spend very long with them at all.

The level of trust at the beginning sometimes isn't as ready as it is if you spend a lot of time with your subjects. Have you encountered that obstacle, and how do you deal with it?

I think it depends on what you're doing or how hard you're coming at them. Sometimes, people are much more revealing at the beginning than they are when they have a chance to adjust themselves. I find that you get much more offhand things from people, much more revealing in the first five minutes than you do when they're all settled down. I'm someone who works off a great deal of adrenaline, I suppose. I like the chaos. I feel that the chaos often reveals stuff at a certain level. It doesn't mean necessarily the most profound level, but it can be very effective in terms of people defining themselves very quickly. I've found that. If there aren't any warm-up questions you just kind of go for what you're after; sometimes you get much more candid answers than when they're all settled in and much more relaxed.

Do you always go into an interview shooting?

Yeah, I pretty much do. I don't say that I may arrive and I might be filming. And what I normally do after the first magazine is spend a bit of time saying hello and all the rest of it. But I do think, particularly with the sort of stuff I've been doing where you're moving from house to house, you're moving from person to person quite quickly, you sort of want to see where they live and how they are and what it's like to meet them. You don't want to start with them sitting on a couch. I think it's important not to do it in such a way that it's rude; you don't want to be rude or disrespectful. I don't think it is.

How do you choose your film subjects? Are you commissioned mostly?

I didn't choose *Fetishes*. I've chosen pretty much everything else. I guess, just look for a subject that kind of has a resonance and lots of life to it and is a kind of microcosm of something, is indicative of a particular place or a particular society or a particular group or something.

At what point in the process do you know the scope of your film?

Well, I think you have to get a sense of the size of the subject. I don't think you ever really do. I think you pick up your characters along the way. I never really ever, ever have any permissions before I start. I really don't have anything. I guess it adds something. It's not necessarily a very comfortable way to work, but I do think it produces something much bigger than the imagination. And generally, with a great deal of persistence, you're normally surprised at what you get. I think it's important to know why you're interested in the subject. I think it's very important for me, anyway, not to know what I really feel about those people, and to discover that in the process of making the film, because I think that's what the film is about. And you hopefully take the audience on that journey. You hopefully tell a very complicated story, not a simple story. I think these stories are all quite complicated and hopefully it's that complication that will give the film some kind of longevity.

Do you think that you make the same film each time with different subjects, or do you push the envelope in some way and challenge yourself in different ways?

I've certainly made different films from when I started and gone through different styles. I think at a certain point I discovered a style or a form that kind of worked. And then, I applied different subjects. And maybe there's a similarity in the subject, too, in that the subjects were all very complicated and they had lots of different layers and they were a combination of: sometimes the people were dead; sometimes there was a lot of archive stuff; sometimes there was a lot of disparate information I was pulling together. And to that extent, stylistically, I would say that I've developed a formula. Which actually hasn't really made it any easier to do. I think, maybe, I've gone for more and more complicated subjects. *Heidi Fleiss* was complicated but not as complicated as [the film about Tupac and Biggie], for example.

So maybe that's how you push yourself?

Yeah, I think distilling massive amounts of information and, yeah, maybe it's taking more hardcore stories. I would think of this story as being much more hardcore, in a way, than the Heidi Fleiss film, which is more a study of a set of relationships which were indicative of the city in a way that was kind of neat . . . which I'm sure I didn't set out to make, necessarily, but which evolved. Maybe it seems, now, because we've sort of resolved it, a much more complicated story. It certainly has been very challenging. They're all challenging, though. You just tend to forget in between what a pain in the ass they all are.

Do you ever find yourself in a situation where you have to artificially create drama?

I think if you think you can get it by doing something else, yeah, you do it.

So, are there boundaries?

Well, sometimes it's just a question of moving things on a bit or someone's backed up against the wall and you know you're not going to get it because it's constricting and restraining. And if you create a bit of activity . . . a lot of interviews are dependent on energy and keeping the energy going and not allowing it to dissipate too much. And sometimes you get in a situation that's absolutely flat and you know that you're not going to get anything because it's just too flat. And I don't know what it is . . . you know, everyone's sitting in a chair or something and it's just flat. And you just need something to happen, you need someone to fall over a table or someone to drop their drink or anything that's going to create something else.

So that kind of thing is acceptable?

Well, I don't necessarily fall over tables and stuff but sometimes, if it's just really awful, I just say, "I don't think it's working." I mean, I can think of an interview I did this time, and ostensibly it was a great interview but it was flat, flat, flat. And I don't know if we did something wrong or it was one of those situations where we went in and then it was too dark and we had to put lights up or something, which I never normally ever do. And by the time we actually got around to doing the filming, the person was an inhibited sort of person, anyway, and I could never eke him out at all. It's just flat, so it won't be in the film. Occasionally that happens. I think part of being good at what one does is that you throw away what doesn't work.

Ethical boundaries, levels of involvement in subjects' lives. . . . Are there lines you won't cross because that would make you part of their story as opposed to documenting their story? Or do you create the rules as you go?

Well, I think you do have to, yeah. I always feel, whether I'm comfortable with it or not, or whether I feel it's the right thing to do, you know, with the empathy you have with that person, I think all those things are important.

So ethical decisions are made on a case-by-case basis?

Yeah, I think so. I mean, of the people you film, some people you really like and some people you don't. I mean, I just recently was subpoenaed to appear in this court with Aileen Wuornos to testify on her behalf, or what I thought was her behalf, but it became more complicated. Her best friend was there, who was really poor, and I ended up giving her money. I guess because I liked her and I felt that the film had made money and it seemed kind of weird not to. It's strange that you make films about people, some of whom don't have any money, and you make money on the film. It's an odd thing.

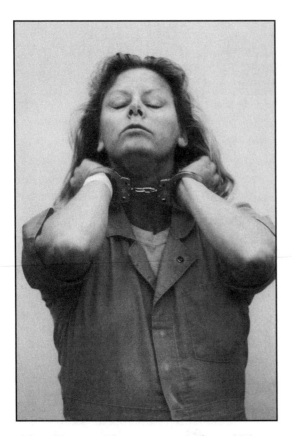

Aileen Wuornos. Photo courtesy Lafayette Films.

Do you pay people to be in your films, and does it violate anything?

In the Heidi Fleiss story, I made a point of letting everybody know how much everyone was being paid, and I kind of did the same thing in the Aileen Wuornos film. I think it is a reality of filming today that people want to be paid, and if you want to make the film you kind of have to pay them. Otherwise, I don't think you will be shooting anything. And ideally, I don't think you would want to pay them. But I guess if you're doing iconic, mainly mainstream subjects, you know, people treasure every little thing they have, and this is their big payday. It's like you're actually sharing some of the money you got and it's kind of nice to be able to pay back a little, to arrange to have benefits and stuff from the film later. I don't think it always has to be a negative thing.

I always think that the way people present themselves and the [subjects] that they choose to take issue on are very important.

They tell you a lot more about the person than they think they do.

I think so. In a way, I always think those things are kind of a blessing in a film, because if someone sets themselves up like that it's a great help, really, in defining who they are. Is it because they are really hard up, or is this how they set themselves apart, or is it how they value themselves—I think that's kind of useful.

What kind of ratio do you shoot?

I think it's about 40:1, or something.

After shooting, do you figure out the film in the edit suite, or do you know where you're going before you start editing?

Well, I think I know where I'm going, but it does take me lots of different passes to get it right. I do seem to need to recut and recut and recut, and there's a fine line between working and not working. When it's too long, it's not very amusing and enjoyable to watch. So I think they're just strange things, films—aren't they? They just take a lot of working on, and I've been cutting this [Tupac film] now for three months and I've probably just about got a decent structure, but I'm sure there's lots of internal editing I've got to do.

Roughly how long do you take in editing?

I think *Kurt and Courtney* was about eighteen to twenty weeks. This, I've been on twelve weeks, and I work really long hours. I work from nine to eight five days a week, and I work half days on Saturdays.

Do you do test screenings?

Yeah, I do. I do lots of that when I think it's at a point where it's kind of working. I think it's useful if it's just . . . like sometimes, people just don't understand things or they need more information or they just don't understand the significance of something. Because I think often, one is close to the material and it's often to do more with setup than anything else. And that's useful.

Do you think there is a type of person better suited to documentary filmmaking than another?

I do think one needs to be pretty fit, and I think you need a lot of stamina. And you need to be genuinely interested in people. And to have that sort of curiosity—I think there has to be that thing of just going out and doing it even if all the funding isn't in place and you have to go on shooting for several weeks longer than is budgeted. I think that's all pretty important. It's very rare that it all sort of works out. There has to be a certain, that kind of slight madness to keep doing it, to go on and on and on and on and on—that sort of passion.

Where does your funding come from?

I had funding from the early days—it was PBS and people like the British Film Institute, and I've had funding from HBO—that was more lately. And I've had a kind of deal with Channel 4 England, which is how I came to do this last film. Of course, the funding when you begin is terrible; you have a pain in the ass doing it, and then, of course, as you get more successful, it's easier to be funded. But there's a sort of expectation of you. I guess it's all to be expected. I think your freedom diminishes in one way and it expands in another. It's funny; it's quite hard for me to do just a local story and I think they wouldn't fund me. They wouldn't fund me at the budgets I've been getting. And there's an expectation that you're really gonna come up with stuff and that's hard, too. And it's pressure, and so on. So, you know, you kind of get one thing and you lose something else.

But I think what I really love [is] looking at people like Pennebaker and Fred Wiseman and Leacock and that lot. They're such great people and they're so devoted to things and I like that. There is a kind of family there. Maybe I'm on the commercial end, in a way. But I actually like Michael Moore's stuff. I really like the documentaries. I'm a big fan of a lot of people's work and I'm just pleased that people are still making them and being funded and it isn't all crap.

You made a fiction film. Will you make another one?

Yeah, I'm actually going to New York this weekend for a meeting on another feature. I think my mistake on the last one was to make it before the script was right, and I am absolutely not going to do that this time. So I don't think the script's right; we'll see what happens.

Is it fiction you want to get more into?

It took me awhile to find a kind of niche in documentary, and I think if I could find that in feature I would love it. I actually love, this sounds really stupid, but I love laughing. I love comedies and I just think I could do it. I would just enjoy doing it. For me, one of the by-products of doing documentaries is, I've discovered all these things I could do that I never knew I could.

Do you make your living doing only documentaries?

I've done a few commercials, but I've really made my living with documentaries.

If you weren't making films, what would you do?

I'm not actually trained as an architect, but I think I could do that. I'm actually quite good with design, although I couldn't draw to save my life. I'm kind of fascinated with people and houses—what kind of spaces people like living in and the way in which design influences behavior. Then again, it gives you a great opportunity to go out and rummage around, look at things, cause a lot of chaos. That's probably what I would do. I think if you just do what you enjoy, it's always a good indication of what you'll be good at.

Do you watch your films after you've made them? Do you watch your first film ever?

Yeah, I do watch my first film. I hardly ever look at them, although if there's a screening or something and I happen to walk in, I'll generally sit down and watch it. But most of them . . . probably a couple of them, I have a problem sitting through, but most of them I like, just because they remind me of those characters, they remind me of that time, and I don't wince in pain. Wild horses couldn't drag me to see my first feature. I've watched it once with an audience, and I didn't think anyone would know who I was and it was just the worst experience that I had in my life. It was just awful. It was so bad.

It wasn't well received, or you were just uncomfortable?

I just wanted to die. I just knew it was terrible. And knowing that I had something to do with it, it was just hell on earth.

Chapter 9: Joe Berlinger
Journalist Storyteller

Berlinger began his career in advertising but made the transition to filmmaking after working with David and Albert Maysles on an ad campaign. Berlinger cut his teeth in verité filmmaking at Maysles Films, where he met his frequent co-collaborator, Bruce Sinofsky. Their films, verité portraits of people and communities, often in crisis, consistently place in critics' top ten films of the year lists.

Berlinger and Sinofsky's first feature film, *Brother's Keeper* (1992), garnered several major awards, including 1992 Best Documentary from Directors Guild of America, National Board of Review, National Film Critics' Circle, and the 1992 Sundance Film Festival Audience Award. In 1996, the duo released *Paradise Lost: The Child Murders at Robin Hood Hills*, which was a year-long examination of a small town split by the murders of several young boys in what was alleged to be a Satanic ritual. *Paradise Lost* won a Primetime Emmy and numerous Best Documentary awards for 1996 from the DGA, National Board of Review, and Peabody. Their follow-up, *Paradise Lost 2: Revelations*, was a look at the aftermath of the trial. They also collaborated to make *Where It's At: Rolling Stone's State of the Union* (1997), a celebration of the thirtieth anniversary of the magazine.

Berlinger went on to write and direct *Blair Witch 2: Book of Shadows* (2000), the sequel to the film phenomenon *Blair Witch Project*. He has also helmed shows for television, including *The Wrong Man* for Court TV and *The Begging Game* for PBS.

How did you get started in documentary filmmaking?

I've had a very circuitous route to becoming a filmmaker. I feel I fell into documentary filmmaking by accident, but [I'm] thrilled that I did. And as I get older, I feel more in tune spiritually with what people are supposed to be doing, so I clearly feel now I should be doing this, and doing a very specific kind of documentary. At the time, it felt like happenstance, but now, I see that certain doors open at the right time. And when a door opens and you step through . . . I was a language major in college and always imagined myself having some kind of international career. I was always interested in the media and always loved film, but never imagined I could actually make a living in the film industry.

Right out of school, for a year, I worked at McCann Erickson in New York, advertising. I got that job because I was a really good amateur magician and I turned my interview into a magic show. They couldn't believe I had the nerve to do that, so they hired me to be in this account management training program even though I had no M.B.A. and I was way younger than anybody else.

And then within a year I heard about an opportunity to work overseas at Ogilvy [& Mather], and because I now had advertising experience at a major New York agency and had gone through their account management program, and because I was fluent in a number of languages, particularly German, I got hired by Ogilvy to go to Frankfurt. By the time I was hired— this was the mid-eighties and there was this big movement . . . for a particular client like American Express or British American Tobacco or Mattel, they tried to come up with concepts that were generic enough that they could shoot one commercial that all the countries in Europe could use. The globalization of advertising was the big buzzword.

My job in Frankfurt was to coordinate all these pan-European shoots— I had zero production knowledge, had not gone to film school, had gone to Colgate and was a language major, had very little advertising background— I sort of bluffed my way into the middle level. So I found myself, at twenty-three, living and working in Frankfurt at Ogilvy & Mather coordinating these big TV commercial shoots as a producer, and that's when the film bug hit me. I stumbled my way through and figured out how to be a producer and, all of a sudden, realized I loved film, and that's when I started thinking, "This is what I want to do for a living." I spent a couple years in Europe as a producer and found my way back to New York and was producing American Express commercials at Ogilvy & Mather in New York trying to figure out, how can I really get into the film business, when I had this idea to hire the Maysles brothers.

Again, everything seems like happenstance, but when I look back on my life, it seems the route I was supposed to take. So I guess now I'm about twenty-five. American Express wanted to do a documentary-style TV commercial campaign, unscripted, which was unusual for ad agencies. Now, real people is very popular, but at the time, it was the odd project that was an unscripted, real people project. So I hired the Maysles brothers to do this commercial campaign which turned out well, but the client didn't like it and it never aired. But in the process of hiring them, I hit it off with David Maysles. David was much more attuned to and interested in business than Albert is. He and I just started talking, and I wanted to get into the film business and he wanted to develop their advertising business more. Up until my arrival at that company their presence on Madison Avenue was, more or less, if someone thought to call them, they would come in for a meeting, and every now and then, they did a commercial. I was hired to really develop that business.

I went over to the Maysles because I thought this was my opportunity to get into the film business, but even at that point I didn't necessarily want to be a documentary filmmaker. They hired me to become their executive producer for commercials, and I spent five years there developing their TV commercial business, and I used it as my documentary film school and learned all that I could. Made a couple of short films, which did very well, which encouraged me. And that's where I met Bruce Sinofsky— he was an editor for the Maysles. Bruce had helped me cut a couple of my short films, and Bruce and I had become very close and realized we liked working together and shared a similar aesthetic.

Bruce Sinofsky (left) and Joe Berlinger. Photo credit: Gannett Suburban Newspapers.

So, in '90, we started making *Brother's Keeper* sort of on the weekends, and, in '91, when we had all the material, except for the trial material, for *Brother's Keeper*, we presented that to American Playhouse, and Bruce and I each left the Maysles to dedicate ourselves to finishing *Brother's Keeper* and starting our own company, and I've been a documentary filmmaker ever since.

How do you characterize yourself in terms of style?

I hate labels and I hate categorizing because I feel documentary film-making is so ghettoized in terms of people's perception of what film is. To me, there is one giant spectrum of what film is. On one end is the talking head, scripted or heavily narrated documentary, and on the other end is the biggest budget Hollywood feature you can imagine. It's all one big spectrum of filmmaking. And I think all filmmaking is extremely subjective. So to me it's all one continuum, as opposed to documentary filmmaking being its own separate category. And along that continuum, I feel I fall into the verité camp, although we are not classic verité filmmakers like Pennebaker and Maysles, because I do believe that the films we make are subjectively objec-tive instead of objective. I don't believe there's any objectivity in cinema. So I consider myself a verité filmmaker, but I also philosophically believe I am a storyteller as well as a journalist.

I don't believe some of the things Bruce and I do in our films would be embraced by an Albert Maysles. We do use interviews from time to time. We use music to underscore the mood. We are not afraid to withhold informa-tion in the film until the right dramatic moment, but I think it's all okay. When I say I am a storyteller as much as a journalist, it's important to note I take the journalism responsibility very seriously. I don't challenge obvious conventions of journalism—like, you would never put words in people's mouths. We would never set up a situation that would never happen in real life. We would never so manipulate chronology that you're totally changing the meaning of the event.

However, I believe that any documentary maker who tells you they are presenting you with the objective truth of a situation is kidding themselves. For example, particularly with verité—*Paradise Lost*, we shot 150 hours of material, so the selection of 150 minutes of that is inherently subjective. The movie took place over a year, so twenty-four hours a day times 365 days means there were many hours that we weren't around to shoot. All the obvious arguments you always hear . . . I really believe where you point the camera, or whether it's a tight shot or a wide shot, or how the material is edited—filmmaking is an inherently subjective medium. So I don't take our responsibilities as journalists lightly. And certain rules that we've been accused of—frankly, we've been accused because our films are so visceral. We've been accused of telling Mark Byers what to do and what to say, for example, which is totally false.

But here's the key—I feel the only thing I can promise an audience is to present them with my very subjective view of what I experienced and what Bruce experienced. My experience in *Paradise Lost* was that there was this incredible miscarriage of justice—that the case had so many holes and yet the three kids had certain characteristics that the townspeople found offensive, so you had to include some of their "weirdness"—I don't perceive it as weird, but they perceive it as weird. And there were certain questions that I had, like, why aren't these kids pounding on the table more loudly about their innocence? I still believe they're innocent but I always wondered why they didn't . . . so when I say we selectively withhold information until the right dramatic moment it's because that's how we perceived the experience. As a journalist I'm presenting to an audience my perceptions of what I experienced in Arkansas for a year covering this strange case. That's the most I'm going to promise an audience and what I'm going to be true to. Other filmmakers, I think, would have spent a year down there [and] would have made a very different kind of film.

Any good film, whether it's a fiction film or a nonfiction film—to me, the film that works the best is the one that reaches into your soul and causes that "aha" experience that you have in a movie theater when you become totally lost, or on TV or watching a tape or whatever. Certain films, for certain people, feel emotionally truthful, and as a documentary filmmaker, I'm looking for emotional truthfulness where I register something with somebody. When you first start watching *Brother's Keeper*, the film works so well because for the first twenty minutes, I think, most audience members are laughing at the brothers, just like Bruce and I were. We couldn't help but laugh at these guys. We liked them and everything. But until you get to know them they seem laughable. But you come to recognize their purity and their specialness, and you're no longer laughing at them. You're laughing with them when they do something funny, and you start to care about them, and that emotional shift is the kind of emotional journey that I went through, and that Bruce went through, and the kind of emotional journey that I want to give to an audience.

It's a different kind of filmmaking than news reporting or traditional talking-head interview kind of style, which I'm not knocking. But I would not do a Ken Burns baseball film or Civil War film. I think he's a master at it. I like to tell real stories as they're unfolding, and only those stories in which I can, for myself, discern what is the universal message, what is the revelation about the human condition that I can present to an audience. I've occasionally done other things simply for a paycheck, but in terms of my art I only want to do one kind of documentary, and that is a nonfiction feature film—that's what Bruce and I like to call our work. Artistically, I'm only drawn to those stories that can't be reduced to black and white, that have multiple sides to them, and I don't want to tell the audience what to think about them. I'm so attracted to the form because they're great life experiences for us while we're making the films.

While making *Brother's Keeper*, Bruce and I vacillated. Is he guilty? Isn't he guilty? Maybe he is and we should be more critical of him, or maybe he is but he is such an innocent that we have no right to assess or judge his life. Or maybe he did but he has limited intelligence and so many people have been telling him for so long that he didn't do it that he's come to believe it himself. We kept going back and forth. And that's exactly the experience I want to give the audience and let them come up with their own conclusion. From a pure journalism standpoint, a pure TV news standpoint, some people don't understand our work and find it really sloppy and [ask], "Why don't you tell us what to think, and why don't you give us the answers?" That's not the type of film I want to make. I want to give the audience the same type of emotional journey we were on, and if they don't want that kind of emotional journey, they don't have to watch the film.

That does come across for me. They are challenging. They raise more questions and make you think and involve you on that level. What is your level of involvement as you are making the film? Do you consciously maintain a distance, or is there a certain level of involvement that is acceptable?

It's a very difficult question and a very fine line you have to walk. I think the type of films Bruce and I make are chock-full of ethical dilemmas that I wrestle with all the time. Ethical dilemma number one is, we enter people's lives at a time of crisis and tragedy. And while I think we are good stewards of that responsibility, and people generally come away liking us or feeling like we impact their lives in a positive way, I am inherently and constantly aware of the hypocrisy, frankly—that we use a lot of persuasion power to let people allow us to film—hypocritical because God forbid I ever have a tragedy of the magnitude that we have filmed. It took six or seven months before two of the three families in *Paradise Lost* agreed to talk to us. Three victims' families agreed to talk to us, just by being courteous and polite and telling them, "When you're ready, we'll film you." We never ambushed them with the camera, so we are very respectful. But I am constantly aware of the personal hypocrisy of convincing people they should allow us to make the film while knowing that if I was ever in that situation I would never allow filmmakers into my most personal moments. So I'm aware of it, and because I'm so aware of it, it makes me feel I need to be a good steward of that responsibility.

The other ethical dilemma is the issue of compensation, which plagued us on *Paradise Lost*. I don't believe that it's bad to give people a small token of your appreciation, because of the type of film that we make. We have been accused of checkbook journalism—paying for our access. I know in my heart that that is not true. In *Paradise Lost*, for example, we gave each family an honorarium of $7,500, and only gave that money eight or nine months into the process, long after we had established a working relationship, long after we had started filming them. It's a tricky issue. I know in my heart we didn't buy access. The amount of money isn't life-changing, and for the money that we gave them, we did not lay any expectations on them as to what they should say and do.

This film was three and a half years in the making—and I feel like, when people because of a crisis, are unable to work because of the murder of their children or the prosecution of their children, and we are coming down—and they see that each roll of film that cranks through the camera, by the time you get it through the lab and onto your Steenbeck [it] is about $350—and they see the kind of money we're spending, and I certainly made a nice living making the film—we're not a TV news crew coming down for a quick hit—our whole style of filmmaking is predicated on an intense investment of time with these people. When we arrive and people need assistance I'm not afraid to give it. As long as it's clear that it's not buying access, and it's not buying words out of their mouths. But I think it's hypocritical for us to come down and spend lots of money and film and make a living and not offer any kind of assistance. I'm asking people to invest a tremendous amount of time in a project. I think it deserves to be compensated.

Also, in this day and age, people are so media savvy and aware of what people make from movies that I think there's a certain expectation which is difficult to deal with. So that's yet another ethical dilemma that I feel I have to deal with.

Do you get involved in your subjects' lives? Yes, we do get involved. We become their friends. We hang out. That's how we get such intimate material. It's so intimate and personal and so revealing that people think we stage it. No, it's not because we stage it. It's because we do get involved in people's lives. The Ward brothers—they were totally impoverished and we gave them a percentage of our profits at the end of the film. Does that mean those guys did what we asked? Of course not. I think the Ward brothers were the purest subjects we will ever have because those guys truly did not understand what making films was, [about], and they were exactly the same when the cameras were on or when they were off.

In *Paradise Lost*, I felt there was such an investment of time that deserved compensation. But the reason I feel it's okay to get involved in subjects' lives is, I believe all filmmaking is subjective. I believe the camera is sometimes a recorder of objective reality, like in the courtroom. That's

(Left to right) Delbert Ward, Joe Berlinger, Bruce Sinofsky, Douglas Cooper (cameraman), filming Brother's Keeper. *Photo credit: Derek Berg, courtesy Creative Thinking International, Ltd.*

clearly objective. I don't think there's one easy answer. The camera is an objective recorder but, then, what does the filmmaker do with that footage that makes it a subjective process? Sometimes the camera changes the nature of events. Mark Byers shooting the pumpkins—clearly, he was mugging for the camera. We didn't say, "Hey, go shoot pumpkins." He told us they were going to do some target practice, so we got in the car, so the event was legitimate. But, especially in *Paradise Lost 2*, his reaction to the camera, his reaction to the event, was clearly manifested for the camera. I don't think that's a bad thing because in that scene, he's revealing things about himself unwittingly, and the audience is learning things about his character and about him that he's not intending to reveal, even though he's mugging for the camera. When he's spitting into the camera in *Revelations* at that graveside talking about getting even, I think it communicates a whole other thing about him that he's not intending to communicate. Clearly, he's mugging for the camera—he's performing, but that still has documentary legitimacy. So I think it's okay to get involved in your subjects' lives, and that raises yet another ethical dilemma which causes pain from time to time.

First of all, I say it's okay to get in your subjects' lives so long as you don't set events up that wouldn't normally happen or tell people what to say or do for the film. That's where I draw the line. For example, the Ward brothers lived in a shack. It was cold. There wasn't a week that we came up that we didn't bring them some extra food, some clothes, some kerosene for their kerosene stove, because that's the way they heated their house. A cynic could say you are buying your access. To me, it was, here are impoverished people who . . . I go back to my nice home in the suburbs and I, relatively speaking, don't want for anything and I make . . . well, back then I wasn't making money. It was all a crapshoot. But I felt it was just human kindness to bring some comfort to these people in our own small way. But the downside of creating a relationship with people and the ethical dilemma it raises is, even though you have a relationship with people, you can't be afraid to do the job at hand. The families of the victims felt somewhat betrayed by us when *Paradise Lost* came out because it was not a searing indictment of the defendants. And that took a lot of preparing and hand-holding when the film came out to explain exactly what we explained when we started the film, which was—this is what we say to anybody we're making a film about—"We can't promise you one point of view or the other. We're going to be truthful to the situation. And whatever the truth of the story is, that we perceive is gonna be what the film is gonna be about."

Now, meaning the subject of a film, if you believe your cause or your point of view is the correct one and you hear a filmmaker say, "We're going to tell the truth about the situation," your belief is, the film will adhere to your point of view. So we'd never say to the families of the victims, "Those rotten bastards killed your children. We're going to make a film about how rotten they are." We'd always say, "We're going to follow a story until its outcome." Ironically, we started off *Paradise Lost* thinking we were making a film about guilty kids because that's what we had read. Our initial reports were that these kids did something terrible. And I think Bruce and I were interested in making a film to try to understand that mentality . . . to try to understand disaffected youth. How kids could be so cold and heartless that they would kill three eight-year-olds in a Satanic ritual, which is what the news reports were. That's what attracted us initially. In other words, we thought we were making a real-life *River's Edge*. It wasn't until three or four trips down after reviewing the evidence and meeting the lawyers for the defendants and meeting Damien [a defendant] for the first time that we started to say, "You know what? These kids are probably innocent, or something is not right here." Which actually is the most exciting kind of film—you start off making something about one thing and it becomes something else.

The commitment to your story and to your film necessitates being on location for extended periods of time. Do you think you have to be a special breed to make the time investment you do to get the stories you get? It can be difficult to take time off from family to make films. Do you see this as a hardship? Exciting?

I don't want to use the word *special* because certain people are suited to certain things. I don't want to set myself apart from other people. Now, having experience in Hollywood . . . I have enjoyed making a feature film, I have enjoyed and done a couple episodes of *Homicide* and lots of commercials. I don't want to undersell my enjoyment of that kind of filmmaking. But it taps into a whole other part of your brain. The great thing about documentary filmmaking and why it's been my first love and I would never give up what [it] does for me—I consider myself incredibly blessed that I get to travel the world and enter into people's lives, learn things about life that you would never learn—just hang out in Munnsville . . . One of my great disappointments in all of our films—this is a big challenge for me and my career—I don't think the films even come close to capturing the real-life experience that Bruce and I have had in making these films. It's why Bruce and I are very close friends. It's very hard to imagine working as a team in feature films or in dramatic fiction filmmaking, but working as a team is very important and rather standard. Most documentary filmmakers work in teams because you go out and battle the world on many fronts and you have these incredible life experiences that you want to share with somebody of a kindred spirit. I can't describe to you what it's like to be at the murder site with somebody you think might have committed a murder, ranting and raving, and feel the death hanging in the air, as clichéd as that sounds, where you know these bodies were dumped. Or to be in this shack in upstate New York with smelly people from another time and place who you've come to love. If you were on a trip and you lost your way on the highway and you came driving down Johnson Road, which is where the Ward brothers lived, and you saw a pig that had just been slaughtered hanging from a tree and rusted stoves strewn in the high grass and beat-up tractors and these smelly old guys who haven't changed their clothes, you'd be scared shitless. You'd run for the hills. You wouldn't have the nerve to

Bruce (left) and Joe on the Ward brothers' farm during the filming of Brother's Keeper. *Photo credit: Derek Berg, courtesy Creative Thinking International, Ltd.*

get out of your car. And yet, we took the time to get out of the car, and to sit in that living room and open up a can of beans and eat with them. And to this day, they're probably my most favorite people and the kindest people I have ever met.

And the experience of breaking down that stereotype and realizing that these people are just so special and so interesting and that experience of hanging out in that town as it displayed the best of American values and human values . . . I mean, there's nothing like that experience that you could ever imagine . . . whatever that experience is has made me a better person, has made me in my everyday life not so judgmental. So that kind of experience, to me, is what documentary filmmaking is all about.

Does that take a special person? Well, you have to want to have these kinds of experiences. You have to not be judgmental. It is very hard on your family. I think it takes specialness of the spouse or girlfriend or boyfriend or whoever your other half is. My wife puts up with a lot of absences. . . .

And those real-life experiences are what make it all worthwhile. That's why I can never imagine not doing these kinds of films anymore. I feel privileged. I dreamed of making a feature film . . . I had my trailer and my food, and nice catered lunches, and everything was so comfortable, but you know what? I would trade that in a minute for the experience of walking in mosquito-infested, poison ivy–infested backwoods following the father of an eight year old who has been slaughtered, and wondering if he was involved. And following him to the murder site and watching him burn three kids, who you think are innocent, in effigy. That, to me, is a much cooler, life-enriching experience than directing a feature film, although I loved that because it tapped into some other part of my brain—a purely storytelling part. You have to be up for it. You have to be less concerned about money and you have to be okay with longer absences from home. You have to have that spirit of adventure, and you have to want to meet people in new places in new situations. And the most important thing is to not be judgmental.

Would you do another fiction film?

I want to do another fiction film, but the big lesson of *Blair Witch 2* is, I was not passionate about it and I allowed the studio to change the movie. If you look at my director's cut, I did a great job of delivering exactly the script that I wrote, and that was approved. If you look at the final movie, it bears little resemblance to the movie I wrote and directed and handed in. Because it was uncharted territory for me, I allowed myself to lower my standards and not stand up for what I believe in. I should have walked off the movie at that point, which I was afraid to do. The *Blair Witch* sequel— they came to me and it seemed a good opportunity. I was not passionate about the project. I allowed myself to be manipulated. I will only do a feature film if it's on my terms and if I'm passionate about it.

Tell me about editing. To what extent do you know what your film is going to be when you start editing, or do you find the story as you edit?

I'm very involved in the editing process. *Brother's Keeper* and *Paradise Lost*, Bruce and I edited. *Paradise Lost 2*, we hired an editor. Actually, *Paradise Lost 1*, we hired an editor because there was so much trial footage, we did have an editor roughing out the trial sequences while Bruce and I edited all the verité material. We oversaw the editor's trial editing, then Bruce and I edited the entire film. And then, in *Paradise Lost 2*, because of the nature of our growing business and our multiple commitments, we experimented with having someone else do the physical editing, but we were extremely involved in the editing room for major periods of time.

The editing process, to me, is everything. That's the equivalent to the script process, where you discover things you may not have noticed before. The key to verité filmmaking is not having any preconceived notions about your subject. As a human being you can't help but have some preconceived ideas, but you have to be open to changing those ideas. The most dramatic example would be going down to make *Paradise Lost* thinking that we were making a film about guilty teenagers and disaffected youth, and exploring how three teenagers could be so rotten as to slaughter three eight-year-old boys, and to discover the possibility that, in fact, it just wasn't adding up, and ultimately it's a film about the miscarriage of justice. That type of openness to your subject matter on every level is critical to this type of filmmaking, because the films are very much about the process of discovery. For me, anyway, the films are as much about the journey that we take and reporting the emotions of the journey as it is about the story itself.

So you have to be open. That extends into the editing room. You have certain ideas about where the material is going to take its shape, but the reviewing of the material and being very intimately involved in the editorial process is critical because I feel not walking into the editing room with too many ideas is very important. And the story changes many, many, many times. Of course, by the time you've shot your material you have a better idea of what your story is than when you started the film. It's not like you have no ideas about what you want to make the film about, but you're open to certain possibilities and certain structures. I would say when we started *Paradise Lost 2*, it was clearly a follow-up film to keep the flame of hope alive for Damien to follow the appeals process. It wasn't until we got into the editing room that it became evident that it was a meditation on the nature of documentary making in general, and specifically the film was about the impact of the first film on the case. And that we only discovered as we were watching the footage and it manifested itself as a theme. So we started to chip away like [at] a sculpture. The story is in this big block of granite and we started chipping away in the editing room. It's why I don't like making films about past historical events because it's just not as interesting to me as the whole process of discovering what your story is about and being open to letting that story lead you to some emotional truth. And often, those truths don't come out until the editing room, which is why I would never abdicate the editing responsibility to someone else.

Do you find the end to your film when you are shooting or when you are editing?

I think it's a little of both. I think you know you have great moments that are the conclusion . . . In *Brother's Keeper*, we knew generally the story was over because the boys were acquitted. However, we had invited them to come to New York. At the end of *Brother's Keeper*, Roscoe says, "Come back up in the spring when," I forget the words, "when the green leaves come out again." We see them broken down by the tractor and have this conversation with Roscoe the day after the acquittals. And a few weeks later, when we were reviewing our material, we got a call from John Teeple saying that the boys wanted to take us up on our offer to come to New York. So these guys loaded up into a rusty old van that John Teeple had, and it was amazing that they even made the trip. And they put these lawn chairs in the back because the van had no seats, and we gave them a tour of Manhattan. And we filmed it and it was just this great footage that we never used because, I think, it's not until you're in the editing room you see emotionally what the end of the movie is. We had always imagined this New York footage as being the epilogue of the film, and not until we cut the film and experienced it did we feel like there's no better ending to this film than the boys saying goodbye to us and getting the tractor going and riding off into the sunset. So we never used the footage. The tractor footage that is now the end of the film, we always knew that that would be close to the end of the film. We didn't know it was the perfect ending until we actually saw it. We have this great New York footage, that I guess will be on the DVD, of them taking the Staten Island ferry and the Empire State Building and crossing Broadway—great footage but, somehow, it diminished this fairy-tale quality that we had on an emotional level. We realized the New York footage was counterproductive to the emotional content.

Bruce and I have a very odd way of working in the editing room. Editors always scratch their heads as to how we don't have a preconceived structure. Generally, what we like to do is . . . we know any number of great scenes, and where they actually fall is a question we leave open. Our procedure is, we cut scenes regardless of structure. From certain material, we cut multiple scenes because sometimes something will happen in the two hours we cover that ultimately we can only use for one or two moments. In the old days with the Steenbeck we'd have what we call lifts, which are literally scenes that we put in this box while reviewing our material, and then, a structure would start to emerge and suggest itself. That's one of the things we are maybe criticized for, that we selectively withhold information until that dramatic moment. If we didn't know something in month two of *Paradise Lost*, say, about Mark Byers, but we know it by month eight—some documentary filmmakers believe you should present all of your knowledge at the front. We don't believe in that. We believe in presenting the experience as we experienced it so the audience can have the same emotional journey. That can be misunderstood as manipulating chronology, but it isn't. Our films are the experiences that we had. If we thought Damien was guilty the first month we met him, then we don't make it so clear in the film that he's innocent. And, at first, our viewership should have the same feeling. . . .

What we like to do is cut scenes, and, then, a structure starts emerging so we can recreate the feelings we had while making the film. It's a fine line. It can't be all about our emotions and what we feel. It is journalistic. You have to tell the facts. If you know something . . . if stuff is clearly not true but we thought it might be true at the beginning, it needs to ultimately be balanced. You don't just wildly invent a story that doesn't exist. We do try to create a film that has all the dramatic tension of any kind of fictional story in terms of its structure, of having a beginning, middle, and end, and having some kind of dramatic arc, but not at the expense of the truth. Obviously, we have to pay very close attention to honoring our journalistic responsibilities, but also make it an engaging storytelling experience, as well as present what we experienced covering the story from an emotional standpoint. For example, in *Paradise Lost*, Mark Byers talks about how they find a jar of testicles of one of the kids under the bed of Damien. And when we first shot that, we hadn't met Damien and we hadn't been able to confirm that we had looked at the evidence yet so when we first heard it, we thought it might be true. It was shocking. And so it's legitimate to put it in the film early on because, even if it's not true, ultimately it demonstrates the level of hysteria and rumor that was swirling about the case and helps to explain how these kids could have been convicted without any real evidence. Of course, you can't leave that in the film uncountered. Damien counters it when we finally get to him later, and we find no evidence from the police, but again, that's a balance you have to find between dramatic storytelling and the responsibility to tell the truth, which in my definition of filmmaking is the subjective truth of what the filmmaker is experiencing and acknowledging that—not trying to present a film as being the absolute truth.

Now we're at that stage in our careers that we don't edit our films, because we are involved in too many projects. But let's just talk about *Brother's Keeper* and *Paradise Lost*. We screened selects; we would cut from each situation as many truthful scenes as possible. It's not like we cut different versions of the same event. For example, in *Paradise Lost 2*, one of the core things we kept returning to is the discussion the West Memphis Three's extended supporters have with that journalist, and we probably cut ten scenes from that, all truthful because that was a three- or four-hour filming situation. Sometimes certain situations yield ten scenes. Then, we start playing with structure and we start seeing what sort of scenes are emerging.

And eventually, Bruce and I say, we have to slay our babies—sometimes in and of themselves are probably the best of the four or five that we cut from a situation, but as themes started to emerge as the film suggests what it's about, they don't fit into the grander scheme. I can't explain how you make that decision—you just feel it. So you start building different sections of the film. Juxtaposing different things, and certain scenes just drop out because you don't want to return to the same setup too many times, because it feels inelegant or it doesn't fit the direction the film is going. The hardest part is recognizing which of the scenes you have to dump that you've fallen in love with, and not being afraid to dump scenes that you love. And sometimes you regret those decisions.

There's a scene we took out of *Brother's Keeper* that, to this day, it pains me that we took it out. We came to Sundance with a 120-minute film and, of course, we thought we had the perfect film and the feedback was it's a great film but it's a little too long. So we cut fifteen minutes out of it. And some of the stuff I don't miss, but there's this one scene. Bruce and I always talk about it. Why did we cut that scene? It's just one of my fondest memories, and, to this day, I still don't know why we dumped it. Sometimes you make the wrong decision. It's a scene where Roscoe takes us into the woods. When he was younger, he used to go there to drink beer and whiskey and he tells the story about how Bill cut himself with a chainsaw and used to poke his tongue through the hole—it's just this incredible scene where you get this glimpse of Roscoe as a young man . . . Roscoe always had chewing tobacco in his mouth and was starting the process of senility, and to hear him as a young man drinking beer and listening to the waterfalls. . . .

This was a different time, but this scene reminded me of an experience I had. One of the first times that we met the guys, Roscoe specifically wanted to take me into the woods and show me something, and I was a little nervous because he made it very clear he wanted me, and we had heard rumors which we learned were just rumors because people said nasty things about these guys all their lives in town until this happened, and then the town loved them. But the rumors were that these guys were gay and with each other and also, when Roscoe was younger, there were rumors Roscoe was involved with younger boys. When you're first meeting these guys you don't know what's true and what's not true and, of course, we've all seen *Deliverance*, and these are exactly the stereotypes the film attacks and breaks down. When you start watching *Brother's Keeper*, you think you're watching *Deliverance* and by the end of the film you love these guys. And that's the experience I had in real life.

So one of the first times I met Roscoe he specifically asked for me. Why? We don't know, because the guys liked Bruce as much as me. But Roscoe wanted to take me to I don't know where. He just said he wanted to show me something, so I went trooping into the woods with this old guy I had met a few times. And generally I trusted the situation, but who knows? We walked about a half a mile in the woods and he brought me to the very place where we later filmed the scene and he wanted to show me the waterfalls and the ridge. And he just wanted to show me the most beautiful, in his mind, piece of their property—they had about one hundred acres. And the whole experience taught me a lot about not being judgmental and trying to believe in the fundamental goodness of people, because here I'm spending my whole walk figuratively looking over my shoulder, a little nervous, wondering what's happening and this incredibly innocent, beautiful moment when he just wanted to share something with me.

The first couple times the house smells and you're sort of grossed out by the sanitary conditions, and by midway into the film you almost look forward to that smell. You aren't grossed out. You walk into the room and you're greeted by that smell that reminds you of that incredible life experience that you're having. And so when he took me to that ridge, it was a real turning point for trusting that experience and trusting these guys and not having a rush to judgment, which is also very much what *Paradise Lost* is about.

And so this scene that we cut out of the film was an important scene for understanding Roscoe as a younger person. And for me, personally, which the viewer would never get, it reminds me of this turning point that I had with these guys. Sometimes you cut stuff out of a film and make decisions that you are not entirely happy with, and sometimes, there are scenes that remain in the film that, reviewing later, you wonder why they're there.

You assume when you edit a film and present it that, by and large, the scenes that are in the film are the most important to tell the story. And as we were editing *Paradise 2* certain scenes, those lifts that we had chosen to discard either for legal reasons or editorial reasons—maybe a dozen scenes deemed five years earlier as not making the cut for one reason or another— all of a sudden, with the new film and new footage, took on greater importance. In *Revelations*, there's two kinds of flashbacks. There are flashbacks to scenes that were actually in the first film, so we obviously found certain scenes in the first film were important to highlight on the second film. But what people may not realize, there are probably a dozen scenes that never made it into the first film that now, all of a sudden, are important enough to make it into the second film.

Do you do test screenings, and do you think they are important?

I think test screenings are really important. Our films are very complex. The main reason I believe in a test screening is, after you have been locked in a room for sometimes as much as a year and a half, there is nothing like projecting it, and that's how we do our test screenings. I don't believe in bringing a bunch of people in front of the Avid or the Steenbeck. I believe in doing an interlock screening where you project the work print. There's nothing like sitting with an audience. You see things you never saw before. Just sitting in a theater and watching something projected with an audience, whether it's an audience you know or don't know, I don't know how much the knowing matters. But generally you invite fifty to a hundred people whose opinion you respect. Films change drastically after those screenings, not because of the particular comments that people make but because Bruce and I are sitting in the audience seeing the flaws and seeing the opportunities. We always give out questionnaires, but I never pay attention to individual comments. I read them and if they ring true to me I pay attention to them. But if enough people say the same kinds of things, a certain comment, it may be a very specific comment, or maybe the spirit of the comment all adds up to the same larger conclusion . . . at some point, if you read enough people saying the same thing, either directly or indirectly, that will rise to the top and obviously that's a comment you should pay attention to. But major structural changes and major changes to a film are usually just a process of seeing with new eyes. I find that an essential step to our process. And all three films changed drastically after the screenings.

Do you go through multiple screenings?

It's generally a one-time thing. Generally, right at the end of the road, and we're pretty close . . . I would say it's not more than twice, and probably just once.

Where are you headed?

I consider myself a documentary maker first and foremost, and mainly a verité filmmaker. I had this *Blair Witch* experience—first of all, the movie I wrote and directed is not the movie that was released, and that was a source of great pain to me because I pitched them on a very risky approach, which was not to make a teen slasher movie but one targeted to a slightly older audience, and not to do a sequel to the story itself but to do a sequel to the phenomenon. It sort of honored my role as a documentarian by making a comment about the dangers of blurring the line between fiction and reality. My script of *Blair Witch 2* was a parable about exactly that—if you so blur the lines between fiction and reality, someday you won't know quite what the difference is—because I was actually quite offended by the *Blair Witch Project*'s marketing approach, that it was a real documentary. There were some people in the theater thinking they were watching the truth. The scarier part was people walked out of the theater still thinking they had seen a real documentary; according to the marketing department at Artisan, 40 percent of the people who walked out of the theater still thought it was real and they descended upon the town of Burkettsville insisting there was a real Blair Witch. And while I found the film itself to be a really impressive, innovative storytelling experience, I found the marketing of the movie by both the filmmakers and the studio offensive to a documentary maker like myself, as well as the overreliance of fiction filmmakers on using bad documentary technique to wallow in the clichés of bad documentary making as a way of communicating reality to people. The purposeful shaky cam and the loss of focus—all the things that Bruce and I strive to leave on the editing room floor.

So I pitched Artisan on doing a film. In fact, they approached me. I wasn't passionate about doing it; in fact, I never thought in a million years I'd be doing a sequel to that movie. The idea hadn't crossed my mind that I'd ever be in that situation. So I decided if I did the movie I was going to do a very gutsy original approach and make a comment on the things that bothered me—shaking the camera does not equal reality, which is why I chose to film it like a traditional movie and also to make it about, like in *Paradise Lost 2*, the impact of the first movie. And to talk about the dangers of blurring the lines between fiction and reality. Now my script totally adhered to the concept that I pitched and my director's cut totally adhered to my script. Literally in the twelfth hour, two months before release and when it should have been locked, the studio lost its will because the marketing department had a different vision for the film late in the movie and inserted all this gory footage that I find repellent and turned it into a teen slasher movie instead of this intelligent Hitchcockian parable that I was endeavoring to make.

That whole experience of losing control and doing something you're not passionate about has reaffirmed my independent roots like nothing else. I have been sent dozens and dozens of really bad horror scripts that I couldn't be paid enough to do. But my future is to continue to tell stories where I am in control of my creative destiny, and most of the time that will mean nonfiction. I will never put myself in a situation as a hired gun working for people who just care about the bottom line, which makes me a good candidate for documentaries.

Chapter 10: Bruce Sinofsky
Experiential Filmmaking: Bringing Us into the Story

Sinofsky began his filmmaking career at Maysles Films, where he met Joe Berlinger. The two collaborated on a documentary short, *Outrageous Taxi Stories* (1989), and thus began their filmmaking partnership. *Brother's Keeper* (1992) was their first feature-length documentary endeavor, and it became a much-lauded film and one of the most successful self-distributed documentaries at that time. Their next coproduction, *Paradise Lost: The Child Murders at Robin Hood Hills* (1996), began as a chronicling of a triple murder allegedly by three Midwestern small-town teens, but became more an exploration of stereotyping and local mentality. *Paradise Lost 2: Revelations*, their follow-up film, was a look at the effect of a film on that situation and an examination of the execution or misexecution of justice. Most recently, Sinofsky helmed a project for PBS's *American Masters* series on Sun Records. *Rockin' Good Night* is part documentary and part performance film, looking at the history, present, and future of the famed recording label. Star-studded, it features recording sessions from such legends as Jimmy Page, Bob Dylan, Elton John, Paul McCartney, and Robert Plant.

What was your background in filmmaking?

Well, I went to NYU film school—I came there in 1976—how I really got my break in the film business is that my grandmother knew Albert and David Maysles's mother—they were both in organizations in Boston. My grandmother is now ninety-seven—and kept on pestering me to go see the Maysles brothers. So I went up there on Valentine's Day, 1977, and met David, and they hired me that day and I ended up working with the Maysles for fourteen years.

As . . .

I was an apprentice editor, I was an assistant editor, then I was an editor. Joe Berlinger and I met there in '86 and later on in the story, in '90, we went off to do *Brother's Keeper*, and then we left and formed our own company.

Would you consider yourself a cinema verité filmmaker? And what does that mean to you?

Well, I think the Maysles approach, at least in principal, is that there's a line you don't cross. And I, frankly, don't believe in that line. I believe that's a line that's in the sand and it should be crossed when it's necessary. I mean, I do have relationships with people that I've filmed over the years that went beyond just the filming period. I'm still very good friends with people up in Munnsville, who I did *Brother's Keeper* with, and the people with *Paradise Lost*. This film I'm just finishing now on Sun Records, I'm very good friends with a lot of people that I've met there. And I think that if you're a good filmmaker you film everything, you get close to people, you dump that baggage of not being part of people's lives on a personal level. And then when you get into the editing room, you just have to be able to put on blinders when it comes to your feelings towards people, so you don't let that impact how you edit your film.

So I am a verité filmmaker. I'm not a lover of interviews, but sometimes you have an obligation to your audience to get some information that is very difficult necessarily to get from a scene, so you do interviews. Both Joe and I have tried over the years not to do interviews, but sometimes when it's a complicated murder case or a complicated story, you have to. I would love to do a film like *Salesman*, which I think is the best of what documentary and nonfiction has to offer. But it was a much more lyrical story and didn't cry out for long explanations as to what it was to sell a *Bible*. The story is really about these four remarkable men who traveled from Boston to Florida and it's really, as Albert used to love to say, a real-life *Death of a Salesman*. But I would never consider myself a purist. I'm not afraid to use fictional sorts of elements—not recreations, but helicopter shots, to have your film scored, to cut it and shoot it the way you would a feature so it cuts like a scene. I think those elements just add to what tends to be a very, very well-crafted story. What I really like about *Brother's Keeper* and *Paradise Lost* is that they have a clear beginning, middle, and end. They've got their heroes and villains. They've got rising and falling action like you'd look for in a dramatic picture, and I think that's why people embraced our films on television and in the theaters, because they felt like something that they were very familiar with, which was a movie that they would pay $8 to see—as opposed to . . . many documentaries are sort of illustrated lectures that are well-made. I would put Ken Burns in that category, because I admire his work, but I find the films to be rather static and stilted. The Maysles and Pennebaker and Leacock and Drew—that's where I cut my teeth.

Are there rules that exist in documentary filmmaking that you wouldn't break?

I would never recreate something, and I would never tell somebody to say or do something. But there are subtle ways of getting people to give the information that you need to tell your story. You put them in situations that are comfortable to them where they can talk about certain things. But I would never say, "Here, I need you to talk about this, that, or the other thing because I need that material." When I'm working on a film, whether on my own or with Joe, we would do these story conferences every night. "Okay, what did we get today? What did we film tonight?" We'd be sitting in our hotel rooms at the Ramada Inn or something on some dumpy highway. "Okay, we got this, this, this, and this. That moves the story in this direction; that helps solidify this point we're trying to make, or didn't help clarify it for an audience." And we would have a road map of what we've gotten and what we need to get. And if we were doing an interview or if it was a situation that was conducive to getting the information that we needed to complete the story, then we would be able to do that. But we would never say, "Do this or do that."

What I mean about crossing the line is the bond of the relationship that you have with people. In *Paradise Lost*, it wasn't unusual to have some of the mothers of the victims call me at two and three in the morning, or to call Joe. Because, like in any death situation, for a week after the death of somebody there's casseroles and coffee cake and conversation, and then it disappears. And then, they feel uncomfortable talking about it because nobody wants to talk about it anymore. But by calling us at home in New Jersey—they're in Arkansas—we could be a release for them. We could talk to them if they had a little too much to drink, or they were just feeling sad and they missed their child and they just didn't have anybody anymore to talk about it because everybody had talked about it too much, and they knew that we were there to listen.

Now, is that crossing the line? Pure documentarians, I think, would say so, and we've been criticized very loudly by the International Documentary Association. Frankly, our films have never really been embraced by pure documentarians, who somehow feel that the films, as good as they are, as entertaining as they are, can't have been done without some sort of collusion with our subject. We've always sort of pissed on their parade because it's just not the case. There are certain documentarians who believe you can only make films in a certain way. And if that were the case we would have just biographies with stills, classic interviews with the wilted palm tree or the wilted potted plant behind the person with a badly lit slash across the back, and that's all we'd have.

We'd never be able to get into the field, into people's lives, which I think is an amazing phenomenon. I think you have to be responsible enough to say that if it wasn't for the Ward brothers letting us into their lives in *Brother's Keeper*, or the six families in *Paradise Lost 1* and *2*, or *The Begging Game*, which we did for PBS about panhandlers and people who lived on the street—if they hadn't let us into their lives I wouldn't have the house that I have, the life that I have, the reputation that I have. I've somehow taken advantage of their misery or tragedy in those cases and used it to my benefit on a personal level. Sometimes that's a little thing I have trouble wrestling with. Not that we coerced them or forced them to do it . . . I think oftentimes people who are sort of disenfranchised, who are poor, who live in trailer parks—sort of the leftover people that people don't usually give airtime to or even ask their opinions—are usually people that are not anxious and want to be filmed or want to be involved in the film because, in many ways, it's their fifteen minutes. I know for a fact that if any tragedy ever happened in my life, I can promise you I would never let anybody like myself in my own home.

I'm really thrilled that this project I'm just finishing on Sun Records was fun. Dealing with Paul McCartney and Plant and Page, and Matchbox 20, as well as Sam Phillips and a lot of legends, like Jerry Lee Lewis, from Sun Records was fun and nobody got killed. Nobody's angry. It tells a wonderful story about music, which is a passion of mine. So were *Paradise Lost 1* and *2*—those two films are a constant in my life because I'm constantly being called for interviews. So that tragedy, that difficult film, that difficult experience is something that stays with me.

Doing documentaries is disruptive to your regular life more so than fiction films, especially films like *Paradise Lost*, with such grim subject matter. Is it difficult on your psyche?

Definitely. Films like that . . . it's your responsibility to be a sponge and to soak up the emotions and what these people are going through on either side of the issue. Because we were just as time-intensive with the families of the victims as we were with the accused's families. And your job is to hold in, and you become like a water balloon and you can't let that water out until you get into the editing room. These films that we made are really impressions of what we experienced. It's what we felt. We can never say it's the definitive truth because I'm not one of these believers that you can ever have the definitive truth on film, because as soon as you edit one frame, what your cinematographer chooses to shoot and what you choose to shoot have an effect on the reality's perception. I believe that it's an impression, never the defined truth.

I think filmmakers that go out there with a mission oftentimes don't make the best of films because they have a blind spot to things that they want to avoid. I'm wide open with the iris. I'm looking for everything that I can find. Every day, you go back to your hotel room. Every day, you would commiserate with your crew about how depressive and the sad state that these people live in. They live in a trailer park, they live on about $8,000 a year. Three families—their eight-year-old child was killed. My son Alex is now turning eighteen, and he was eight at the time. Over the years, there have been odd moments when I've looked at Alex and imagined that, my God, these kids would be seventeen, eighteen years old. Would they be going to college or would they just be working? What would they be doing? Other things that the Byers and the other people would say: "Oh, we're never going to be able to buy him his first car," or his first dance, the first date, all those things they lost—they still haunt me today. So you have a responsibility when you make films. If not, then it really does become strip-mining. You go into a town, you strip them of their story, and you walk away. Then you go onto another one. It's what news-gathering groups have to do. They don't have the time or the resources to do due diligence to people's lives. Filmmakers who don't do that—I don't have a lot of respect for them.

Do you think there are certain traits that are beneficial to doing this work?

I think you have to have a thick skin and you really have to persevere, because getting permission. . . . With *Paradise Lost*, we had the benefit of making *Brother's Keeper*. And the idea of cameras in the courtroom—we could have the judge call the judge up in Munnsville, New York, and tell him we weren't going to be disruptive and things like that. But in terms of the people you meet, you have to be patient. You can't force yourself. We always say that the work we do before and after we film is much more important than the time we're actually filming. So in a day, we might go to somebody's house and just spend a day with them. Go out for lunch and hang out and talk and get to know them a little bit before we do any filming at all. And so there's a bond and a trust. In some cases, it takes six, seven months to get somebody to finally say, "Yes, we see where you're coming from. We see what you're doing. Although this is the most personal, most devastating moment in my life, and I never talk about my dead son, you're somebody we feel we can do that to."

That work you do, it's very human. You have to be able to talk, you have to be able to understand other people's ways of life. You have to be able to sit down with somebody who doesn't have a pot to piss in over a beer, and there can be no differentiation between you and them. There shouldn't be, anyway, but there is in society, unfortunately. If you're making money and you're educated, there is a difference, but it shouldn't be one that's palpable. And I think that that's something Joe and I did very well. Time has treated the relationships well because we're still connected to almost everybody that we've filmed. You have to do that; you have to work hard at it, too. We always talk about jumping off a cliff, and hoping that there's a mattress or a parachute involved, because you're venturing off into. . . . You know, when Joe and I went down to *Paradise Lost*, it was me, Joe, Doug Cooper, and a local sound guy. So it was, like, New Yorkers—leather-clad, long-haired New Yorkers—parachuting into Arkansas, and the reception was hardly warm. But over time, we found a common bond with these people, a common ground.

And you have to have a small unit that's indestructible. It's like an army platoon and you go off and you get to fight battles and you have to know that the people you're working with are going to be there for you. And that gives you a sense of comfort and trust. You know that you're going to be dedicating a lot of time and energy. Documentaries are long—two- to three-year commitment for a long-form film—and you just have to be able to have that dedication. Because sometimes you're going to have multiple days where nothing's cooking and you're gonna start losing your drive and energy, and it's like, "Well, jeez, do we really have a film here? Should we be doing this?" And then it's like you're a fireman and an alarm goes off and something's there to capture and you know that you're on the right track.

What excites you about documentary filmmaking?

Part of it is that I'm fascinated by environments and places that I don't normally frequent. We've always loved subcultures and things like that. I'm always interested in the human condition, so I'm always fascinated to live, in some ways, through other people's experiences. I've never been on trial for murder and lived in a trailer park and all those things, but I am fascinated by the human condition and love spending time with people who walk in different circles. So I get to hang out in the studio with Paul McCartney, and I get to hang out with Damien's family, and I get to take Delbert out for his first Chinese food in Munnsville. That whole experience, I found incredibly rewarding; almost as much as the filmmaking itself is the life experience that I have in making it. I suppose it's like a sociologist and anthropologist, in that you're almost put into a time zone. Who thinks about being in Arkansas and covering a murder case, or hanging out with Plant and Page in a studio in London, or sleeping in a box with homeless people to see what it's like to spend a night in the dead of winter and how they have to exist on a day-to-day basis? I think those kinds of experiences are phenomenal, and I embrace them.

Left to right: Roscoe Ward, Michael Kraus (soundman), Joe Berlinger, Douglas Cooper (cameraman), and Bruce Sinofsky shooting on the Ward brothers' farm. Photo credit: Derek Berg, courtesy Creative Thinking International, Ltd.

Every time I look for a new filming subject, it's gotta be something that intrigues me because I'm off at work a lot. It has to be something I really like and really feel strongly about. I just did my first shoot last week on the Steppenwolf Theatre Company in Chicago. They were doing *Cuckoo's Nest* there, so I did a little shooting around the theater with Gary Sinise and some of the cast members. They've sort of revolutionized theater. And I like theater, and I said, "It's a good opportunity—I'd like to venture into that," and that's worked out very well.

Is that a topic you chose yourself?

I was approached by Steppenwolf and we met for dinner with a couple of the people and I said, "Yeah, this would be something that I'd be interested in." And for every one film I do there has to be two or three that I don't do because the dedication of a year or two is, like, "Shit, I'd better do something I really like." If I'm not interested in the subject of the film, then my audience will never be interested, either. So I know if I'm interested in it then I can make an interesting film.

What percentage of your films were your original idea versus those that someone approached you with?

Well, *Brother's Keeper* and *Paradise Lost* were from articles that we read in the paper. I was approached about the Sun Records film. We pitched the *Begging Game*, which was the homeless people's film, to ABC at the time, and the *Rolling Stone* magazine anniversary show, we were approached. I'd say it's fifty-fifty. I think usually American Masters, or PBS, or HBO—they have very powerful people who run these departments—they often have a lot of good ideas. *Brother's Keeper* and *Paradise Lost* had to be pounced on almost immediately just because of the subject matter and the urgency, but [with] others, there can be a much more leisurely pace.

Can you characterize your style as a documentary director? Do you think you make the same style of film each time, or challenge yourself consciously or unconsciously to do something new, discover something new . . . ?

Every film is an exploration. I don't even use the "documentary" moniker. I've always said *nonfiction*. And I've always said that all filmmaking is storytelling. We are in the nonfiction arena. Joe did *Blair Witch 2*, and I'm involved with a project with Warner Brothers, so there'll be some fiction work in the future, but I love doing nonfiction. I love the unexpected that you can get from going into a place that you know nothing about. So it is about discovery.

I've always felt that fiction is handed the same set of paints, but just a different aegis, and a different piece of canvas. I like to challenge myself. How do I make this look different, feel different, seem different than what I've done before? I think the limitations with what Ken Burns does is, every film is the same. And I find, as interesting as the subject might be, he hasn't challenged himself at all filmically—maybe the research stage, finding people, and the access that he gets is great, but I find the work to be tedious after awhile because it's not challenging to the audience on a visceral level or a visual level. And you could take a look at *Jazz*, then flash back to *Civil War*, and you wouldn't see much difference in style. They're good films; I'm not criticizing the films, I'm just saying that they're more like illustrated lectures as opposed to the films that I admire that are much more experiential. I'm quite fond of what the Maysles did and Leacock and Pennebaker and Drew, and I like the work that Michael Moore has done. There are really talented nonfiction filmmakers, but it's hard to make film after film.

I consider myself a nonfiction verité filmmaker who embraces some of the artifice of fiction in using helicopter shots, and scores, and the way you shoot, and the way you construct, and the way you tell your story with a beginning, middle, and end. I like that about fiction film. I think we all do. But too often documentaries tend to be films that have a point of view from the director, that they try to drag their audience kicking and screaming to their position.

I think of the bigger films—like *Paradise Lost* and *Brother's Keeper*—that there's a certain ambiguity that allows the audience to think and to make decisions and to question things. Because when people say to me, "Well, you know, you were wrong," or, "You were right," I say, "You know, I don't think there's a right or wrong answer in the films." If you think that scene was this or you feel that meant that, then you're right, because it's interpretive. A good nonfiction film that doesn't take a point of view on something is like a great piece of art. If you go to the Museum of Modern Art and look at a Monet, no two people see it the same. So why shouldn't you see a film the same way? That's what I love about the art form. Nothing gives me more pleasure than after a screening of a film that I've done that, three or four days later, I see somebody or overhear somebody in the bus or the coffee shop talking about this film that they had seen, and each saw something completely different in the same frame, and to me, that's like, "Wow, then I did alright."

To what extent do you think about the audience when you make a film, and does that at all affect how you make films? How do you feel about test screenings?

We do test screenings in the sense that we'll show a rough cut and an advance cut to friends and family to get some feedback. And you can actually watch and get a sense of what's working and what's not working just by the way people are breathing, how they're reacting—things people laugh at, things you didn't think they'd laugh at, or don't understand. That's helpful, and I think Joe feels pretty strongly about that. I've always been a little less in that department because I feel that you can get pulled in too many different directions by people feeling that they have to say something, because they've been invited.

But I don't think I make films with the audience in mind, ever. When Joe and I are working together it's really what Joe and I think about the film, and if we're not editing it ourselves, what the editor thinks about it. If you start making films with the idea, "what's an audience going to react to?" and "what are they gonna want to see?" you're not letting the natural material that you have dictate what you're filming because then, you're thinking, "We should really get this because our audience is gonna want to see that," so I never even worry about an audience.

After *Brother's Keeper*, I stopped even caring about critics. I mean, it was the first film out, and it got amazing reviews. We must have had three hundred great reviews and one bad one. After that, you're never as good as the reviews and you're never as bad as the reviews. I just stopped caring what critics had to say about it. I was much more interested about the person down the block or the stranger on the train that saw this film. I would read reviews and they were reading into things that Joe and I had no intention of. You end up taking credit for it, but they were putting us on a pedestal for things that other people were saying. "Wow, these guys made a great film about poor man's justice," and this and that and this, and it's all very flattering and you stop thinking about your filming and you start worrying about critics, and you're dead. The film is very personal for me and I'm very fortunate in most cases. I wouldn't say I've ever had final cut, but I'd say that in almost all cases, 98 percent of the film is exactly the way I wanted it to be. There's always compromises on certain issues—it could be for language, it could be for legal reasons, or whatever, but the films are usually just the films that I want them to be. I've been lucky with that.

What kind of ratio do you shoot?

I know in *Paradise Lost* we shot 150:1. Ninety-nine percent of what we shot, we didn't use. That's how much we shot. And there's a lot of trial material that we didn't use. We were there for five weeks of trial and we basically taped everything. *Brother's Keeper* is probably a 50:1 ratio. You shoot a lot when you have to shoot a lot. With the Sun Records project, I never shot more than twelve, thirteen a day. When you're shooting film it's so expensive that, honestly, I was very well organized on what I wanted to try to get in any given day . . . didn't shoot everything that moved. I think sometimes people who are shooting Beta, or, even worse, now with DV, they just shoot so much that the editor is going to go crazy because they've got seven hundred hours' worth of material. It's amazing—we accumulate it but then, all of a sudden, you stack it in a room and the editor's going nuts, like, "What am I going to do with all this? It's going to take me a month and a half to screen it." And then, how do you screen it and have some game plan, the way you want to go with that big lump of clay and mold it into something that you fancy?

To what extent do you know what the big picture is before you go into the editing room?

They evolve once you're editing, but I leave every filming situation sort of knowing what the scene is, and I think Joe feels the same way. When you get into the editing room, obviously, the film takes on many lives, and any documentary film can be cut fifty different ways. But if you're instinctive in your editing and your craft, you go with your gut instinct and you start cutting the scenes that you can cut, and you start figuring how you put this jigsaw puzzle together. Most films, most good nonfiction films, are created in the editing room. The Maysles always said, "Content dictates form." So, depending upon what you accumulate and what you have available to you when you start editing over that six months to a year, it's sort of like being one mile away from this huge totem pole, and as you get closer and closer and closer and closer, and it gets clearer, and, all of a sudden, it's like, wow, you're there, it's like, "Okay, this all makes sense."

Bruce (left) and Joe on the Ward brothers' farm. Photo credit: Derek Berg, courtesy Creative Thinking International, Ltd.

Some people cut things out of sequence for dramatic effect. Is that verboten?

No. We did flash-forwards, flash-backwards in *Paradise Lost,* and again, embracing the strength of your material if you can come up with a clever . . . it's not to manipulate your audience to think this happened beforehand, like Barbara Kopple did a couple of times in *American Dream,* and I don't think it hurt the film. I think she took stuff that she got afterwards and made it earlier, which raised the dramatic tensions. But I don't think we consciously ever tried to put anything in and out of sequence for those purposes. *Revelations,* we just flashed forwards, flashed backwards, but we never did anything that manipulated the facts of how events took place, put things in the wrong light. That's a mistake.

Do you ever have an underlying hope for some of your films? To effect change, for example?

Well, it's hard to say that you have that kind of hope when you're not sure what the film is gonna be. I must say that for *Revelations,* we did hope that this was gonna help Damien. Because by then, we could fully articulate that we felt that these kids hadn't done the crime. That's one where we sort of skewed from the path that we normally take by being ambiguous. We were very pointed in saying that the system didn't work and that these guys deserved a new trial. I'm not saying that they should be set free that day, but I really think that those guys are innocent; they do deserve another trial.

And yet, we were allowing Mark Byers enough rope that if he wanted to hang himself we would be happy to film it. In the literal sense. So, in that sense, we did have a mission. We did feel like part of the failure of the first film was that it never got onto the editorial pages. It was only on the entertainment pages, and it was treated like entertainment. We felt that it should be embraced by editorial pages with the issues of poor man's justice and that sort of hysteria and witch-hunt kind of thing that was going on. So we felt that we could make the next film, because of the momentum of the first film, the attention it got—we could make a film that had a bit of a mission statement. Again, why make another film that the audience just makes up their mind about? We sort of pushed a little bit on this one.

I never am aware of you as filmmakers in your films.

We work really hard. It was a little difficult in *Brother's Keeper* because sometimes, we felt by including our voices you could understand what they were talking about—we didn't want to subtitle them. Even the little thing where they named the turkeys after us—there was a larger scene where you actually physically saw us and both Joe and I said, "Let's lose that. It's too much about us." Films shouldn't be about the filmmaker. I'm not Nick Broomfield. It's obvious that he wants to be on film and he sort of loves the attention. That's his style of filmmaking—same with Michael Moore. That's their way of . . . I don't want to call it ambush filmmaking because the people they're ambushing pretty much deserve to be ambushed. But it's a style that allows them to be part and parcel of it.

My feeling is that we're sort of there, but we're not there, and the audience is almost seeing it firsthand, as close to firsthand as they can. And it shouldn't be filtered through the voice and the actions of the filmmaker or the cameraman. Like the Maysles in *Grey Gardens*, they're clearly there and there are times when Big and Little Edie talk to them and dance with them. If Albert says that they didn't cross the line in some way with that, because he's a bit of a purist, I think he's wrong. I think they did cross the line because clearly, there was affection and there was a relationship between the four people. Sometimes, Albert will pooh-pooh that but I really think that he got close to these people. It's okay—it's a good thing—but sometimes, he'll talk about, "You don't cross the line," but that's the line I was talking about, that Edie continued to have a relationship with Albert and David well after the shoot.

Critics have said Nick Broomfield's films are as much about his pursuit of the story as they are about his subjects. And he becomes part of the story.

A lot of times it gets in the way of what the story is. He clearly has an agenda and he has an opinion, and he's not subtle about it. That's one of the other canvases that we have to work with. That's the one he chooses and is most comfortable with.

I think what happens often when you do verité and you let people talk to each other and interact with each other—it's their feelings that are coming across. When you do an interview, they are responding to a question, so it's not coming directly from their heart, it's not coming from them of their own free will. They're being asked something, so they have to respond to it. And then you do a follow-up to it if you haven't really gotten what you wanted. When you allow people who have been friends and worked together for forty years to get together in a room or a bar or a backyard barbecue . . . you start them up. You push them down the hill a little bit so they have some momentum, and they just go. And your job is to stay out of the way. At the end of the day you've shot fifty minutes, and you've got a wonderful three-and-a-half-minute scene. And the rest was just getting to that point. Look, I admire all those other people; it's just the style of filmmaking—being on camera—I don't want to be on camera.

There are lots of offshoots from verité. How do you see documentaries changing or evolving?

Those offshoots are still there and strong. One of the good things that Ken Burns has done is he's gotten mainstream America to watch documentaries. And with cable—*Biography* and all these other things—more people are watching them, but how many people are going to the movie theaters to watch a two-hour piece of nonfiction? Not that many. They're still always going to be the bastard child of Hollywood. They're never going to really be embraced on a large, large scale. But I think a great documentary is as good as, if not better than, a great fiction film any time, just because there is no script. There's no net. People will watch films like *Brother's Keeper* and *Paradise Lost*. I run into them or they call me and they say that those films changed their lives. It changed their lives in terms of what they want to do with their career or how they perceived humanity on a certain level. You don't often get that with the fast-food kind of entertainment that Hollywood tends to put out.

But it's getting harder and harder to make films like *Paradise Lost* and *Brother's Keeper*. One, because the competition is harder because unfortunately with the plethora of cheap video equipment, where you can go out for $3,000 and have a digital camera—it somehow gives license to people that think they can make films. And, unfortunately, often people with the equipment go off and make films and they stink. I think maybe 10 percent of all documentaries in long form that are made are good, and the rest of them stink. That's being maybe a little hard on the form. You know, making a film about Joe's bagel shop or very personal films about a relative or this or that—often they're just so personal that they don't hold as much weight as other films. That's one of those offshoots you're talking about—the personal film—the person who's ill with AIDS, or somebody who has cancer, or the aging grandfather who was at Auschwitz—I mean, they're all personal films and they all have great subject matter, but I think sometimes there's just too many of them. Because they're personal, that doesn't mean the person making the film has the ability to make a really good documentary.

The difference between chronicling and telling a story is the critical difference between amateur and professional....

You can see the same parallels to fiction films. There are several dozen really talented, great fiction filmmakers, and I think there's the same amount in the nonfiction world. It costs a lot of money to make fiction on a certain level, because they're so much more involved. You can go off on any corner of Manhattan and make a film about something in a documentary. That's good and bad because a camera should be in the hands of people and people should go out and tell stories. But there's a glut of bad films out there. Look, I can be honest and critical because I think I've done some good work and I've seen—people submit work to me all the time. More often than not, I see very bad work, but the heart's there and the desire's there, but the skill is not. It makes me feel good, because a lot of the people I work with are really gifted cinematographers, editors, and directors, and you see the talent that they have. It makes you appreciate what you've done yourself with other people, because I really do feel that what I learned from Albert and David, and what I learned from Charlotte Zwerin, has been used well. And what I try to instill in people that I work with, either in the editing room or on location, is that I want everybody to feel that they're part of a filmmaking team. It's not Bruce's film, or Bruce and Joe's film. It's everybody's film. It's as much the soundperson's film as it is the PA's [production assistant] film, in a certain way, because without all of those people nothing gets done. Although you get the lion's share of the credit publicly, internally you'd find that the people I work with and Joe works with all felt that they were very much a part of a collaborative effort. If you surround yourself with really good people—who have a good visual sense and a good sense of themselves and filmmaking—then it only makes what you do better.

Are you and Joe partnering still?

Yeah, we're doing a film together with Metallica. We're doing a feature with those guys, with Elektra Records, and we're doing a film with a Mercedes group. We're always looking for projects. I'm helping him out on an HBO project. I'm meeting with Fleetwood Mac next week about a film. When Joe went off to do *Blair Witch* [2], it made sense that we'd do different things. But we love working with each other. I think he appreciated the experience he had on *Blair Witch* . . . but also appreciated that he and I made really good films—he was needing an identity of his own, as opposed to being just Joe and Bruce, Joe and Bruce. And I think that was something that I understood and I respected, and now we're back together doing certain projects, which is great.

We made these films together and we are a team, and the work that we did together should be talked about in those ways. But the Sun project, which I absolutely adore, is being shown to the television critics next week as PBS's and American Masters's showpiece for the year. That's been a great film for me. It was good for me to go off and do something like this to make sure that . . . without really thinking about it when you always work together, there's always that shoulder to lean on. When you're alone you want to make sure you can do it in a vacuum like that. It was a fun experience and reinforced the lessons that had been taught to me over the last twenty-five years.

The reality is that in filmmaking . . . you never know more than you don't know. I really believe that. I'm forty-five now, and I don't think until I was maybe forty that I really felt I had a grasp on the work and what I did. I really felt that all the life experiences that I had—like the death of my father, divorce, five children, all these different things, remarriage—all those things just made me a better person, but also made me, I think, a better filmmaker because I had a much more varied life experience and I was also sensitive to a lot more things that maybe I wouldn't have been when I was twenty-five, thirty years old.

Funding—is it easier to come by with a track record?

It gets easier. I know it's difficult, and I know that money is tighter and budgets are getting smaller. We had the benefit with *Brother's Keeper* of funding it ourselves. I don't think second mortgages on homes are benefits.

What was your budget for that?

Well, we spent a couple of hundred thousand dollars on our own and then, when American Playhouse came in, I think the ultimate budget was a little less than half a million. But based on that success—it did, like, a mil-

(Standing, left to right) Lyman Ward, Roscoe Ward, Joe Berlinger, Delbert Ward, Bruce Sinofsky, and (seated) Douglas Cooper (cameraman) in the Ward brothers' home. Photo credit: Derek Berg, courtesy Creative Thinking International, Ltd.

lion six, we distributed that film ourselves and it did really well, and reviews were great, and it was very well respected—then HBO, all of a sudden, was interested in us. So every film I've done since then has had a minimum budget of $700,000—usually a million, million one, $900,000, which is a lot of money for nonfiction. So I've never had to fund-raise, I've never had to do a grant proposal or anything like that. Thank God NEH grants and all those other grants are available, because not everybody has the luck. Again, I owe it all to the Ward brothers. If it weren't for the Ward brothers, I wouldn't be sitting in an editing room here at PBS looking at Jerry Lee Lewis. Because those grizzly old men gave me life, I think I've been very fortunate. I demand a large amount of money because one, I also demand a lot of salary—not huge, but enough that I can live very well on one film if I have to for a year. I'm just not one of these people that believe that documentary filmmakers have to be living in the East Village on nothing but old pizza and three-day-old bagels. You can make a living and you can have a life.

Do you make a living solely off of documentaries?

Well, I do commercials, or corporate film from time to time, but largely, it's the long form . . . something in the documentary realm.

What appeals to you about doing fiction film?

Storytelling. It's also a different experience. The film that I want to make is a very personal film, something I feel a deep passion for, and I feel if I can shoot it in a realistic way to make you feel like you're really a part of it, it will take some of my documentary skills, and it'll also take those documentary skills of working with people to working with actors. Because, if I can get actors to not act or not feel like they're acting, then I'm gonna get an honest performance that the audience is gonna embrace. And I think that's something that I'll bring to the table.

Is this your first fiction piece?

It'll be the first major fiction piece. It's something I'm under contract with Warner Brothers on. We actually will start the writing process over the next couple weeks—the script. But it's been a four-year process to get a lot of parties—because it deals with John Lennon and his death, so you're dealing with Yoko, you're dealing with music, and it's taken me a long time to get everything going. But Warner Brothers is fully behind the project, and I'm hoping to be shooting spring or fall of next year. I'll be the director and I'll work with the writer—the story is by me, but obviously, Warner Brothers wants a skilled writer. Documentary filmmakers don't get the shot at the brass ring of Hollywood very often, and I'm only gonna take one shot, because if I do it and I do it well, then there'll be life after it. If I do a bad job, it'll one, kill my film career in terms of the fiction arena, but it will also hurt other nonfiction filmmakers who are hoping that they get a chance to use the other canvas. Joe, unfortunately, had a bad experience with *Blair Witch* [2]. Michael Apted, who's done *Coal Miner's Daughter* and also great documentaries, is one, but there aren't that many.

If successful with this project, would you seek a balance between nonfiction and fiction filmmaking?

Oh, yeah. I would never abandon nonfiction because that life experience of going off with people and sharing their lives, their real lives, is much different than being on set in an artificial environment that you're creating. I imagine as long as I'm making films, my heart will be in the nonfiction world. The unknown is what my feelings would be to fiction, but I would never stray that far away.

How have you changed since your first film—do you have more or less anxiety or have you changed in terms of how you handle your subjects?

I think, actually, there's more—not more anxiety . . . we did *Brother's Keeper* and there was nobody watching. And then, when the film came out and it was a big hit, every film you make after that, you have your name. It used to be just Bruce Sinofsky; now, it's Bruce Sinofsky and, in parentheses, it says, *Brother's Keeper, Paradise Lost*. So there's always a little bit of extra weight, that every film I make has to be as good, if not better. So I think, sometimes, that's a good drive to help motivate you.

But I'm always a little nervous before every shoot, not in the editing room or anything, but every shoot, every day that I go in, my wife always says, "You didn't sleep well last night. You always have to go to the bathroom before you leave," and I think that's just nervous energy that I bridle. I take that nervous energy and it's a good nervous energy, and I use that to just keep me going through the day. It's like Bill Russell of the Boston Celtics—he used to throw up before every basketball game, and then he'd be ready to go. For me, it's always just a little nervous anxiety, even if it's the most simple situation, or maybe something I've already filmed or some-body I've interviewed before who knows me and is very comfortable—I always still have that little bit of nervous energy and I like it. I never go on to any filming situation so prepared that I think I've got it all figured out. I think that nervous energy always just guides you into an arena; it helps you get the best, and you'll never be satisfied until you've gone to dinner.

One thing David Maysles taught me . . . he said, "If, on every shoot, you go out and you get five good minutes, or five great minutes, and you have twenty shoot days, you're going to make a great film. But you have to make sure that you walk away each day knowing that you've got the cover-age and you got the material that you need to continue the process." That's something that I've taken to heart over the years.

If you didn't make films, what would you do?

I'd be in the South of France drinking wine. Since the age of twelve I've wanted to be a film editor and a filmmaker. That's thirty-three years. I probably would have been a pretty good politician, or a very good social worker. But there's not much else that really interests me, because I think, when you find what you really like, it's like breathing. I don't have a Monday through Friday. Life is just . . . there are 365 days of the year whether I'm working or not working, on a project or not. Every day is the same to me. I never wake up and say, "Oh, I gotta be there by 9:30." I don't dread anything. All of it's enjoyable to me. I've never had a nine-to-five mentality. Since I was nineteen years old I've worked in this sort of wonder-ful world of creativity with amazingly creative people around me, and it's fun. I laugh every day, I have wonderful kids at home and my wonderful wife, so my life's really full. The only thing I would like to have is, maybe, twenty-six hours in the day.

Chapter 11: Irving Saraf
Recreating Emotions

Saraf was raised in Israel and moved to the States to earn a degree in film from UCLA. He was the founder and former head of the KQED-TV film unit, and then became manager of the Saul Zaentz Production Company, where he served as postproduction supervisor of *One Flew Over the Cuckoo's Nest*. He has worked in feature and documentary film as producer, director, and editor with over 150 films to his name, many for TV.

With his filmmaking partner, Allie Light, Saraf won a 1991 Academy Award for Best Documentary Feature for *In the Shadow of the Stars* (1991) and a 1995 Emmy Award for *Dialogues with Madwomen* (1993). Their other films together are a series of portraits of folk artists, *Visions of Paradise* (1979–1982), *Mitsuye and Nellie* (1981), and their latest films, *Rachel's Daughters: Searching for the Causes of Breast Cancer* (1997) and *Blind Spot: Murder by Women* (2000).

How did you get your start in film?

The way I got into film altogether is very strange. It's kind of silly. I came from Israel. I came here to be a student and I ended up at UCLA. And they told me I had to get a major. I knew nothing about what to study, so I looked through the book and I decided to get a major in movies. I thought, "That's great, my parents will be happy that I'm going to university and getting a degree, and I will go and sit and watch movies." Which I liked to do. I knew nothing about filmmaking, nothing. I took some still photographs when I was a teenager, but I knew nothing about film. And I got totally hooked. I think I was the only student in my class who wasn't connected to some kind of a Hollywood family.

As soon as I graduated, I came to San Francisco and I was looking for work, and I heard about a new station that just started, public television station KQED or Channel 9, and I volunteered there. And in a few months I was hired part-time, and a year later, I was head of the film department. Which didn't mean much. It meant I cleaned film. But then my father bought me a Bolex camera and actually the first national project was a

Irving Saraf filming a KQED-TV project in 1969.

series of five films with Ansel Adams, which I mostly shot and edited. And from then on, a few years later, we started a special projects unit, and we did only national programming for public television. We had to turn a profit for the station, which we did, and it grew over the years to be the number-one producing station for public television. We always beat Boston. I ended up with a department of forty-two people. The station decided to get out of national production behind my back, so I quit and went to work for Saul Zaentz.

What excited me about documentaries. . . . I got interested already in documentaries at UCLA by seeing all the classics, like the British Crown Unit, and these were the documentaries that really excited me. Then we saw the very beginning of cinema verité. No, the cinema verité was later; I was already working at KQED. And then, the sixties exploded. Late in the fifties, I already had a feeling that something was happening in the world. There was this urge that Dick Moore and I talked a lot about, documenting the history of our time, like being a witness of what was going on and showing it to the world, so we just started mapping them out all over the world. We made films about the civil rights movement, we made films about jazz, we made films about rock—this was the San Francisco rock 'n' roll explosion. We got tear-gassed in Louisiana. Then, later on, in '67, we made a film in Cuba about Cuba that was shown all over the world, and then, in '68, we made a film about Castro [*Fidel*]. And then, when KQED decided to close shop, I had an offer from Saul Zaentz to start a film department at his record company, so I did, and then, the second film he made was *One Flew Over the Cuckoo's Nest*, and that made us big.

Would you say that you began in documentary as a cinema verité filmmaker?

Oh, yes, oh, yes. I remember in 1963 we were filming a series called the *Anatomy of a Hit*, about how a film becomes a hit. That's how I met Saul Zaentz. And I ordered a lightweight camera that the Maysles brothers were using and I just unpacked it right on the set and put it on my shoulder and went crazy. Here was something you could run around with. And at first it was crazy because we were running around with it rather than letting the action unfold in front of us, so it was useless. I said "we" because by then, there were five of us.

Irving filming Fidel Castro in Cuba for Fidel *in 1968.*

Then later on, in 1966, I believe, we had an assignment, actually, from the headquarters in New York—at that time it was called NET, not PBS—to make a film about southern blacks in northern cities, and we concentrated on one family—it was a mother and ten children who were on welfare, an awfully good-looking family. And we interviewed a few and they caught our eye. They had certain interesting ideas and manners and we started filming. And we realized that verité-only is going to be a totally superficial film—it'll show the mother and ten children sitting in pajamas watching television because that's what was on the surface. And we realized verité is great when it captured an event that placed itself out in the street, like what we filmed in the South about the voting rights struggles, competition—things like that.

But when we need to deal with real life, with inner life, we had to develop certain devices in order to get at the dream life, and inner life of people. But we even did it a little earlier by, for example, suggesting to a composer that he start playing his piano, and pretty soon he forgot us and he started composing something right on camera. So in this film we asked people about their dreams, reenacted those dreams, then played to them. We used each other's interviews as a catalyst to evoke something. We hung around the place to see what was going on, but we also did a lot of, well—I'm going to use a negative word—manipulating. The agreement was that we would develop the craft with them, with the mother and the older kids, that we will always tell them after the fact what we have done, and it will be up to them to decide whether it should be included in the film or not. And we kept that agreement.

So the oldest boy was saying all the time if he only had a job, he would buy a car, and then, he will get a girl. That was the sequence; he was sixteen, I think. That's pretty typical, I think, of adolescent boys. Well, he was sixteen, he could get a driver's license, he already knew how to drive. So we talked him into going to the employment office and signing up during the summer. And then, we arranged with a friend of ours to call him up at a certain time and ask for an interview, which was manipulated, right? And the call came from this guy's secretary and said they got his name from the employment office—would he come for an interview? And we followed him to the interview—we actually filmed the interview secretly but we decided that wasn't right, so we threw it out. And he did well in the interview—he got a janitorial job. And we filmed him at the job and everything. At first, it was big excitement in the house that Robert had a job and all that, but then, eventually, the mother says, whether he has a job or doesn't have a job, he will be losing just the same.

So the film evolved. We had certain plans as to how the film would go, but the film took a life of its own. And that's when we started using catalysts—I shouldn't say manipulating. I would say catalyst.

Then, when I got together with Allie and we started making films together, first of all, my filmmaking took a leap in terms of education and depth. And also, because of my years with Saul Zaentz, it got much more polished because I worked with feature films. So I still believed in using catalysts. And between Allie's poetry and verbal background, although she did a lot of still photography, and my background, we evolved into a style of our own.

Was it difficult to stray from your roots in verité? Was it difficult to start using catalysts to move the story along?

No. I was never a purist. By nature, I'm a nonreligious person. I don't believe in any dogma. So, anything to tell a better story. And it's interesting, when I was a student, Hollywood people would come and give lectures, and directors tell us that you have to tell a story in a film. I thought, that's old stuff. We don't need to tell a story; we have to show tension in the film. And then, when I started working and making films, I realized that that's all we are doing—we have to tell a good story and tell it well, no matter what it is. Even if it's a so-called experimental film.

How do you characterize yourself as a filmmaker? Because you constant-ly experiment, is that your style?

There is a style there now in the last ten films that Allie and I made. People tell us they can tell our films. I guess it's interview-based. We got to be very good interviewers and people open themselves up to us in a way that sometimes scares us. I remember a number of interviews—it was after the interview that the person says, "I didn't know I was going to say all that—very intimate stuff." There was stuff that we decided not to put into the film because we found it was too personal and it could be damaging to the person if it got out.

But I became very interested in seeing the inner life of people. And after I left public television I stopped going after famous people and got interested in what we call ordinary people. And we said that we will make films about the extraordinary lives of ordinary people—the inner life of most people is fasci-nating. But the limit of it is casting—some people just don't work well on camera, they don't have the facial expressions, the body language, to express inner life. They don't have the storytelling abilities to express themselves as well, so we have to pass on these people because they wouldn't make a good film.

I hate the word "documentary" because it's derived from the word "document," which means it's something that can be taken up in court to prove somebody's guilt or innocence, and it's not. But I don't have a better word. I don't like "nonfiction" because it is such a negative term, so I don't know. I say I'm a documentary filmmaker who makes films about people's lives.

Are there rules for you in your filmmaking? Is there a line you wouldn't cross?

I would never lie or bend the truth, as I see it. I'm very faithful to what I think is the truth. That, to me, is the criteria, the line that I'll never cross. And I believe that there is no such thing as an objective truth. People say that you should never show anything that you didn't film, or you shouldn't edit, or whatever. We always edit—we always point the camera where we feel it's right to point the camera. And we turn it off. We are manipulating whatever we see according to what our inner voice tells us to do to capture the truth. I am very careful not to exaggerate somebody's act. I like to present people the way I think they are. I'll never betray people. I always believe in the practice that the only subjective in the film is to be revealed by the subject—they're part of the film. But I do believe in using actors; I do believe in reenacting. I would like to stretch it as much as possible.

Do you continue to try new things with each film?

I don't know. It's hard for me to judge. We start with the old framework, and then we expand it, because we keep filming during editing. We have our editing set up in the dining room, which is next to [the] kitchen, and the camera is also sitting in the editing room, and during the editing we see that something is still needed; something will work nicely here, and we have to film it and put it in.

Talk about some of the devices that you have come up with in your filmmaking that allow you to present things differently. How do you capture parts of the story that happened in the past or different ways of seeing the truth without having someone talk to the camera?

Well, the device of reenactment or an actual description of what's being said is something that we didn't invent and a lot of people use filmmakers a little differently than other people, but I think it's a technique that's highly controversial. *60 Minutes* won't have anything to do with it, but we're not unique in using the reenactment device. We try to illustrate the emotion that people express. It's not interview-based, because when everything is interview-based, people tell us and we try and visually express it and make it more coherent or more lively or more dramatic or more meaningful. Anyway, film is a visual medium, so it's very important to try and portray things visually as much as possible. So I'm sure Allie talked to you about visual equivalents trying to illustrate the emotions expressed. And for us it has been very successful with audiences. We find that the more realistic we make the presentation, the harder time critics and maybe audiences have.

The more abstract, the more successful we are. Because to, especially, critics and film people it's the line between fiction and nonfiction that cannot be crossed that we are manipulating.

So that's why critics might not be receptive to that?

I think so.

But audiences seem to think that that's a good thing?

No. I think that even with audiences, I can't tell. I get responses from audiences from friends, acquaintances, or people who followed our films, and a lot of them are very surprised that our last film [*Blind Spot*] was not a big hit. I still love it and I think it's wonderful and we expanded the language of documentary film. And I still think it's going to find its place in the sun or in the darkroom. The marketplace, the festival directors and critics—well, critics didn't get a chance at it—turned it down. So both Allie and I are trying to figure out why, and maybe it was too representational. Not abstract, not as abstract as our previous films, like *Dialogues* or *Rachel's Daughters*, which had a huge audience. Or even *In the Shadow of the Stars*; after all these years, we meet strangers who say, "You made that film?" And that was over ten years ago. They still remember it. It was a wonderful film. That was a real beloved film. It was funny, it was poignant, it had all the elements of a good film. And it played in theaters a lot. So here, we went forward.

Perhaps the appeal of the abstract is that you could reach different levels of understanding with more abstract representation?

Probably. I mean, even with *Dialogues*, there were people who said, "You're not supposed to use any reenactment. This is a documentary. What you film is what it is." I don't know. I don't believe in purists, purity, or anything like that.

What's exciting in the documentary field is, it's changing. There are lots of offshoots from verité. Lots of people have philosophies about what can be documentary and how to push the form. But there are purists who believe you shouldn't do this or that. Even interviewing, for some, is verboten.

The Maysles wouldn't interview. They would just hang around and not say anything—they were purists. I admire the work of the Maysles and Pennebaker and that early crowd. They're only a few years older than me. And one of the things is, they were terrific cameramen. They really told a story with a camera, and Pennebaker still does. And they really dump their editing off on some poor soul who has to struggle with these incoherent films and make it into a story. These are really the unsung heroes of the cinema verité movement.

But that just isn't a way that works for you as a filmmaker, correct?

Well, it worked for me in the beginning. What happened is that the filmmakers in the early days . . . I was such a purist, that I believed what you shoot, you edit. And at KQED, at one time I was head of the whole film department, and that was my rule: you shoot, you edit. So even the newspeople worked four days a week; they finished their filming by 5:00 or 4:30, they made arrangements with the lab, they had something to eat while the lab processed the film, they took it to the station, they watched it with the reporter, they striped the sound at the same time, and they edited it. They learned to shoot in such a way that it took four or five cuts to make the news package. So I came from that school, that you had to go all the way. And it improved our filming, it improved our shooting, because we knew that it had to be edited. So I think it had a big effect on the way I work.

In terms of your editing and shooting, when do you know that you've got the end to your story? Can you preplan it, or is there an epiphany moment in the process of filming?

Both. We always plan. In fact, we even set it up. I remember in *Fidel* we set it up, but the ending became the beginning and the beginning became the ending. And I know that epiphany usually happens not for the ending, but for the moment of truth of the film, that exciting moment, which usually happens about two-thirds, three-fourths into the film. At that point, we grab each other's hand, if I'm not shooting, or look at each other because we know we have a movie now. We do plan for beginnings and endings because we feel this is where we say hello and set premises of what to expect from the film and what is the basic style of the film. And the ending is where we say good-bye, and what you are left with. Endings are difficult. A lot of terrific filmmakers have a hard time ending a film, by making too many endings or just, all of a sudden, boom, turning off the projector. We plan for the endings.

How would you say you have changed as a filmmaker? Has your experience changed as a filmmaker with respect to the process?

Well, I really am comfortable in the film world more than in the non-film world. I'm sixty-nine now, and I started at twenty-three, so I went through a lot of technical metamorphoses. Technically, evolution doesn't phase me at all. I was always comfortable with it. I don't like to do the camera work as much as I did. I have friends who are so good. And I've done enough of it, and you really have to specialize in it.

Do you still shoot some?

Yeah, I shot the last two films. I don't like the responsibility of the film on my shoulder because it's really hard to concentrate on three different things at once. I try to interview from behind the camera, and to be the interviewer from behind the camera, I find, is extremely difficult. Or, rather, ineffective. As a secondary, it's great, because if you have an idea or there's something that's been missed, it's natural to ask. We use the principal interviewer and secondary interviewer technique. One of us—in the case of *Dialogues*, it was always Allie—is the principal interviewer who gets the questions together. She's the one who has the eye contact and who creates a conversation—we don't ask questions; we create a conversation. Questions are guidelines, so all subjects are covered. The secondary interviewer listens to what is happening and doesn't have to concentrate so much, and sees, all of a sudden, that there's some words that can open the floodgate. And it's hard to come up with this when you're the primary interviewer. But that's the way we work in interviews. I once tried to interview myself in the mirror from behind the camera. That was a disaster.

Do you have a favorite part of filmmaking?

The one that I think I'm really good at is editing. I feel very, very confident as an editor. I've had jobs where people filmed a lot, not a lot, but some, and to take that and make something out of it and end up with a good film. . . . I like to make films in which you are not aware of the editing at all. They just progress naturally and they go down like a good meal. You're just in the story and you're not aware that's it's not just one shot. So that's a fun process. And it's really cheating. Editing is cheating. There are all kinds of things to have to cut. It's fun. Oh, it's like cutting and pasting time.

Do you cut multiple versions of a film?

No I don't . . . I think the downside of the Avid is that you can be cutting fifty different versions, and then decide which version is best. There's only one good version.

Do you do test screenings?

Yes.

Do you do them to take a pulse, then make changes accordingly?

No, we don't make changes. We do work-in-progress screenings, not finished films. That's almost impossible. Certainly difficult. The way we show it in the state that we think there is a story, in the rough cut, the story is coherent. The way we show it is one or usually two screenings, and we try to include as many strangers as we can find because we know that friends are going to be a little biased. If something is not clear, or something seems to be out of order or something is kind of over the top, we pay attention to it. It's terribly important that we are communicating with strangers—it's fantastic. One of the most wonderful experiences of my career was sitting on opening night in New York and watching *In the Shadow of the Stars* in the company of three hundred strangers and my son, and I was watching people. And they were listening, and the body language and they were loving the film. I can't describe the experience. It's fantastic. It's wonderful—the smiles on their faces . . . it was just wonderful.

If you weren't making films, what would you be doing?

I don't know. There's part of me that is very lazy, and I want to do nothing but be a country squire. I don't know if it's guilt or something that drives me to put in twelve- to fourteen-hour days in films. But in between, I try to postpone work as much as possible.

Is there any one thing that you can capture or articulate that keeps you coming back and making films? You obviously have a passion for it.

Yes. Because it's fun. It's really fun. It's like still playing—it's like a three-ring circus, with a complicated shooting schedule. And on *Shadow*, we had sixteen people and we had a tight, complicated schedule. It was great. And we filmed everything we wanted. That's wonderful. I like to work with a lot of people. I like to see a lot of talent contributing to the film. The wonderful thing that I saw, especially when I worked on some dramatic films, was many people

Filmmaker Irving Saraf. Photo credit: Stella Kwiecinski.

working so hard, with such devotion in their small tasks and creating such a . . . it's such a joint effort, to create a work of art. You see it in the theater a lot, and any public performance; you don't get that with documentary because documentary is usually three or four people. But I love the circus.

You've worked on fiction films.

I was postproduction supervisor on *One Flew Over the Cuckoo's Nest*. I was an editor of another film that Saul made.

Do you ever think about doing fiction films?

We did. We just said that we didn't have enough passion to really go through with it, dealing with all the obstacles. Actually, I was supposed to make a film with Saul, and we came very close, and then when we started talking to studio people—it was mixed, and I just didn't have the drive to push for it.

Do you contemplate trying fiction again?

Not at the age of sixty-nine, no. You have to have the drive at the age of twenty, twenty-five.

Documentaries take a lot of drive and energy, too, don't they?

Yeah, but it's different. You don't have to raise ten million dollars. But I think the money makes a big difference. We make our documentaries very cheap, but we always compete with films that cost five times as much as ours. So *Dialogues with Madwomen*, which was one of our most successful films of all time, cost $62,000. That includes transfer to 16mm.

Do you have favorite filmmakers?

When I was young, I loved the work of Bela Lorenz. People said he was a nut and egomaniac, but I didn't care. I wasn't a Flaherty fan. I mean, they were okay, but they didn't turn me on. Then, when the verité people came, the whole Bob Drew group, I was flabbergasted, I was crazy about that stuff.

Every once in a while, I come across a film where I say, "I wish I could do a film like that." I really love good work and I am expressive about bad work, which gets me into trouble, because you're supposed to be very polite. But I do say, "This is crap," if I think that way. And I see gems that never got their due and it breaks my heart. Some films are exquisitely made. There are really unexciting films that get nominated, and often win, versus some beautiful things that just get left behind.

Your win for *Shadow*—did that change anything for you?

Change in that people take me seriously. Not in fund-raising, for sure. If you apply for a grant, they still ask you to send your previous film, to make sure you know how to do it. In the whole media world in the United States, it's all what you did last year.

In Hollywood, if you're young and you made one moneymaker, they give you two, three more chances. I don't know, it really didn't. More respect and, especially, self-respect. Little things. People who put us down . . . when they watched the film really sunk in their chairs. That was nice to know. We had some witnesses to that. And getting telegrams from all over the world was incredible. And getting champagne and flowers from all over the world. But if people put us down now, like one guy said to a friend of ours about us trying to make a film, "Well, they're amateurs," and then that friend of ours said, "They got the Oscar." And he said, "Oops, I'm sorry," and that's about it. It didn't transform my life.

Where do you think documentary films are going?

I'm not very good at predicting because I'm wrong so many times, but I think the fly on the wall, the pure verité, is going to expand tremendously. We just saw a wonderful film on public television. It was about four or five taxi drivers in New York, and it was all shot in taxis at night. Without the new technology it couldn't be done. And it was wonderful. So the verité is going to evolve fantastically. But the limitations of it, of being able to portray only what's public—there's going to be a fight and a struggle all the time—yes reenactments, no reenactments, what kind of visuals?

In the interview, here's the problem. I used to believe that you had to interview only when people were moving, working, driving, and cooking, not sitting down. But they never get the kind of intimate situation unless you just face each other, so how to reconcile the two? I don't know, I think the language is evolving. Luckily there are a lot of good documentarians working right now and developing and searching.

What are you working on now?

We are making now a film that we are . . . we bring our commitment to the public good, I would say. The film's about children's health, because there is a rise in the incidence of asthma and cancer and birth defects and obesity, and we want to find out why and what can be done about it. So we are making these four films, starting with asthma. They are destined for PBS. We are filming the pilot about asthma and I would say we are nearing the halfway mark of principal photography, and we have enough money to start hiring videographers, so I don't have to do it. We never do sound, because neither one of us is good at it. We know how to operate it—we put earphones on and, you know, turn the knobs; we know how to run a Nagra, but it's a real skill that I have a lot of respect for, and I like people to understand every word in our films.

Do you have a favorite film that you've done?

In the Shadow of the Stars. Because it broke all the rules that we made for ourselves. We used to teach; I taught for eighteen years, one course, and I always told my students never to make a film about more than three people—there are about eleven principals [in *Shadow*]. It moves so beautifully and coherently and it has so many subplots that work so well. It's an intricate film. It flows like a perfect drama. And as I say, it has pathos and humor and all the things that work well in a drama and, to me, a satisfying film, and it evolved so beautifully. It's the first long film that Allie and I made together—we made half-hours and hours before—and it turned out magically. The *New York Times* called it close to magical. And that's why I think I love it. Magic.

Chapter 12: Allie Light
Searching for Metaphor

Light brings to filmmaking a poetic sensibility and a background in writing. When she began partnering with her co-filmmaker, Irving Saraf, she brought that sensitivity to the moving images, which, she says, are a search for metaphor. From her first film, *Self Health*, to their Academy Award–winning *In the Shadow of the Stars* (1991), to their Emmy-winning *Dialogues with Madwomen* (1993), and, also, *Rachel's Daughters: Searching for the Causes of Breast Cancer* (1997), Light strives to push the form of nonfiction filmmaking by finding new ways to communicate emotions in her very personal film journeys, sometimes as both subject and director. Light has also published a book of poetry, *The Glittering Cave*, and has edited *Poetry from Violence*, an anthology of women's writings.

How did you get into filmmaking and, in particular, documentaries?

With filmmaking, Irving and I are truly partners. He was a filmmaker before I was. When we got together I had just gotten my degree in poetry writing from San Francisco State. So I was an artist, and I've always felt that that's what I was, from the time that I was a small child. But I didn't know a lot about movies, and I actually didn't know a lot about visual arts. So after I finished with my poetry, I felt that I really needed to do something else with my poetry, which would be visual, like putting it on the wall in some way. I began working in a program at San Francisco State called the Pegasus Program, which was poetry in schools. It involved having kids write to imagery and it was done with big projectors on the walls so the images would be gigantic. That was a way for me to enter into the visual world. And I was such a reader. Readers, although we range far, are also blocked in a lot of ways because we don't look at things. I actually learned to look at things after I got together with Irving.

We began in a funny little way. I would write a poem and he would make a little film about it. And I would write a little poem about the film that he made. We did that back and forth. And at the same time we were falling in love, and that was thirty years ago. When we met, we were actually each married to someone else, and I became a widow, and he eventually was divorced, and we got together.

How did you expand your involvement in filmmaking after you got together with Irving?

When I got into graduate school, I got into a department called interdisciplinary arts so that I could make that transition. And I made my first film with my ten-year-old daughter, which was a nude study of her. I suppose now I would get arrested for pornography. It was a beautiful portrait of her. That was the very first film that I made.

And then Irving encouraged me to get together with other women filmmakers. At the same time I had been moving towards feminism and I eventually ended up as a women's studies teacher. The very first film that I made was called *Self Health*, and it was about how to do your own cervical exam. It was a very interesting process for me because I found that you can think you're working with feminists, and you can encounter the same problems that you have if you're working with a male crew. I thought we could do this—this was a very egalitarian way—and it didn't work out. But it worked out enough to get me into the area of making movies. And that film went a long way. It actually was translated into Japanese, won a number of prizes. It was a very much in-your-face film, but it was a good time for that because it was right in the middle of the women's health movement. Women were learning how to do their own cervical exams, learning what our bodies were about, so that was a really good introduction. And it was after that that Irving and I made our first film.

Was your first film commissioned, or did you come up with that on your own?

Maybe one time I've worked on a film for someone else. But no, it's an idea that I had. I was, I think, thirty-five at the time, and I wanted to learn, actually, how to do my own cervical exam. I was older than other women at the clinic, so I felt embarrassed to go in there and take off my clothes and use a speculum. And so, I thought, let's make a film about it; so that way, I could do it and still maintain some control. That's one of the things we set up as a crew, that we didn't want to be voyeurs. So we would do this process first, and then we would feel that it was okay for us to film the process, and we did do that. It did work. I was the director. That was my first real film.

What about the process kept you coming back?

It was incredibly exciting. It's just like writing poetry, except your tools are different. It's the search for metaphor, which, for me, is a lifelong desire. I look for it everywhere.

After *Self Health,* what was your next step?

We made our first film about a naïve folk artist that I found. I went on a trip with my daughter, who was around fourteen, and it was one of those wonderful trips where you don't have an agenda. We saw a freeway sign in the Mojave Desert that said, "Ghost Town," and we started toward the ghost town. And here, by the side of the road, was this very weird yard with almost life-size figures. And we stopped and I talked to the woman. It was really my first introduction to what's called naïve art, art that has no training behind it. And when I got home, Irving and I talked and we said, "That would make an interesting film." He was dead, the artist, but his widow was there alone with all these dolls.

So we got married at the end of '74, and on our honeymoon, we went back. The place was called Possum Trot and it was out in the high desert.

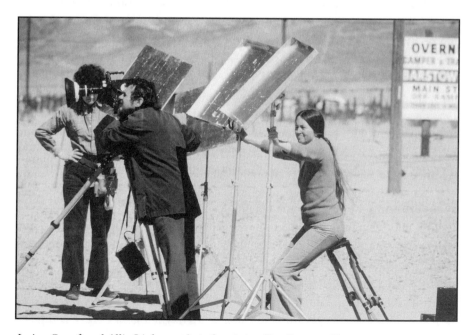

Irving Saraf and Allie Light on their first joint film, Possum Trot.

We shot some footage, enough footage to go back and make a little clip and write a proposal and apply to the NEA, and we got a small grant. And then, we went back and shot *Possum Trot: The Life and Work of Calvin Black*. We took mostly students with us. We were both teaching, and we spent a whole week there and documented the whole place. It was a wonderful time.

That film was twenty-nine minutes, a standard half-hour. And it introduced us to the whole world of folk art—it's really quite a remarkable field because our impression is that, with a naïve artist, the whole creative process is much more obvious. It's there because there's no disguise, like there might be with a trained artist. You can really see the process. And that's what we wanted to show.

And then, we made a series of films. That was the first one. And there were four more. The whole series was called *Visions of Paradise* (1979–1982), and they were of five folk artists, half-hour films. All but one was broadcast. We ran into trouble with those films when we tried to market them as a series because nobody was interested. Folk art wasn't all that appreciated, I think. The one called *Grandma's Bottle Village* is very popular in public broadcast, and it's been broadcast the most.

Where does the art come in, in terms of documentary filmmaking?

Well, for me, it comes in in a number of ways. It's another way of writing poetry. That's probably, for me, the most exciting because you emphasize life in a particular way. But it's also the greatest way there is for me to tell a story. And a storyteller—filmmakers are storytellers just like writers are—it's the whole excitement of how to tell a story. It's a reflection of life, but it's not a document. You know, it takes life a step further. A narrative tells a story, and it stands alone by itself without having to know anything about what went before or after. It's not like a news report, where it relies on what you already know about the subject in order to put it all together.

What are some of your favorite films?

It's like asking a person to choose their favorite child. They all have their own strengths and their own magical moments for me. *In the Shadow of the Stars*—I love it because I feel connected with my own life. It was a way of saying good-bye to my first husband, who was a singer. My husband was a member of the San Francisco Opera chorus and he always wanted to be a star. He had a wonderful voice, but he died when he was very young, of cancer. And he never had a chance to achieve stardom, but one of the things that he did was carry a camera, a little Bolex black-and-white silent camera, under his costume, and he filmed a lot of the opera stars of the fifties. Irving and I had all this footage at home and we said, "What can we do with that—a silent opera?" We decided to make a film about a star, what that drive is, and what it looks like. And so, we started by using quite a bit of the black-and-white footage and slowly got rid of more and more of it as the other film built around it. It became, for each of us, the start of our own lives, too. It started for me as my past with my first husband, but it evolved into other things. In that respect, that's one of my favorite films.

Dialogues with Madwomen was even more connected to my life—I'm in the film. It took about twenty-five years to be able to really come out as a madwoman, so it started with a desire to tell my story—I had been in a mental hospital. But, by then, I had been teaching women's studies for a long time and I had heard stories of so many other women. So, actually, two of the women in that film are former students of mine from those years. So it evolved from just being my story to the stories of six women. And I love that film because I love the metaphor in it.

Is there a way that you could describe yourself as a documentary film-maker? For you, is it a search for self, or is there a common thread among them?

I can tell how I feel. I'm scared every time. I never feel like I have the capacity or the ability to do it. So each time, it's going into a really scary foreign country for me. I have a wall of . . . just like of power, not my own power, particularly, but a balance of power, I guess. I have to always remember that I'm helping somebody tell her story or his story, that this is not my story. There are elements and seeds of my story in everything I do because there's always a hook, a personal hook, but it has to go beyond that. And so I learned a tremendous amount with *Dialogues with Madwomen* because I was on both sides of the camera. I learned what the hot seat is really like. I hope it made me a more caring and vulnerable person as a director. I don't want to ever forget how vulnerable you feel, but I also found it disturbing, too.

As you're filming, do you know what the film is, or do you discover your story in the editing process?

I think the latter, probably, although you have to start with something, some kind of script, and then hopefully it's gonna enlarge and be greater

Allie at the AVID editing system, working on Dialogues *with* Madwomen.

than . . . you can have those moments that you never would have thought you had. You see the crew at the end of *Dialogues with Madwomen,* the crew working on the beach because I felt that I had tried so hard to demystify what's mad in these women and what happened to them in their lives, and to me. And if you could demystify that, then you should demystify the process by which you get that. And so, it was a way of showing, yes, this is a film, and there's more to these women's lives than what you've heard, but this is really a film; this is not real life, and here's proof of it.

How was that, directing yourself?

I couldn't fall back on Irving and say, "You know, it's gotten so complicated." Irving was there the day on the beach and we had worked it out—I had really scripted that very carefully because we were going to use two cameras, so each camera could reveal what the other one was doing, and we had to stay out of the shots. It was hard for me to do that because, basically, I'm a shy person. But the camerawomen who I've worked with so many times—they were so supportive, and I felt that I could really fall back on them.

How do you think you push the medium of documentary film?

Sometimes I wish I did cinema verité because it's the only process that happens in the present. As Irving says, "Documentary film is about the past," because they're usually about something that's already happened.

The other thing about cinema verité is that people think it's the total truth, and it's not. There's much more to truth than what you see happening in front of you at the moment. This is an example: In *Dialogues with Madwomen*, there's a three-minute sequence in my story where I use three or four different versions of myself. So you see me in a little interview at my present age, and then, you see an actor portraying me running down a hill with a baby in her arms, and then, you see a piece of archival footage with a woman whose name is lost and is probably dead—a madwoman, a mad-woman without a name—and that's me. To me, that's much more honest than if I try to be the only one who is me. You know, it's not honest if I—I was fifty-one when I made that film—if I, as a fifty-one-year-old woman, was sitting naked on a table being examined by a doctor because that happened to me thirty-some years ago. It's better to find a woman who's that age, who can be me, who can be my stand-in, because that seems more honest to me than if I try to reenact myself. All of the reenactment and everything, in my estimation, is trying to get at the truth, and there are many, many ways to commit a truth, because, I guess, there are many kinds of ways of saying what's true.

How do you think you've changed as a filmmaker in terms of your feelings?

Well, I have more anxiety about approaching new projects. I felt that the old nemesis of shyness and one-on-one encounters that I always had—they always lurked in the back of my mind, but that, I could overcome. Somehow, the armor has worn more thin, so there's that problem.

I think that I'm a better interviewer than I was, by far. I think I care much less about what the rest of the crew thinks about me. At the same time that I have more anxiety I am able to be more risky; I plunge in. I will say things in an interview that are only meant for the person I'm talking to, and I really don't give a shit about what the crew might think. I don't care that much about protocol, I guess, anymore. So that comes, I think, from being successful in some ways. I feel more able to be myself, and, at the same time, I have a lot of anxiety.

And the camera is extremely isolating at the time that it's on you. *Dialogues with Madwomen*, of course—the aftereffect of that film was that

I didn't have any more secrets in the world. For three or four years after the film came out, people I had never known thought they could ask me anything—that's what's so awful to me. They could say anything to me, like, "How do your children feel knowing that their mother went through this?" or, "How were you going to hurt your children? What kind of medication were you on?" There was no barrier. I was in therapy for the last four years because my oldest daughter was diagnosed with breast cancer and I was so afraid of losing her that I had to get some support. And I would say this to my therapist—suddenly, everyone thought they had a right to be a part of your life—and she was very helpful. She said, "You have to learn to say, 'No.' You don't have to go on every radio show; you can say, 'No.'" And that was very helpful to me. That helped me separate my personal life.

How do you find your end?

Well, I think that a documentary, a nonfiction film, has to have a beginning, middle, and end. And the seeds of the end have to be in the beginning or the middle. It can't come out of the blue. In life, it does come out of the blue, but in a documentary film, which is about life, you can't do that. The other thing is, a film has to have a beginning to start at the beginning, and so, in *Rachel's Daughters*, it starts with Jenny's funeral and then, right away, it moves backwards and maybe people will say, "Oh, maybe one of these women will die because we just saw the funeral, we don't know which one." But already, by the time the film has moved that far forward, the seeds of the end are there because toward the end, with the women in black on the hillside, they are the mourners from the funeral made into a metaphor, so you could not have any other ending, as far as I'm concerned, once you have that beginning.

At what point did you come to that ending?

It was an evolution, but it really began before the film began, because I was on a television show with a number of women who had breast cancer in the Bay Area. And one of the women, she's actually in the film, died before the film was finished. But she said to the interviewer that day that she's been fighting cancer for so long, and she said, "I'm alive now but behind me are four women who've died and behind each one of those are other women." I haven't forgotten that and it was so eloquent and so simple, so those are the last words that were spoken in the film. And then when she says, " . . . and behind me are four women," the camera tilts up and you see this vast number of women dressed in black. And so they are my secret chorus and they're there to remind you of what life is about, and they're also there as mourners for the deaths of the women. So it's sort of become one of the four women behind the next living woman waiting to die, and that's what the end of that film signifies.

What kind of shooting ratio do you have?

It varies, but with the digital camera now it's much higher. All I remember is *Self Health*, the very first one, which was 6:1.

How do you like DV?

Well, I like it, but I miss those beautiful images, although they're gonna get better, I guess. But our last two films, we shot on a little 1000.

Do you find that you can make films differently with DV?

Well, in some ways they're more relaxed in front of the small camera. We've been able to be very portable with it, and it's very good for interviews

The chorus on the hillside from Rachel's Daughters. *Photo credit: Delligatti.*

but it's not good for landscapes. We use all kinds of stuff; we use a lot of our Bolex 16mm when we want to shoot something to make it look more beautiful if we don't need sync sound.

How do you like nonlinear?

It's wonderful. *Dialogues* was edited on one of those early things that you can't get frame perfect—it's always three off one way or the other—and that was just maddening, but the AVID's terrific.

How long to edit one of your films?

About eight months. We spend a lot of time. Well, *Rachel's Daughters* was very long. It was 106 minutes. But I would say that we spend six to eight months.

Test screenings?

We have done them with the three long ones. We do it with questionnaires because we don't want one or two people to monopolize afterwards, so we just tell everybody to do them there, or they can drop them in the mail.

Funding?

It doesn't get easier. We're not good fund-raisers. So what we mostly do is, we start the project with our own money and then, we'll limp along and we'll get a few grants and we'll make films on incredibly small budgets. *Dialogues* was ultimately ninety-three minutes long and cost $63,000—that was cheap. *Rachel's Daughters*, I think, was $280,000, or was it $180,000? *In the Shadow of the Stars* was just under $200,000. We eventually get our money back, for the most part.

We have a new film that has not done well at all. And we're trying to figure out what's wrong with it and what went wrong. I don't think we'll ever make our money back from that one. We have about $50,000 of our own money in it. It's a film about women murderers. People just have a really hard time with it.

That's interesting. I wonder why?

I think, maybe, because it's not about victims—I mean, the women are victims, in a way, but this is not a film about victims, it's not about murdering your husband because he beat you up. It's called *Blind Spot*, and I really like it and maybe, in a way, it's the best time, if we're gonna have a failure, to have it now because we've had some good ones under our belt. I felt the film will find its place, find its market, but, so far, it hasn't. We finished it in 2001. HBO turned it down we sort of expected that would happen, but it's like dropping a stone into a deep pool and it just went away. It's too painful for me to spend too much time thinking about it right now, but I know that Irving was doing a transcript the other day on the AVID, so I was listening to it and, all of a sudden, I said, "You know, I really love this film. I don't know what's wrong with it, but it's a good film." So far, it's been turned down by a number of festivals. We did a long version which was ninety-one minutes and we're not totally happy with some of the reenactments, but some of them are great.

Reenactments really do bother people, and that's probably where we do push the envelope. But I really do believe in them, because I think that you're dealing with a medium that is really about action and about picture and if you don't have them, you have to make them. And those women, none of them had any home movies as kids, there was no way of visualizing—most are in a cell and you have an hour to do an interview and you can never go back, so how are you gonna flesh out these women's lives unless you recreate them? And I feel that we were totally true to the women. But then it turns out, people say, "But that's what they do on Fox TV," or these other shows. I hate the reenactments they do, but there's got to be room for good ones, as well. Especially when you think that the very first documentary films were scripted and did have reenactments and did have dramatically done pieces—there's a precedent.

You've had success with films with reenactments before.

But, this time we did much more with acting and with little scenarios, whereas before, we did a lot with metaphor and what we call emotional equivalents. We would call these little things we do emotional equivalents because they are not exactly what you're hearing, but are a metaphor or an illustration for what's being said—the emotional thing that's being said. Like, in *Dialogues*, when the woman runs down the hill with the baby in her arms, what I was saying was that when I was depressed I was afraid to go to sleep at night for fear that the baby would die, and so I slept with the car keys under my pillow. You're not going to put somebody trying to start a car, but a woman running through the night is the emotional equivalent of what's being said. And so I think those are much more acceptable than where you actually are trying to do an entire scene.

Do you work on multiple films at one time?

With *Shadow*, we ran out of money two years into making the film—it was a five-year project, and so we started *Dialogues with Madwomen*, so each one of them took five years but overlapped, and we were working on both—going back and forth for part of the time. And then, with our new films, we're doing four films called *Small Bodies of Evidence*, which are about children's health and the environment. So we're shooting a lot of those at the same time.

How is it working on multiple films at once? Is it difficult to maintain focus?

When you're doing a series, in this case, it's easier. It's easier and it's cheaper, so if we have a pediatrician who knows about asthma and cancer, we can get stuff for both films. *Shadow* and *Dialogues* were very different. We needed much less money for *Dialogues*. We could do a lot of that without any money, so when we didn't have money to go to the opera and film, we could go and do this, the other. For the *Paradise* films, we shot all those, then edited them over time. We shot them all first, and that's a kind of combining, too, and that was easy because, although the artists were all very different and in different parts of the country, it was about the creative process. I guess I've never done it in such a way where I really had to stop thinking about one in order to think about the other because there was always some relationship.

Do you want to direct fiction films?

No. I'd like to write them and get a really good director who knows what they're doing in fiction. No, that's too big a project. I would just sit there, but I'd like to be on the set, of course. I'd like to see what happens with my writing and how it would come to life.

Do you think you have different experiences as a woman filmmaker that a man doesn't have?

I think that either man or woman, you cannot be afraid of your subject. If you are afraid of something like incest, you can't do a good interview with somebody who's been in that experience and wants to talk about it. And the best example that I can think of happened with *In the Shadow of the Stars*, where Irving and I were interviewing an African-American opera singer. And in the world of opera, there was a time when there wasn't any place for a black singer, so we wanted to talk to him about this. We got to the point in the interview where I felt that we could do that, and he just opened up and what tumbled out was wonderful, and I was so thrilled with this interview. And when we got the footage back and looked at it, I couldn't believe what I saw. The cameraman was a white guy; as Frederick was talking about what it's like to be a black man in a white world, the camera started pulling back and it just got farther and farther away until you couldn't even see the microphone. He was running away. The cameraman was running away. I cried when I saw that because he ruined the interview. I mean, you want to come closer. You don't want to run away from them, and I learned so much from that, and we did end up using it, but we used it as voice-over. You see him being made up, and it's a real close-up on his face, and the makeup being put on, and you hear his voice. So it turned out okay, but what an illumination for me it was to realize what was happening. And it just hit me. If you're afraid of the subject, you're not going to get a good interview.

As a feminist, you want to bring all those hidden things out and so I'm not afraid to talk to anybody about anything, and I get a good interview. I think that maybe women have a little more handle on the emotional, so we're a little bit less afraid. We haven't been socialized to be afraid of it.

Chapter 13: Barbara Kopple
Through the Lens Fearlessly

Prolific and *gutsy* are words commonly uttered in connection with the name Barbara Kopple. Her subject matter doesn't shy away from the controversial and even dangerous. *Harlan County, U.S.A.*, her first feature nonfiction film as director/producer, won her a 1977 Academy Award for Best Feature Documentary. It chronicles the violent struggle between coal miners in Appalachian Kentucky and management. Several of her subsequent films look at peace rallies and demonstrations, workers trying to unionize, and civil rights issues. In 1991, *American Dream*, a story of economic crisis in the American Midwest, won Kopple a second Academy Award for Best Feature Documentary.

How did you get into filmmaking?

I guess my first job was with the Maysles, who did *Gimme Shelter* and *Grey Gardens* and many, many others. And I came to them right after school, and they were just finishing the film *Salesman*, and my job was to do everything nobody else wanted to do. Which was . . . one thing was, Porter Bibb, who was one of the producers who worked there, asked me to get the mailing list from the Museum of Modern Art—you can't just get that—so they could send out cards for that. And I did. And at night I would help the assistant editor—the editor would leave the assistant editing work, and I would do that. I was so voracious about learning. I started doing sound, and editing on people's films. And I started my own company.

I also worked on a film called *Winter Soldier*, which was much earlier than the Maysles, with a collective of people. It was Vietnam veterans giving testimony of what they had done in Vietnam. And it was incredible. We did it with Donald Sutherland and Jane Fonda, who were the people who put up the money for it. I think I was probably one of the youngest people who was working on it. I loved every minute of it. I was doing sound. We all lived together in the editing of it. And Vietnam veterans who were out of the war would come stay with us on this fantastic estate that was donated to us to edit the film. And they'd sort of shake us in the morning and wake us up and we'd all talk and look at material. And sometimes, if we woke them up in the morning, they'd think they were still in Vietnam and they'd take their hands as if they still had a gun in it. So it was pretty heavy. It was sort of an end of innocence.

When we were shooting the *Winter Soldier* film in Detroit, Donald Sutherland kept sort of following me around, and I was scared I was going to get fired because I was really young and I looked really young. So I kept avoiding him. I remember I was sitting in a hotel room, and I was loading a film magazine. And I had my hands in the changing bag. And he came over to me and I figured, oh, this is it. And he said, "I've been trying to talk to you for a couple of days." And I said, "Oh, really." And he said, "I just wanted to tell you I've been watching you and you're incredible. You're doing a great job." So that was something that made me feel really good. It was really nice.

Prior to that, had you had any film experience or taken any classes in filmmaking?

No, I studied clinical psychology. And made a little film in college, but not really. I think my first really, really big experience was with the Maysles. That was real.

What attracts you to nonfiction films?

Well, I do both fiction and nonfiction. What attracts me to nonfiction films is the storytelling aspect of being able to go into the hearts and minds of different people and people whose voices you might not have ever heard before and people whose lives you're being allowed to enter into. And for me, it's one of the most magnificent and incredible experiences, to live and see what their lives are, and what the things they care about are, and have people trust you and open up to you, and be able to bring their story back and let other people see it. And it's a life they probably would never see before or feel unless you were able to be in the field.

How many fiction films have you made?

I've done a bunch of different fiction films. I've done mostly *Homicide: Life on the Street* and *Oz*, and we're in the midst of possibly doing something with Anne Bancroft called *In Loving Kindness*, and a few others.

So is there a good balance between the two?

I think I've done many, many more nonfiction than fiction. But I love fiction, also. Doing *Homicide* was so much fun. I just adored it. It was so great. [Producer] Tom Fontana is amazing. Such an extraordinary person, and he's such a good person and gives people great opportunities and helps them in so many ways. And I remember he was looking for something for me for a while, and the first [*Homicide*] I did was called *The Documentary*, aptly. And before I went, he was telling me all the different ways the actors might respond to me. He said that Andre Braugher might give me a hard time and Yaphet Kotto might give me a hard time. And I was thinking, I'd been machine-gunned with semiautomatic Harveys and I can't think they would give me a hard time but, you know, I'm ready if that's what they want to do. So I went, and what this was, it all took place on New Year's Eve. And, I guess, until the ball drops on New Year's Eve, there aren't any homicides. So I had the entire cast in the squad room. And then, I also went out to film the story that was supposedly the documentary [the film within the episode], and little did I know that I had one of the hardest films you had to do on *Homicide* because it was huge. I was doing two films in one. But it was an extraordinary experience. Andre Braugher did give me a little bit of a hard time, but it was sort of fun. We were doing a barroom scene and he said, "Barbara, so is this the documentary section?" And I said, "Yeah, of course it is." And he said, "So we don't have to do many takes on it?" And I said, "Yes, we do. A good documentarian stays until she gets everything." And so he laughed. I just loved them. They were all so great and supportive, and we had so much fun. We'd go to Baltimore, and you're away from home, so your whole existence is doing nothing but *Homicide*. So it's just one of the great experiences.

And then I also did *Oz* with Tom Fontana, and I just loved that. It was extraordinary. It's wonderful. It's so gritty and so incredible, and it was great working with all those men, as well as Edie Falco and others.

If you were to talk about your style as a nonfiction filmmaker, how would you describe that?

I think probably my style is cinema verité. I learned from the Maysles. But I think, also, it depends on what you're doing, and I think different films require different sensibilities. For this film I did called *Wild Man Blues*, which was a film about Woody Allen on a jazz tour, that was definitely verité. We tried to make ourselves guerilla filmmakers. We put a wireless mic on Woody and Soon-Yi and let them run.

Woody Allen with Barbara Kopple during Wild Man Blues. *Photo credit: Myles Aronowitz/Courtesy Fine Line Features.*

But I think some things—like the Mike Tyson film that I did—couldn't be verité because Mike Tyson was in jail. We were able to film in somewhat of a verité style the things around him. But it was much different. So I think it depends on what the content is. I think you should never pigeonhole yourself—it should be the most important thing to allow people to be who they are and to not put a filmmaker's agenda into it.

Are there lines you won't cross in making films? For instance, do you do interviews?

I'm open for anything. I will interview somebody. I will do anything that I think needs to be done to get them to open up, to get a sense of who they are and what they are about. I don't have any what-I-will-do and what-I-won't-do. I think each new project that I do, I do it as if maybe I'll never be lucky enough to do another, so I want to make it as wonderful and as good as I possibly can.

Is it difficult not to become involved in your subjects' lives?

Oh, of course, you become involved in your subjects' lives. I mean, in *Harlan County*, we were machine-gunned with semiautomatic Harveys. We were told if we were ever caught alone at night we would be killed. The coal miners and their wives let us live with them and protected us. Of course, you get involved. If you didn't, why do it? I mean, why make films? It's about the passion and excitement and about being there and being part of a community and part of their lives.

Do you have to hold back from becoming part of the story?

I think the mere presence of you there changes the story. Because you're there. But I think most of the subjects that we do as nonfiction filmmakers,

Barbara Kopple (left) filming Harlan County.

what the people are struggling to do, or who they are, takes over, and after a while, they forget you're there.

Are you commissioned, or do you generate your films?

I do both. Some come from my own heart and soul and others, people ask me to do, and if I like them I do them. I like that because they come with a budget and that makes it much easier—the ones I have to do on my own—some of the worst and hugest struggles that one ever has to deal with.

You are one of the preeminent names in nonfiction filmmaking. Is fund-raising easier now than when you began?

Oh, no. It's terribly, terribly difficult. I think no matter who you are and what you do, fund-raising is always difficult, and it's harder and harder every year. When I first started there was the National Endowment for the Arts and National Endowment for the Humanities and other foundations, and it was terribly difficult, but at least it was out there. But those agencies have been cut back so much.

Also, if you've done a couple of films they think you really don't need it, so they give it to someone else. So it gets more and more difficult to do the things that you want to do. It's very hard, but it's also great and won-derful to be asked to do a film and have somewhat of a decent budget, and be able to use everything you have in your soul and create and tell a story—rather than divide yourself in half, and half of it's fund-raising and half of it's continuing and going into huge debt. I sort of like when people call up and say, "Would you do this?" It's too hard, I think, the other way.

Part of the challenge in nonfiction filmmaking is, you don't have the same schedule that you do in fiction films. For instance, you don't have a firm finish date. Everything is not preplanned for you. Is that difficult?

When you decide to make a film you make an incredible commitment to it. And, for me, I don't want to leave a stone unturned. I want to do more than is expected and think of all the different things that I could possibly look at to illuminate for an audience what the situation is, or who these characters are, or what's happening. And, you know, it's not forever. You go out there and do it. And when you're out there, you're solely and totally committed to it. Even when you're doing a fiction film, the time you're spending on that, you are totally and utterly committed to that. You're on a deadline. You have to do certain scenes by certain times, and there's no stopping. It's twelve to fifteen hours a day, depending on what the project is, and it's nonstop work. You know, you just wear your sneakers and go.

What is the ratio you shoot?

I think it depends on the subject. I don't think like that. You think about who would be interesting. You follow some people, and then some people lead you to other people. We just got back from the Hamptons in Long Island. We're doing a miniseries for ABC looking at different characters—their dreams over the course of the summer. And you never know what's going to happen. And for us, September 11 happened. And so, for me, this piece has now totally changed, and now it's sort of a look at innocence, and it's a look at what life was like before September 11. You follow a lot of different people because you don't know what's going to happen— unlike fiction, where it's written. And you don't know what's around the corner, and you have to be there, to see how someone moves and changes over the course of a period of time. It's not easy, but it's wonderful. You get something that's extraordinary and changes your whole way and your whole sense of being, and you realize why you're doing it.

As you're shooting, do you know in your head how your story is evolving or does it evolve in the editing room?

I don't think you ever have a different story in the editing room. When you're out in the field, if you don't get the material that tells the story, no matter what you do in the editing room you can't put it together to say something. And I think when you're in the field you see different themes emerging, different stories being told. And I think in the editing room you see strong scenes that take you to certain places and how things start to connect. Editing is really intensive and you have to make it seamless and flow like the experience, so you can't weigh one more than the other. Because unless you get the material and it looks good and sounds good and it has all the things that you need to put it together, you can't put something together unless you have all the elements that go into it. They're both so heavily weighed.

How long do your edits take?

I think we edited *Wild Man Blues* for eight months. Some take a lot longer. One reason is, maybe you don't have money. Two, it's a much bigger story. *My Generation*, which was a film that looked at the three

Woody Allen on tour in Wild Man Blues. *Photo credit: Fine Line Features.*

Woodstocks, the money we were supposed to get from the people who were funding it—they decided they weren't interested in it anymore and said, "We're not funding it anymore." So I was left to my own devices. I was so far into it I couldn't stop. So it just took forever because I'd have to go out and do a million different jobs just to keep the editing going. And then, they decided to do Woodstock '99, and we were just about finished with Woodstock '94 and Woodstock '69, and I had to go out and take a deep breath and film Woodstock '99, and had to go back into the editing room. That took an extraordinary amount of time. *American Dream* took quite a bit of time, and *Harlan County* took quite a bit of time. Most of the things are funded and all you have to worry about is the story, and it is not as terrible as it is when you're doing it all alone.

How do you know when you have the end of your story?

In *Harlan County,* when a miner was killed by a company foreman and they came in and signed the contract. And there was one more huge strike when the entire labor force of the United Mine Workers went out, and we knew that that probably wouldn't last more than three weeks, but we had to do that to see how one impinged on the other. *Wild Man Blues*, at the end of the tour. *Mike Tyson*, that was pretty easy to figure out. *American Dream*, at the end of the strike. It's all different. Things happen. The story is told. Stories have a beginning, middle, and end, and they end because people have changed and so much has happened that you know that you have been able to capture that transition. Each film is so different.

Do you have a preference between fiction and nonfiction?

No, I love them all.

Do you have favorite films that you've done?

I think *Harlan County* is definitely one of my favorites. Nobody believed in it, and I was really young at the time I was doing it. I'd come back to New York every now and then and different people would say, "Are you still working on that?" And I didn't know how to explain to them what it was about. And I think, also, understanding what life and death was all about with the coal miners and watching that whole struggle, that that was a really, really important film for me.

I think also another film that I'm really in love with is a film with Gregory Peck that I did . . . to see what a truly magnificent and beautiful human being he is, and like the character in *To Kill a Mockingbird*, Atticus Finch, and it just rejuvenated my hopes and dreams in what people are all about.

Do you try new things in your filmmaking consciously? Do you try to challenge yourself?

I think each story is a challenge in itself, because each one is constructed differently, because they're about different things. So you don't go in saying, "I'm going to try this," or, "I'm going to try that." You go in hoping to uncover things you didn't know before and hoping to be able to take your audience on a journey that you're on. And maybe you find different ways to communicate with people depending on who they are. But, for me, the most important thing is the people and making the situations as comfortable and intimate to allow people to open up, and the camera and everything else just fades away.

Do you ever pay people to be in films?

I don't think you pay people to be in films. Sometimes if somebody needs something and you want to do something on a personal level, at a certain point you might help them. After I did *Harlan County*, for example, different people would call me up and say that they needed certain things. Whenever I could, I would help them because I cared about them, as any friend would do. But I think there's no ironclad rules. Some people might feel that there are. Some places do pay people, and it opens up a whole world, so you just have to weigh those priorities and make those decisions.

Some people have very stringent rules. I think that if somebody makes a big case that this takes away from their lives, I would consider paying something. But I don't know. It hasn't happened yet. But now, if it means something very important to them and they truly needed it . . . but I haven't done it.

What would you do if you weren't making films?

Maybe I'd be writing. I don't know.

Do you do commercials?

Sure. I like them a lot. I have one on now on Paxil, an antidepressant. I love doing them. They're fun and you get paid. And they're done in a very small amount of time so you feel you have accomplished something, so I like them.

Do you edit your films yourself?

No, I have editors. Which is also very important. Because as a filmmaker, you were there and you bring to it so much more. For me, it's really important to have the editors look at the material without me explaining anything to them because they're your first audience. And even though you, as a filmmaker, may have felt this or that or whatever, what's on film is what's there.

Do you do test screenings?

Yeah, I do. I do screenings where I bring my friends in. I do screenings where people who have nothing to do with film whatsoever look at something and give me their opinions. There are no rules, so sometimes people just come into the editing room, or sometimes I like people to see it for the first time on a screen and I invite people to do that. I did that at the very beginning. *Harlan County* was a rough cut and I was so scared. And I invited all these people who I really respected—all these editors and other filmmakers—and I was nervous. And we showed it, actually, at Pennebaker's, and they really liked it but I was petrified about what they would think about it.

Do you take their feedback?

Oh, sure. Absolutely. And I watch them and see when they're looking at their watch or see when they laugh or see what they say.

How has winning Academy Awards changed filmmaking for you, or has it?

Why would winning an Academy Award change filmmaking? As I said earlier, I look at every film as if it may be my last, and to have gotten two Academy Awards was extraordinary for me. And they were both films I had done all on my own—*Harlan County* and *American Dream*. And it was totally difficult and such a struggle. And in a way it was also really wonderful for the people who were in the film. With *Harlan County*, people couldn't believe it. They were running all over eastern Kentucky screaming, "We got an Academy Award!" And it's a really beautiful thing because otherwise, films like this might not be seen, so that helps to let people know that they exist and their stories exist.

Do you have nonfiction filmmakers as favorites?

Sure, I have a lot. I really like Albert—*Gimme Shelter* and *Salesman*. And Pennebaker—*Don't Look Back* and *Monterey Pop*. I'm really glad any time somebody gets excited about this craft and wants to go into it—there's so much to explore out there. And also, nonfiction filmmakers are very supportive of each other and we know each other and help each other and go to each other's screenings. And you really feel as if you're part of a community.

There are a lot of different styles—like, Nick Broomfield and Michael Moore have changed the face of nonfiction film. Is there a sense that people are pushing boundaries? What's going on now?

There's reality shows with sort of manipulated reality. And as much as people might not like that, it's really opened up the whole world of nonfiction filmmaking to show people at networks and other places that they can be entertaining and exciting and interesting and that there are audiences for them. And then there are the ones that are cinema verité that really get underneath the souls of people. And Michael and Nick, who put themselves into their films and they become a huge character, and what they're able to glean from the people that they're filming and their commentary on it. It's all pretty exciting, pretty interesting. I love it. *Sherman's March*—there are just so many. I think it's wonderful.

I think that as many times as people can sort of go around those corners and take risks and do those different things . . . it's exciting.

Index

BOOKS FROM ALLWORTH PRESS

The Directors: Take One by Robert J. Emery (paperback, 6 × 9, 416 pages, $19.95)

The Directors: Take Two by Robert J. Emery (paperback, 6 × 9, 384 pages, $19.95)

Hollywood Dealmaking: Negotiating Talent Agreements by Dina Appleton and Daniel Yankelevits (paperback, 6 × 9, 256 pages, $19.95)

Making Independent Films: Advice from the Film Makers by Liz Stubbs and Richard Rodriguez (paperback, 6 × 9, 224 pages, $16.95)

Making Your Film for Less Outside the U.S. by Mark DeWayne (paperback, 6 × 9, 272 pages, $19.95)

Technical Film and TV for Nontechnical People by Drew Campbell (paperback, 6 × 9, 256 pages, $19.95)

Producing for Hollywood: A Guide for Independent Producers by Paul Mason and Don Gold (paperback, 6 × 9, 272 pages, $19.95)

Directing for Film and Television, Revised Edition by Christopher Lukas (paperback, 6 × 9, 256 pages, $19.95)

The Filmmaker's Guide to Production Design by Vincent LoBrutto (paperback, 6 × 9, 240 pages, $19.95)

The Health & Safety Guide for Film, TV & Theater by Monona Rossol (paperback, 6 × 9, 256 pages, $19.95)

Get the Picture? The Movie Lover's Guide to Watching Films by Jim Piper (paperback, 6 × 9, 240 pages, $18.95)

Career Solutions for Creative People by Dr. Rhonda Ormont (paperback, 6 × 9, 320 pages, $19.95)

An Actor's Guide—Your First Year in Hollywood, Revised Edition by Michael Saint Nicholas (paperback, 6 × 9, 272 pages, $18.95)

The Screenwriter's Legal Guide by Stephen F. Breimer (paperback, 6 × 9, 320 pages, $19.95)

The Screenwriter's Guide to Agents and Managers by John Scott Lewinski (paperback, 6 × 9, 256 pages, $18.95)

Please write to request our free catalog. To order by credit card, call 1-800-491-2808 or send a check or money order to Allworth Press, 10 East 23rd Street, Suite 510, New York, NY 10010. Include $5 for shipping and handling for the first book ordered and $1 for each additional book. Ten dollars plus $1 for each additional book if ordering from Canada. New York State residents must add sales tax.

To see our complete catalog on the World Wide Web, or to order online, you can find us at *www.allworth.com*.